Audits of Meaning

AUDITS OF MEANING

*A Festschrift in Honor of
Ann E. Berthoff*

EDITED BY

Louise Z. Smith
University of Massachusetts, Boston

WITH A FOREWORD BY

Paulo Freire

BOYNTON/COOK PUBLISHERS
HEINEMANN
PORTSMOUTH, NEW HAMPSHIRE

Boynton/Cook Publishers, Inc.
A Division of
Heinemann Educational Books, Inc.
70 Court Street   Portsmouth, NH 03801
Offices and agents throughout the world

Excerpts from "The Waste Land" in *Collected Poems 1909–1962* by
T. S. Eliot, copyright 1936 by Harcourt Brace Jovanovich, Inc.; copyright © 1963, 1964 by T. S. Eliot. Reprinted by permission of the
publisher.

Poems by Marie Ponsot appearing in this volume are from Marie Ponsot, *The Green Dark*, published by Alfred A. Knopf, Inc.

LIBRARY OF CONGRESS
Library of Congress Cataloging-in-Publication Data

Audits of meaning: a Festschrift in honor of Ann E. Berthoff /
    edited by Louise Z. Smith.
        p.   cm.
      Bibliography: p.
      ISBN 0–86709–209–2
      1. English language—Rhetoric—Study and teaching.   2. American
poetry—20th century.   3. Berthoff, Ann E.   I. Berthoff, Ann E.
II. Smith, Louise Z.
PE1404.A9   1988
808'.042'07—dc19   87–37950
                                                           CIP

ISBN 0-86709-209-2 (paper)
ISBN 0-86709-242-4 (cloth)

Designed by Vic Schwarz.
Printed in the United States of America.

92 91 90 89 88   9 8 7 6 5 4 3 2 1

THE SPLIT IMAGE OF ATTENTION
(Trinity College Library, Dublin)

Saints in *The Book of Dimma*
deserve their double-rainbow eyes
for seeing form and structure,
skin and skeleton, both
at once. Great
lovers of instruction,
mouths empty, they tip
their earlobes forward
the better to lock in
the learning,
inviting it as it enters and is intimate
with their diamond-cut holy
double-bolted ears.
I look to the next page where
their eyes irradiate
on their own   full
of fear at hearing the shooting
of falling stars.

MARIE PONSOT

Contents

Foreword

My first contact with Ann Berthoff's writing (I feel more comfortable calling her Ana) was through her excellent book *Forming/Thinking/Writing*. After I had given a lecture in California, a participant came up to me to ask if I had read Ann Berthoff's work. I said no. The next day, he brought me her book, a book which has become my constant companion ever since.

A few years later, I went to Boston to lecture at the University of Massachusetts. After my lecture, a congenial group of professors invited me to dinner at a very nice Portuguese restaurant in Cambridge. There, during a very engaging dicussion with these professors, I asked my good friend and collaborator Donaldo if he had read an excellent book entitled *Forming/ Thinking/Writing* written by someone whose name I could see in my memory, but was unable to pronounce. (This difficulty with the pronunciation of her last name is why I now call Ann Berthoff, simply and affectionately, Ana.) Before I finished saying the complete title of the book, a woman across the table from me began jubilantly waving her hands saying, "It's me, I'm Ann Berthoff." I immediately leaned forward and gave her a hug and thanked her for having written a brilliant book. I then began to see a certain coherence between Ana across the table from me and the restless and provocative thoughts of Ann Berthoff in *Forming/Thinking/Writing*.

After dinner, I told Ana that I could clearly remember even the place in my bookcase where I kept her book. I am sure that my clear memory was due to the seriousness and philosophical rigor of her book, a book which has deeply impacted my way of thinking. While reading this important work, I became so critically engaged that I felt challenged to reread it. What became clear to me is that *Forming/Thinking/Writing* is not merely a text about composition theory, or reading and writing, but is about far more. In this book, Ann Berthoff elevates the discourse of composition theory to a philosophical level with which I completely identify. Her refusal to fall prey to false dichotomies that blindly separate creative and expository prose, her insistence in validating unique and personal experiences, her brilliant elaboration of the important theory of imagination, her courage to take risks, her willingness to constantly question, and her theoretical rigor characterize her as a great thinker who has contributed immensely to the advancement of a theoretical framework which has enabled us to critically evaluate and understand our praxis.

The present festschrift is far more than a book to honor Ann Berthoff. It is a real testimony of the deep impact she has had on the many scholars who have not only rigorously and passionately accepted her thinking, but who have also, at the same time, been challenged by its force and brilliance. Rather than describing here each and every chapter in this festschrift, I will challenge the possible reader to critically read and reread each essay with the same seriousness and rigor with which they were written. For example, the important themes and issues raised by Eleanor Kutz in "The Discovery of Meaning" and by Vivian Zamel in "Thinking Beyond Imagination: Participating in the Process of Knowing" challenge the reader in much the same way as Ann Berthoff's work does. These two chapters are but representative of the other excellent ones in the book, all of which are indispensable reading for anyone interested in pedagogy, composition theory, and literacy. In her essay, Louise Smith insists that teaching is not imparting right meanings but creating them through, in Gadamer's phrase, a dialogical "fusion of horizons." In so doing, she captures the essence of Ann Berthoff's philosophy.

The importance of this festschrift emerges in many ways. It emerges in the words of Judith Goleman, who reminds us of the Marxian dialectical procedure "of looking for the logic of a text's representations—the relations of the said and the not-said, the seen and not-seen, the known and the not-known—in the context of specific overdetermined social contradictions." Through their exceptional contributions to this book her colleagues and friends have more than raised themselves to Ana's required methodological and theoretical rigor. I need not reiterate the importance of this festscrift. Its importance stems from the brilliance of Ann Berthoff's philosophy and work and is reflected in every chapter in this book written in her honor.

I cannot think of a better way to continue to honor my friend Ana Berthoff than to critically immerse ourselves in the brilliant methodological and theoretical discussions throughout this book. Over and over again in this festscrift I came across themes that are very dear to me. These themes remind us that literacy is not reading and writing words in and of themselves, as if the reading and writing of words did not imply another reading, anterior to and simultaneous with the first—the reading of reality itself.

Paulo Freire

Acknowledgments

This festschrift celebrates the work of Ann E. Berthoff, whom its contributors have known as scholar, writer, mentor, friend. She has taught all of us, some in her NEH Seminar held at the University of Massachusetts in the summer of 1980, others at professional meetings, others in hallway conversations, almost everyone in her honest red jottings in the margins of our works in progress. Our first acknowledgment, then, is to her.

Most of us have exchanged drafts of these essays with fellow contributors, and we are thankful for one another's help. For the authors' graciousness in receiving my questions and suggestions and for the advice of John Brereton, Donaldo Macedo, and Debra San, who know how things should be done, I am especially grateful. The College of Arts and Sciences, University of Massachusetts at Boston, provided time for me to correspond with the authors. I thank Peter Stillman for helping with editorial matters, and, most of all, Bob Boynton for not only welcoming the project, but patiently seeing it through.

Introduction

The poems and essays in this book are meant to be, as George Herbert wrote in 1633, "a wreathèd garland of deservèd praise," one we offer to Ann Berthoff in homage to her intellectual integrity and to the vitality of the issues she addresses. We invite you to read it as a garland, following the strands you see. The six poems may be read together in order; each may also be read individually, as an epigraph to the cluster of essays it precedes. The first cluster considers how academic and political institutions shape meanings. The second examines how meanings emerge—out of chaos, out of presupposition—in the mind's eye; and the third describes creation of meanings through the acts of individual and collective minds. The fourth cluster presents multiple perspectives on how meaning affects, and effects, language change. The last tells of the fluidity of meanings, how our letting go can help us hold them.

But strands reach into neighboring clusters, too: James Slevin's with Robert Holland's and Susan Wells'; David Bartholomae's with Angela Dorenkamp's and Sandra Schor's; Philip Keith's with Paul Kameen's; Mariolina Salvatori's with Eleanor Kutz's; and so on, in ways that might be traced here were it not for the danger of taking the garland out of our readers' hands. Instead, we hope that reading this book will be like teaching writing, as Marie Ponsot describes it in "Keeping the Door Open," the introduction to her poems:

> Teaching writing is very like writing a poem. Both acts require us to take all the elements into account at once. Nothing comes first; everything is central; everything matters. All the electric connections of the mind are switched on—and, in a good class, that current identifies the workers as it both individuates and unifies the work.

I

Not Academic

Teaching, of course, is holding open
the door and staying out of the way.
Knowledge, its long wandering, brings the stubborn
human love of learning into play.
Sun beyond the door empties the cavern;
a healthy animal hates idleness.

For me, it's not that easy, I confess.
Though I keep hands off the landscape, I invent
local names for the grace the air deflects.
Yes, perception is a private instrument;
each mental sun illuminates a text
that recombines all letters of intent.
Yet, at threshold, I talk talk talk, to ignore
the cure for talk beyond that other door
we students are all headed for.

MARIE PONSOT

1

Genre Theory, Academic Discourse, and Writing Within Disciplines

JAMES F. SLEVIN

Georgetown University

A particular function (scientific, technical, commentarial, business, everyday) and the particular conditions of speech communication specific for each sphere give rise to particular genres, that is, certain relatively stable thematic, compositional, and stylistic types of utterance.

Utterances are not indifferent to one another, and are not self-sufficient; they are aware of and mutually reflect one another. These mutual reflections determine their character. . . . Every utterance must be regarded primarily as a *response* to preceding utterances of the given sphere (we understand the word "response" here in the broadest sense). Each utterance refutes, affirms, supplements, and relies on the others, presupposes them to be known, and somehow takes them into account.

M. M. Bakhtin, "The Problem of Speech Genres"

The questions that I want to consider are these: How are individual acts of producing and reading texts related to one another? How do genres, discursive institutions, make these relations possible? What values, beliefs, and ways of interpreting the world inhere in the discursive forms students practice and in the process of learning them? And what *kind* of

critical awareness of these values and interpretive strategies do students
need in order to produce and not just parody these forms?

I will address these questions by exploring the obstacles that confront
current efforts to establish the importance of writing and the respectability
of its teaching and scholarly study. I will begin by considering the problem
inherent in developing systematic investigations of *particular* uses of language, and I will suggest a solution derived from genre theory. My purpose
here will be to situate the activities of writing and the teaching of writing
in a more central position within our educational aims. I will then look
at some recent trends in literary theory, examining the post-structuralist
interest in the rhetorical tradition. Instead of rejoicing at the apparent
promise of a blissful union of literature and composition, I want to examine
carefully this "literary appropriation of rhetoric" and its marked neglect
of textual production. To establish further the teaching of writing as
central to our larger educational goals, I will examine the nature and aims
of university-wide writing programs in the light of the genre theory that
can enrich our understanding of their purposes. Finally, I will return to
what post-structuralist theory *can* contribute to a conception of writing
as the foundation of critical education.

Genre and the Act of Writing

A genre is a received form, part of a cultural code, that synthesizes
discursive features (e.g., subject matter, meaning, organization, style,
and relations between writer and implied/actual audience) in recognizable
ways. These features, which in terms of the "rhetorical situation" we
would describe as *ethos, logos,* and *pathos*, are united within the relatively
stable discursive "type" to offer us a form within which we can locate
ourselves as writers—that is, a form which serves as guide to invention,
arrangement, and stylistic choices in the act of writing.

In "The Problem of Speech Genres," Bakhtin has undertaken a systematic inquiry into "genre" as a concept and the cultural arrangement
of all genres (not just literary or rhetorical, by far the dominant preoccupation of genre theory) as they affect the production as well as the
reception of discourse. He is concerned with "utterances," and their types,
for he understands that "all our utterances have definite and relatively
stable typical *forms of construction of the whole*" (78). Bakhtin's most common
term, "speech genres," may seem restricted to oral types but actually
includes all utterances, written as well as oral. As we will see in a moment,
he is using "speech" in the sense of *parole*, in contrast to *langue* and the
categories used by linguists to analyze systems of "language." Every ut-

terance, all discourse, proceeds from, and is made possible by, the generic resources of the culture inhabited by a speaker or writer, listener or reader. We acquire speech genres as we do the vocabulary and grammatical structures of our native language, not through dictionaries and grammars, but from receiving and producing discourse.

Tzvetan Todorov emphasizes that this process needs to be understood in "institutional" terms:

> In a society, the recurrence of certain discursive properties is institutionalized, and individual texts are produced and perceived in relation to the norm constituted by this codification. A genre, literary or otherwise, is nothing but this codification of discursive properties. (162)

That is, a genre is an inherited social form, a "discursive institution," within which a writer fuses meaning, structure, linguistic features, and pragmatic purposes and effects. Genres establish rhetorical situations, including relations of power between writer and audience. Understanding them and their institutional contexts is thus indispensable to the teaching of writing.

Such understanding of the activity of writing and its generic underpinnings is often frustrated, however, because we have come to accept uncritically certain views of language and speech that remove the study of discourse from its cultural and interpersonal context. It is precisely that context, and its powerful force within discourse, that Bakhtin seeks to restore through his interest in genre. Stressing that "the *sentence* as a *unit of language* [is] distinct from the *utterance* as a unit of speech communication [*parole*]" (73), Bakhtin argues that this confusion has led us to ignore the situational constraints on our actual efforts to compose and construe discourse:

> Thus, a speaker is given not only mandatory forms of the national language (lexical composition and grammatical structure), but also forms of utterance that are mandatory, that is, speech genres. . . . Therefore, the single utterance, with all its individuality and creativity, can in no way be regarded as a *completely free combination* of forms of language, as is supposed, for example, by Saussure (and by many other linguists after him), who juxtaposed the utterance (*la parole*), as a purely individual act, to the system of language as a phenomenon that is purely social and mandatory. . . . (80–81)

The Saussurian model suggests that only *langue*, and not particular acts of speaking and writing, can be understood systematically; *parole*—writing and speaking as they are actually done—is completely open, free, and so

not susceptible to systematic examination. The best we can do is prescribe
rules or describe discrete practices or proscribe certain infelicities; and all
this, it is assumed, occurs usually at a fairly low level of intellectual
sophistication.

In contrast, Bakhtin argues that conventions and genres of discourse
are social institutions that exercise normative, both constraining and enabling, influence over individual acts of speaking and writing. He focuses
on the inherited system of discursive practices and the actual uses of
discourse. So writing itself becomes theoretically central, and not some
tangential attachment to thought or some arbitrary exercise of competence.
Bakhtin's view of genre helps to establish the study of writing as respect-
able in two crucial ways. First, it offers a basis for the systematic study
of *parole*, of the orders of actual speaking and writing. It can thus enable
a theoretically coherent investigation of how writers choose, emphasize,
and integrate discursive properties according to established and publicly
available codes. Second, it restores language to history, locating it in
typical uses of discourse, which are always historical. In doing this, it
challenges the assumption of conventional linguistics that only language
as a system can have a history because individual acts of speaking and
writing are too promiscuous to be classified or to suffer even narrative
arrangement.

Academic Genres and the Literary
Appropriation of Rhetoric

By focusing on utterance and the system of genres from which each
utterance proceeds, we gain a clearer sense of how university writing
programs can best empower students to understand and master their
writing and reading. In this regard, we share a common interest with
many in literary studies who have long concerned themselves with genre,
and more recently with the genres of academic institutions and the initiation of students into certain discursive practices. Literary scholars interested in contextualizing not simply the literature studied but the
contemporary institutional site of that study have begun examining how
training in literary criticism proceeds, examining the conventions and
aims of critical discourse.

For literary theorists, however, genre categories serve primarily to
explore acts of reading. They are concerned with how genres enable readers
to set interpretations within literary-historical contexts, guiding our response to, and in some ways our evaluation of, literary works. This goal,
however worthy, is limited in its usefulness. First, we need to be concerned

not just with literary genres but with the whole range of discursive forms, literary and non-literary, elevated and popular. Second, most contemporary genre theory is concerned almost exclusively with interpretation, the processes of reception, and the grouping of texts by critics. Considerations of how *writers* use genre are scarce, primarily because it is a difficult process to trace but also because this kind of investigation is not much encouraged within the current practice of English Studies.

Moreover, recent ventures by literary critics into the tradition of rhetorical study discourage rather than assist our understanding of textual production. Terry Eagleton's *Literary Theory: An Introduction* can serve as a familiar example of this tendency. In his conclusion, he sets forth a representative version of this view, parts of which are quite satisfactory, as here:

> Becoming certificated by the state as proficient in literary studies is a matter of being able to talk and write in certain ways. It is this which is being taught, examined and certificated, not what you personally think or believe, though what is thinkable will of course be constrained by the language itself. You can think or believe what you want, . . . provided that [it is] compatible with, and can be articulated within, a specific form of discourse. It is just that certain meanings and positions will not be articulable within it. Literary studies, in other words, are a question of the signifier, not of the signified. (201)

In various parts of English Studies now, one can find this concern with education as an apprenticeship in discursive practices. Teachers so concerned assume that *what* is learned is less important than mastering the genres of academic discourse, especially written genres. Because academic success much depends on how you control this standard discourse, such teachers concentrate on the development of students' powers to handle the genres and conventions of those discourses common to their particular discipline.

For Eagleton, to teach English Studies demands first an ideological choice about your own and your students' relationship to dominant forms of discourse. But since, in his view, "established" literary criticism, as a social institution, generally aligns itself with reactionary discursive practices and educational goals, he proposes a theoretical and pedagogical alternative to this dominant model. I have called this move the "literary appropriation of rhetoric," for Eagleton's alternative

> is, in fact, probably the oldest form of "literary criticism" in the world, known as rhetoric. Rhetoric, which was the received form of critical

analysis all the way from ancient society to the eighteenth century, examined the way discourses are constructed in order to achieve certain effects. It was not worried about whether its objects of enquiry were speaking or writing, poetry or philosophy, fiction or historiography: its horizon was nothing less than the field of discursive practices in society as a whole, and its particular interest lay in grasping such practices as forms of power and performance . . . largely unintelligible outside the social purposes and conditions in which they were embedded. (205–6)

In Eagleton's hands, Aristotle, Quintilian, and Cicero have served human understanding primarily to the extent that they have anticipated Foucault. Others—many interested in deconstruction and semiotics— undertake a similar "rescue" of rhetoric, and for some of the same reasons as Eagleton offers. But even Eagleton's style here, particularly his reliance on personification, unintentionally exposes what is missing from his approach. In his summary, it is a personified "Rhetoric" that has acted, that has "examined the way discourses are constructed," that has "worried about" and "grasped" the forms and power relations of language use. In personifying rhetoric, Eagleton not only states but dramatizes a removal *from* rhetoric *of* real, live, practicing writers—and how they practice and how they learned to practice so. Ironically, Eagleton's book has been well received by those who are primarily concerned with teaching writing, presumably because any privileged discourse or discourser seeking to resurrect the rhetorical tradition might be seen as an ally. But perhaps we should be more alert to what is missing in Eagleton's work, what he barely touches upon.

There was, of course, a reason why rhetoric bothered to analyze discourses. . . . Rhetoric wanted to find out the most effective ways of pleading, persuading and debating, and rhetoricians studied such devices in other people's language in order to use them more productively in their own. It was, as we would say, a "creative" as well as a "critical" activity. (206–7)

What seems a bow to the "creative" practice of effective discourse is actually little more than a nodding off, and the subject of how and why real people actually go about producing real discourse, by far the dominant concern of traditional rhetoric, is dropped in Eagleton's literary version of a recovered "rhetoric." (He devotes barely a paragraph to it in his lengthy concluding chapter.) While he and other literary figures interested in rhetoric concern themselves with the social origins of texts, they are not so concerned with how individuals work to originate them. While they study how texts affect readers, and to some extent how social contexts determine these works, they rarely consider how writers actually produce their texts within these powerful social and cultural constraints.

And why, really, should we *expect* Eagleton to address these matters? His own status in the profession of English Studies confirms his analysis of normative discursive practice within it: his concern to analyze and contextualize the process of textual reception, his concern, that is, with "reading," inhabits forms of discourse, signifiers, that are entirely (to use his felicitous term) "certificated" by the institution of English Studies. As Raymond Williams has noted in characterizing current trends in criticism, "it is significant that the tolerance accorded . . . 'reading-public' studies is usually *not* extended to studies of the economics and politics of writing, . . . " (216). Indeed, Eagleton has no interest in writing or "composition" because the discourses about these subjects are generally *not* "certificated" and thus remain entirely beyond his range of awareness. So Eagleton's research and writing function in some ways as a custodian of established, normative discourse, because, if only by his silence on the matter, he excludes the process of constructing, learning to construct, and teaching others to construct texts. As a result, his conception of a rhetorical education, and perhaps even his understanding of the origins of discourse, are impoverished.

I am making the institutionally discreditable claim that, given their own positions, Eagleton and others like him have much to learn from research devoted to these issues, research that originates from within the academy's classrooms and that concerns the educational practices of discursive initiation and apprenticeship about which Eagleton only speculates. Composition researchers, especially those directing or participating in university-wide writing programs, have studied and assessed the normative discourse of various disciplines, deriving their generalizations from faculty (and their writing) in different fields. Others have examined papers written by students and how they compose them, studying how these "apprentices" try to approximate academic genres and where and why they succeed or fall short. They also have gone on to study the educational process whereby students actually become—or fail to become—competent in the various genres of academic discourse. This ample body of research looks at the specific discursive norms of institutions and the actual practice of young writers who experience, day to day, both the intimidations and the intellectual possibilities involved in meeting those norms. In short,

they explore precisely the area of rhetoric that Eagleton and other literary theorists currently neglect—the concern of rhetoricians "to find
out the most effective ways of pleading, persuading and debating, . . .
in order to use them more productively in their own [discourse]."

Theories of Genre and University-wide Writing Programs

These research activities are important in themselves, but they are
important as well for what they contribute to contemporary investigations
of academic genres, institutionalized learning, and the larger relationship
between discursive modes and the social structures they inhabit. It is
crucial for everyone in English Studies to understand more fully that the
central concerns of post-structuralist critical theorists have also been addressed, and their findings can be enriched, by the work of many composition specialists. This is especially apparent in university-wide writing
programs, where the diversity of disciplines and pedagogical approaches
has virtually compelled a critical investigation of all our assumptions
about writing and its place in the life of academic disciplines.

But, if the literary appropriation of rhetoric minimizes the traditional
concern of rhetoricians with the act of writing and the process of learning
to write, many writing programs de-contextualize the practice of these
genres, and so discourage the critical examination of them that is at the
heart of post-structuralist theory. What we need is a theory of genre that
retains the concern with discursive types and cultural and institutional
contexts, but which attends as well to the production of these forms.

Such concerns with genre have a direct effect on how we conceive of
and implement a university-wide writing program, because they bear on
certain fundamental attitudes that faculty members in all disciplines generally bring to the question of *student* writing. The problem here is essentially theoretical, having to do with the relationship between writing
and reading and the place of both within those intellectual communities
we call "academic disciplines." Most university teachers seem to build
their conception of student writing in ways that separate it from their
own writing and from the other activities in their courses. Student writing
is perceived, simply, as a neutral means toward the expression of thought.
What counts is *what* the student knows, as if *how* she knows (the way of
reading that becomes the way she writes, the way of writing that so
profoundly influences the way she reads and thinks, and the "responsive"
situation that precedes and follows her discourse) were a problem different

in kind. Such a view of discourse removes writing from the context in which it occurs.

A distinction will clarify the problem here and the way some writing programs often perpetuate rather than address this problem. I take it that the notion of a *curriculum*, developed to meet the needs of *learners*, is centered on university courses and programs, while the notion of a *discipline* is centered on a sphere of discursive practices (writing, reading, talking) which derive from a shared way of knowing the world and communicating and debating that knowledge. With regard to the teaching of writing, then, I would distinguish between the concept of *writing across the curriculum* and the concept of *writing within disciplines*. Those concerned with the former, writing across the curriculum, look for general practices, common procedures for teaching writing that will work in all sorts of courses; so they offer generalizations about the writing process and cognitive growth. These are, of course, important, but they are also insufficient, for they consider writing solely as it enables students to learn particular material ("writing to learn"). Writing-across-the-curriculum programs respond to the question: How can we help our students successfully master academic genres so that they can learn what we want them to learn and demonstrate that mastery in all areas of the curriculum?

In contrast, the concept of writing within disciplines asks: What would happen if we followed an alternative view of academic genres, one that is centered on the writer's active, contributing participation in an educational community? Bakhtin helps us to construct that alternative when he discusses the "inherently responsive" nature of textual understanding:

> The fact is that when the listener [or reader] perceives and understands the meaning (the language meaning) of speech [or writing], he simultaneously takes an active, responsive attitude toward it. He either agrees or disagrees with it (completely or partially), augments it, applies it, prepares for its execution, and so on. . . . Any understanding is imbued with response and necessarily elicits it in one form or another; the listener becomes the speaker. (68)

In line with this relationship between reading and writing, "writing within disciplines" begins with a different question: When a political scientist, or historian, or philosopher discusses the writing she studies and teaches (e.g., the texts of Locke and Hume) and the scholarly and student writing which intends to say something convincing about those texts, what does she mean by *writing* and how are these various texts related to one another? When we talk about "writing" in philosophy, we mean not only student papers on Locke or on the epistemological issues

Locke raises and addresses, but also *Locke's* writing and the writing of those who study Locke.

All of this writing is part of the system of genres that operates within what Bakhtin terms a particular "cultural sphere." Every discipline constitutes such a sphere, enclosed by the larger sphere of "academic discourse." Each work within a particular sphere has a dialogical relationship, usually made possible by their generic affinities, with other works—not only those that precede but also those that follow it. Bakhtin notes that

> The work, like the rejoinder in dialogue, is oriented toward the response of the other (others), toward his active responsive understanding, which can assume various forms: educational influence on the readers, persuasion of them, critical responses, influence on followers and successors, and so on. [Each work] is related to other work-utterances: both those to which it responds and those that respond to it. (75–76)

Within such a view, a discipline is characterized not simply by its object of inquiry but by principles governing how propositions and questions deriving from that inquiry can properly elicit interest and assent, can legitimately induce in other members of this community the conviction that a particular idea is not only true but also important to consider. To master a particular discipline is to understand how one effects understanding, concern, agreement, and debate there, and the study of writing and rhetoric is thus central to every discipline. To know a discipline is to know, through attention to writing and the disciplinary genres that shape it, how one forms the truth, makes it understood and persuasive, and thereby contributes to the collaborative, historically unfolding inquiry undertaken by the community that is that discipline.

This conception of writing within disciplines embraces student, teacher, and canonical writing, and studies all of it *as writing*. Within such a view, every discipline is essentially historical, and its history is a history of discourse that responds and leads to other discourse. Students thus face these critical questions: How do you learn to read so that you can enter this history, join this dialogue? How do you learn to write so that you can shape this dialogue, effecting assent, disagreement, further questioning, and so on? In other words, how do you learn to write so that your writing elicits other writing? Learning to respond critically and to summon such response from others is what it *means* to learn a discipline, for this is how a student, through such reading and writing, joins the historical dialogue. This theoretical perspective on writing enables a writing program to embrace the whole life of the university and to conceive of it in terms of writing, which is thereby placed at the *center* of its institutional goals.

Within this framework, the scholarly endeavors of a university faculty are not an obstacle to good teaching but a major resource, because the process of writing is at the center of their active participation in their disciplines. University-wide writing programs should be directly related to the research projects and scholarly life of the faculty, exploring the following questions: How does a scholar read in order to respond, and write in order to elicit response? What are the discursive genres and conventions that govern and enable this kind of reading and writing? And (then) how do we involve students in this process and enable them to understand these genres, produce them, question them, and not just survive them? In the context of these questions, the faculty, instead of seeing their scholarship as relevant only to the *content* of their courses, will see that the activity of their scholarly work is directly relevant to the way they can talk to students about writing. They can draw upon their scholarly activity—their writing and reading within a discourse community—as resources in their work with student writing.

Within such a conception of scholarship and teaching in an educational community, the place of writing is altered, serving a function not only in the student's learning but as an activity essential to the advancement of knowledge within the disciplines and within the larger educational community. When writing is in this way made central to the life of a university, students can be encouraged and enabled not just to practice writing within disciplines but also to question the purposes of such writing and to examine critically the institutionalized training in reading and writing that they are experiencing.

Critical Education and the Blurring of Genres

Such a concern with the *production* of texts within particular disciplines and within the academy as a whole constitutes an important supplement to the analysis of textual reception and signifying practices that someone like Eagleton offers. Students need more than inspiring theory and interpretive strategies if they are to become not just readers of dominant signifying practices but also writers who can form—and make persuasive—their own discourse. In the italicized sections of the first passage I quoted from *Literary Theory*, Eagleton describes the constraining power of institutional discourse, noting that "what is thinkable will of course be constrained by the language itself" and that "It is just that certain meanings and positions will not be articulable within [such discourse]."

Understanding and also transcending these constraints are very much at the heart of his project, but neither this understanding nor this transcendence can ever be attained *only* from *interpreting* texts, no matter how attentive that interpretation might be to larger contexts. Such constraints must be experienced and reflected upon from within one's own writing, which requires that student writing be an integral and *equal* part of any course—precisely the aim of "writing within disciplines." Without this attention to writing, post-structuralist educational goals will do little more than reproduce (in a different ideological form, at best; at worst, merely with different ideological terms) the formulaic interpretive ingenuity that marks the educational agenda it critiques.

On the other hand, people in composition, and especially those actively involved in university-wide writing programs, have something crucial to learn from the work of Eagleton. If students are to understand and control their writing, and not just *adapt* it to the signifying system we call "academic discourse," they will need to do more than successfully imitate its surface form or receive instruction in its conventions. That is, they need to do more than simply manipulate this discourse. Rather, they need to engage fully in its production, to question it, perhaps even to challenge its purposes—in effect, they need to become involved in the kind of analysis which composition scholars and teachers themselves often undertake. Students might even be moved to deepen that analysis, questioning the metaphors of apprenticeship and initiation that govern much of our thinking about how they are supposed to learn. In short, students, teachers, and even some composition scholars need to become the kinds of readers (of discourses and institutions) that Eagleton advocates, thinking critically about the situation in which they try to understand and produce the language of currency.

This process of critical examination, combined with the continuing, active production of texts derived from personal engagement in the scholarly life of the discipline, is more important than mere fluency in the dominant forms and is, at any rate, indispensable to their mastery. Such a critical examination does not entail a particular (that is, an "antiestablishment") judgment about these forms. One doesn't, after all, engage in this critique simply because one dislikes the institution or wants others to dislike it, although that might be a "hidden agenda" of some who advocate it. Rather, we engage in this critical examination simply because we *must* if we really want to understand these forms. Students might conclude that apprenticing themselves to these forms, accepting them and using them, is an entirely desirable choice, but it will be a different kind of choice if they are fully aware, through their own active investigation and analysis, of why they decide to do that. It is simply the case that the process of critical education must examine, critically, that education itself as a social and institutional practice among others.

If for no other reason, this enterprise seems to me necessary if we are, in fact, to prepare our students for the world of academic disciplines as they now exist. Clifford Geertz, in his discussion of the blurring of genres in contemporary intellectual discourse, concentrates on what he terms "the refiguration of social thought." Geertz notes:

> This genre blurring is more than just a matter of Harry Houdini or Richard Nixon turning up as characters in novels or of midwestern murder sprees described as though a gothic romancer had imagined them. It is philosophical inquiries looking like literary criticism (think of Stanley Cavell on Beckett or Thoreau, Sartre on Flaubert), scientific discussions looking like belles lettres *morceaux* (Lewis Thomas, Loren Eiseley), baroque fantasies presented as deadpan empirical observations (Borges, Barthelme), histories that consist of equations and tables or law court testimony (Fogel and Engerman, Le Roi Ladurie), documentaries that read like true confessions (Mailer), parables posing as ethnographies (Castenada), theoretical treatises set out as travelogues (Levi-Strauss), ideological arguments cast as historiographical inquiries (Edward Said), epistemological studies constructed like political tracts (Paul Feyerabend), methodological polemics got up as personal memoirs (James Watson). . . .
>
> [T]he present jumbling of varieties of discourse has grown to the point where it is becoming difficult either to label authors (What *is* Foucault—historian, philosopher, political theorist? What is Thomas Kuhn—historian, philosopher, sociologist of knowledge?) or to classify works. . . . It is a phenomenon general enough and distinctive enough to suggest that what we are seeing is not just another redrawing of the cultural map—the moving of a few disputed borders, the marking of some more picturesque mountain lakes—but an alteration of the principles of mapping. Something is happening to the way we think about the way we think. (19–20)

For Ann Berthoff, Geertz's concluding point, that "Something is happening to the way we think about the way we think," is what education *means*. And its meaning is relevant to how we help students to examine and control the academy's discursive practices. Academic genres and conventions are not, especially now, stable entities outside of history. The genres and conventions of academic discourse are themselves historical; they change, and perhaps the change we are now experiencing is the most profound and rapid since the Renaissance. The whole issue of what the academic genres are, of what "the historian does" or what "sociologists do" or what "literary critics undo" is confused and confusing, not just for beginners but for us—or at least for me.

So the critical study of academic genres, a study that questions them as well as masters them, indeed masters them by both writing within them and contextualizing them, is pedagogically necessary for two reasons: (1) this active, productive, writing-centered experience is consistent with how we really learn, as opposed to just absorbing what others give us, no matter how complex and sophisticated the gift; (2) students, to be prepared for the variety of expectations, and even the "blurring" of expectations, they will encounter, need not so much to be told about and practice *our* understanding of academic genres (which might be wrong and will probably soon be out of date) as to participate in their making, examining critically, on their own, the nature of those genres and the generic basis for thinking, reading, and writing in the disciplines they engage.

Works Cited

Bakhtin, M. M. "The Problem of Speech Genres." *Speech Genres and Other Late Essays*. Trans. Vern W. McGee. Ed. Caryl Emerson and Michael Holquist. Austin: U of Texas P, 1986. 60–102.

Eagleton, Terry. *Literary Theory: An Introduction*. Minneapolis: U of Minnesota P, 1983.

Geertz, Clifford. "Blurred Genres: The Refiguration of Social Thought." *Local Knowledge: Further Essays in Interpretive Anthropology*. New York: Basic, 1983. 19–35.

Todorov, Tzvetan. "The Origin of Genres." *New Literary History* 8 (1976): 159–70.

Williams, Raymond. "Beyond Cambridge English." *Writing in Society*. London: Verso, 1983. 212–26.

2

Knowing Our Knowledge
A Phenomenological Basis
for Teacher Research

C. H. KNOBLAUCH AND LIL BRANNON
State University of New York, Albany

Speaking more than half a century ago of Heisenberg's famous "principle of indeterminacy" in quantum theory, the British astronomer Sir Arthur Eddington characterized the "new epistemology" of high-energy particle physics: "the world of physics is a world contemplated from within, surveyed by appliances which are part of it and subject to its laws. What the world might be deemed like if probed in some supernatural manner by appliances not furnished by itself we do not profess to know" (Eddington 225). Heisenberg's principle, the startling insight that it is impossible to ascribe simultaneously both exact position and exact velocity to a particle, derived from his recognition that the *object* of observation and the *medium* of observation in physics are comprised of the same world-stuff: the particle one wishes to "see" is observable only by means of the photons (packets of energy) which constitute the light that enables it to be "seen." The act of seeing, therefore, has a *material* effect on what is observed, altering it in the very process of focusing on it. Heisenberg himself was entirely conscious of this "fundamental paradox of quantum theory," namely, the inseparableness of observer and object observed, noting that the interdependence, the shared reality of instrument and object, necessarily "emphasizes a subjective element in the description of atomic events, since the measuring device has been constructed by the observer, and we have to remember that what we observe is not nature in itself but nature exposed to our method of questioning" (Heisenberg 57). He adds, citing Niels Bohr (the most eminent of the early theorists in quantum mechanics), that "our scientific work in physics consists in asking questions about nature in the language that we possess. . . . In this way, quantum theory reminds us, as Bohr has put it, of the old wisdom that when searching for harmony in life one must never forget that in the drama of existence we are ourselves both players and spectators" (58).

"In the language that we possess. . . ." The pioneers of quantum mechanics understood very clearly the nature of physical knowledge, a manifestation and consequence of symbolic action, chiefly in the medium of mathematics. Although Heisenberg uses the unfortunate word *subjective*, there is no serious question here of "objective" versus "subjective" knowledge, for these terms are meaningless in the context of the new physics, an erroneous "bifurcation of nature," as Whitehead put it, which misconceives the involvement of human beings in the rest of the phenomenal world. The concept of "objectivity" falsely reifies what is always profoundly human (and therefore interpretive) about our understanding. The concept of "subjectivity" falsely encloses consciousness, separating human understanding from the world that conditions its action even as, reciprocally, it is conditioned by that action. Human beings are not privileged observers outside of phenomenal reality but rather participants within it: they share its physicality and to that extent are constituted by it; they also act upon it through symbols, hence constituting it in human terms. Max Planck, another originator of quantum theory, explains the symbolic character of scientific inquiry in his distinction between the "sensory world" and the "world-image" in physics. A "measurable magnitude," a length, a period of time, a mass or charge, is meaningful, not because it is a "sensory" datum, but because it is the product of an instrument, a product that can be "denoted by definite mathematical symbols with which we can operate in accordance with exact rules." The error of classical physics, he argues, lay in the assumption that a wave, for instance, is "a definite physical process," whereas in quantum physics "it really denotes no more than the probability that a certain state exists." For Planck, "the world-image contains no observable magnitudes at all; all that it contains is symbols" (54–67).

These insights into the nature of knowledge are, of course, by no means restricted to the esoteric world of quantum physics. Polanyi has represented the same "phenomenological" point of view as a physical chemist; Geertz has offered it in anthropology; Hayden White has proposed it for history, Alton Becker for linguistics, Amadeo Giorgi for psychology, and Paul Rabinow for sociology. Contemporary literary theory, from reader-response to post-structuralism, applies it as a challenge to traditional historicism and the tyranny of the True Reading. What binds together all of these figures and disciplines is the central assumption of any phenomenological inquiry: the inseparableness of observer and object observed, the inevitable reflexivity of human "research"—where nature is seen through instruments which are themselves part of nature, where some range of psychological or social practices is examined by means of other such practices, where language is studied through the medium of linguistic expression. But we are particularly concerned here to suggest the importance of this assumption in modern physics—surely among the hardest of "hard" sciences—by way of coming to a subject that may seem, but is not, far removed: the philosophical legitimacy of so-called "teacher research" both as a true source of knowledge about educational practice and as a stimulus for educational change. Specifically, we want to cite the example of physics in order to confront some popular misconceptions about "scientific research" which currently feed the charged political climate of educational inquiry, leading not only to positivistic arguments about teaching and learning but also to the subordination of teachers (as, at best, "amateur knowers" who should do what "real knowers" tell them) and their typically narrative, non-empirical means of representing the classroom.

We need not waste time proving that the popular understanding of science is far removed from that of Bohr, Heisenberg, and Planck, that it remains in fact positivistic, a hold-over from Lockean arguments about the nature of experiential "data" and the means of ordering them by dispassionate analysis. Stephen Gould has spoken eloquently of the pervasive Western "myth that science . . . is an objective enterprise, done properly only when scientists can shuck the constraints of their culture and view the world as it really is" (21). And Gould's arguments are about *scientists* who have thought in this unreflective way about their work. It is not surprising that government officials, education administrators, school boards, and parents should welcome the alluringly hard "data" of IQ and SAT scores, "fact-finding commissions," and multi-million dollar "research projects," or the seeming promise of competency tests, behavioral objectives, teacher-proof curricula, and "higher standards," when the research establishment itself so self-assuredly promotes and engages in "the mismeasure of man." A glance through issues of *Research in the Teaching of English* for the past ten years will reveal quickly enough the prevailing philosophical attitudes and the investigative rhetoric most valued in current literacy research.[1] A look at the proposals which have attracted federal funding over the past ten years will reinforce the conclusion. It seems to us that the "objectivistic" bias in much educational research today has led both to intellectual error, when essentially interpretive judgments are mistaken as neutral, indeed ontological facts, and to the devaluing of teachers' knowledge, insight, and practice, when unsophisticated confidence in empirical measures authorizes researchers and administrators to impose uncontextualized or narrowly conceived curricula and programs of assessment on schools. The concept of "teacher inquiry," which we wish to examine in a moment, has become popular in recent years specifically as a corrective to this political disenfranchisement of teachers as authentic makers of knowledge and therefore legitimate agents of educational change. Teachers have been properly inspired by the arguments of Ann Berthoff, James Britton, Dixie Goswami, and others, concerning the power and usefulness of their own narrative reflection upon the classroom world. But they must come to terms with the unreceptive public climate that the myth of objectivity has created, and specifically the self-interest of the educational research establishment itself, if they hope to find an effective voice for themselves in promoting educational change. They must become articulate about the assumptions and arguments that make teacher research—the classroom narrative—a plausible mode of knowing if they are to claim the authority in educational policy that they deserve.

An example will make the point. Three years ago, when the National Institute of Education (NIE) announced its competition for funding to develop a Center for the Study of Writing, a group of instructors in the field of literacy at one university, together with consultants from several others, proposed a Center the dominant focus of which would be teacher inquiry. Their proposal was not the only one to include that form of research (and certainly there were many excellent proposals in the competition), but theirs was the only proposal featuring teacher inquiry as the very theme and rationale for a research center. The proposal was refused, but what makes that fact interesting is not the refusal itself (only one was finally accepted) but the explanation for it. "The conception of practitioners as researchers," the NIE letter read, "and of the related activities involved in empowering teachers and practitioners is an untested idea, one that is labeled an 'ideology.' As such, reviewers feel it to be a suitable subject for research but not appropriate as the guiding assumption on which to conceive a research center." In other words, teachers' activities in the classroom can legitimately be scrutinized by "research experts" who possess the requisite methodological sophistication and "objectivity," but teachers themselves have no equivalent expertise in the making of knowledge or ability to reflect on their teaching practices: "the feasibility of theory and model-building within such a practitioner-oriented approach is, thus, questioned. Discussions about 'research into practice' issues lack sufficient understanding of the complexities associated with improving teacher knowledge, creating . . . change, and improving practice."

Aside from the condescending language of the letter from NIE, several appalling assumptions stand out: that "real" science is invariably comprised of "model-building" and "testing"; that only "real" scientists, not teachers, understand the complexities of the world they study (even if they then proceed to overlook those complexities by stripping context from their carefully controlled experiments); and that teachers are merely "ideological" when they speak of making knowledge from their classroom experiences, while "real" science is intrinsically unideological because its methods and conclusions lie, not just beyond personal political interest (what scientist would vie with another over research funding, or a "first" discovery, or professional image?), but also, like Eddington's supernatural observer, beyond even the messy phenomenal world it undertakes to observe. Teacher research has proceeded nonetheless in the face of such attitudes, yet with only minimal funding, very little recognition from politicians or administrators (still less from sanctioned "researchers"), and, not surprisingly, little if any subsequent change in schools. If teachers are to be heard, they will have to go further, becoming more politically active in an arena where the prestige and access to federal funding that educational researchers currently enjoy fuels an energetic will to maintain the mythology that safeguards their standing. Initially, that activism entails an intellectual consciousness of the foundation on which teachers' claims to authority are based. Organized, repeated, conceptual challenges, framed in the language of academic argument, will not by themselves change the distribution of power. But they can establish a dialogue through which that distribution may be negotiated. The academic world is not always characterized by agreement or even mutual esteem; but it is minimally characterized by tolerance of arguments it is unable to refute.

We would begin an argument for the legitimacy of teacher inquiry by insisting on two points. The first is that, if there is a villain to be unmasked, it is not empirical science, given the proper sense of the term "empirical," but rather the positivistic understanding of empiricism. Physics, after all, is preeminently empirical, though also phenomenological in its regard for the interdependence of observer and observed. Positivism, not empirical science, is responsible for that erroneous belief in an absolute objectivity which gives rise to artificial hierarchies of knowledge ("empirical" versus subjective and ideological); to the privileging of certain methods (experiment, "model-building") because their rhetoric is no longer perceived as such; to unreflective belief in the "scientific" report simply because its narrator lurks hidden in the prose; and to unreflective dismissal of the "story," the ethnographic narrative, the classroom "anecdote," because its narrator is more visible and therefore "biased." Bohr and Heisenberg are acutely aware of the narrator of physics, the "story"-teller who produces the data and interprets it according to the rules of that art in order to produce a coherent "text." Geertz understands the narrativity of anthropology and White that of history. But the educational researcher in these times is not always so self-conscious—and is proportionately more willing to dismiss statements that fall outside the rhetoric of objectivity. Again, however, it is not the empirical researcher, even in education, who necessarily falls prey to objectivist mythology. It is rather the positivist researcher, an individual who need not be pursuing empirical research at all, who may in fact be undertaking what some would call "naturalistic" inquiry (not all anthropologists, for instance, assume Geertz's view of the interpretive nature of field work, even when they style themselves ethnographers). Positivism is a frame of mind, not a method: one can view knowledge as an absolute, "objective" entity and still claim "context" among its elements. One can be positivistic *about* context, regarding it as an absolute form or structure that the dispassionate observer "sees" in the world and labels for what it "is." What matters for teacher-researchers is less their learning of a method than their understanding of a point of view about observation that holds regardless of method and that also validates certain methods, such as story-telling, which would, confronted with positivistic assumptions, remain illegitimate because there are "more reliable" ways to do things.

Our second point, indeed, concerns story-telling as a legitimate mode of knowing. Educational "research," whether conducted by social scientists or by classroom teachers, is finally not the same enterprise as research in physics—a point that neither physicists, however they may value their own methods in their own domain, nor enlightened educational inquirers would have trouble conceding were it not for the prejudices of positivism. If the teacher-researcher is equated these days with "naturalistic" or "ethnographic" narrative, it isn't because that style is appropriate to teachers but rather because that style is appropriate to the object of attention—in the case of literacy classrooms, the use and learning of language—even though most "official" educational researchers commend empirical study alone. We will not take on here the question of a proper place for empirical methods, intelligently applied, in educational inquiry despite their context-stripping tendencies. One political reality is that such methods have broad public sanction, whatever their limitations in the human sciences (see Mishler 1979), so that challenging their usefulness is far less effective tactically than a more modest appeal for the equivalent usefulness of ethnographic and other forms of narrative. In any case, it isn't necessary to deny all stature to one mode of knowing in order to authorize another: that is the very error which has placed teachers so low in the false hierarchy of knowledge. The issue at hand is the appropriateness of story as knowledge, given both intellectual and practical reasons for preferring narrative in teacher inquiry over even the most fully self-conscious and context-preserving empirical method.

The concept of "story" can be understood in different ways. The least helpful understanding is also the most popular: a fiction, amusing but untrue, a subjective account, something made up by an "author" rather than found by a "researcher" (as "facts" are), something articulated by a fallible, untrustworthy teller instead of that omniscient, oracular "voice" that delivers the true knowledge of physics, anthropology, or history. A more helpful, and philosophically sounder, understanding is that story (from the Latin *historia*) is a form of narrative, a verbal memory of human experience, a record—a telling—of what life is like. To be sure, one might distinguish "story" from other narratives, such as "history," which are (sometimes) more analytical in their rhetoric and (presumably) more dependent upon "actual" events. One might also distinguish narrative from other verbal modes, the exposition of philosophy, for instance, which emphasizes argument rather than scene, situation, and action-in-time. But these technical distinctions do not imply degrees of reliability or truthfulness—because they do not alter the essential fact that verbal statements, whether stories in the limited sense or not, whether narratives or otherwise, are all *composed* and interpretive, told by someone to someone for a reason. Any narrative, indeed any verbal account (as opposed to a model—like the atom and the DNA molecule—or a mathematical equation), is a "story" at least to the extent that all such statements have "tellers" and employ techniques of verbal composition to form meanings. Hence, people speak easily of the news "story" or the "story" of the Incas, and even the "story" of DNA, intending nothing explicitly fictive by the name. Certainly, it would be uncritical to erase all distinctions between story and other language acts. But the worse error is to deny similarities in order to imply oppositions of truth, fantasy, and falsity. There is value, in other words, to metaphorical extension of the concept of story as a corrective to hierarchical taxonomies of texts and the knowledge they offer.

"Story-telling," in the adapted sense of a verbal practice of composing our understanding, can instructively be extended, for instance, to include

not only fictional narratives but also biographies, historical and ethnographic accounts, philosophical arguments, newspaper articles, research
reports, many textbooks, and numerous other writings that make claims
to factuality or truthfulness despite the conspicuous artifice of their construction, the interpretive quality of their statements, and the (compar-
ative) visibility of their narrators. Given the rhetorical similarities, after
all, a "fictional" story is not so easy to distinguish from a "nonfictional"
one, nor is its truth-value so easy to denigrate in favor of more "objective"
accounts. Is Boswell's *Life of Johnson* factual or fictional? In what sense is
a colorless psychological report on "the guilt mechanism" truer than
Dostoevsky's portrait of Raskolnikov? The central feature of "story" is
surely its interpretive character: Boswell's Johnson is surely an interpretation, and so too any conclusion about the nature of guilt, whether its
source is data tables or the actions of a human being. By such reasoning,
the notion of "story" might be extended even further, if one wished to
direct attention less toward a particular medium (language) and mode
(narrative) than toward the more general features of symbolic action and
formal design which pertain to all forms of knowing (including those
favored in objectivist ideology)—in which case, the model of DNA, the
mathematical equation, the musical composition, the choreographed
dance might also, metaphorically, be called stories, texts, even fictions,
because all derive from and highlight the human capacity to use symbols
in constituting the world. From that perspective, the empirical account
of quanta in physics is not opposed to story-telling but is a particular
kind of story-telling, a powerfully simplified rendering of certain aspects
of human experience, precisely as valuable for its distinctive contributions
as any other means of knowing, and as dependent as any other on the
presence of a story-teller who monitors the plot and chooses the most
telling incidents to further its action.

   The story-telling of the teacher-inquirer in a classroom devoted to
language practices has its peculiar features and makes a distinctive con-
tribution to our knowledge of school experience. The narrator inhabits
the world of the classroom, knows it from the inside, does not "descend"
upon it for a short time, edit out what has been judged irrelevant in
advance, and test its observed particularities against general hypotheses
that have been formulated without reference to it. The telling aims not
at selectivity or simplification but at richness of texture and intentional
complexity. The telling does not seek to highlight problems and solutions,
or causes and effects, or stimuli and responses, or rights and wrongs, or
heroes and villains, but seeks instead to depict, to evoke, what phe-

nomenologists such as Heidegger and Gadamer have called "the life-world"—that palpable, sensual, kaleidoscopic, mysterious reality that constitutes our material rather than merely intellectual existence. Geertz's notion of "thick description" (3–30) formally characterizes the method of story-telling that Goswami and others have advocated for teachers who wish to understand this world: a close observation of the phenomenal reality of the classroom, what it looks like, the objects that define it as a material and social space, how the people in it look, talk, move, relate to each other, the emotional contours of their life together, the things that happen, intellectual exchanges, social understandings and misunderstandings, what the teacher knows, plans, hopes for, and discovers, how different students react, the subtle textures of the teaching experience, the subtle textures of the learning experience. Much of this information would be characterized as subjective and unreliable, given a positivist vantage point on "research"—it would be, and has been, represented as "anecdotal," biased, soft. Even some advocates of teacher inquiry reject "anecdotal" knowledge in favor of more rigorous observation, including the trappings of anthropological method: field notes, multiple observers, the "triangulation" of perceptions. These more elaborate forms of story-telling can be very useful (though time-consuming for already busy teachers) if the intent is to look more intensively, to withhold easy closure, to preserve multiple points of view. But if the reason for their preference is a desire to approach more "objectivity" in the account, which entails yet another capitulation to the positivist frame of mind, then they only serve the interests of those who wish to exclude teachers from "serious" research. To be sure, the anecdote can be sloppy, self-serving, and unreflective; but so can the official ethnographic narrative. Either can also be disciplined, scrupulously honest, and authentically revealing. The important point is that a rich narrative statement about classroom life suits people's intuitive recognition of the complexity of that life; it creates within itself the contextual subtlety, the variegated meaningfulness that people naturally sense about the world as it is lived, not just as it is studied. The knowledge gained from such a statement is itself partly intuitive, a "felt-sense"; its "softness" is genuine and reliable, where the "hardness" of an experimental conclusion often rings false, feels mechanical or oversimplified, whatever its claims to certitude.

What, finally, is the substance and character—and purpose—of the knowledge to be gained from story-telling as the principal mode of teacher inquiry? If it's "research," what exactly is learned? Answering such a question is very like answering the related question about the knowledge gained from literature—the brand of story-telling that everyone recognizes as such. Literature too composes, dramatizes, and construes the life-world. Its knowledge is about the life-world. It values the concrete, communicating by means of evocative detail. It does not fear the ambiguous, the irreconcilable, the oblique or ungraspable, but instead approaches the most fugitive meanings *through* its detail. It does not compromise the real, as lived and felt, merely in order to save intellectual simplicity. The knowledge that literature offers is not cumulative in the way that physical knowledge is: one does not "know more" as each story is added to the others. But one knows "better"; one's instincts and values, expectations and judgments mature. One's ability to read the world grows. Literature enhances the *quality* of understanding without presuming to add to its "content." Also unlike physical knowledge, literature is not self-corrective: that is, one story does not falsify another. It is instead dialogical: stories beget stories; voices mingle and interanimate. The telling of stories helps with the living of life, makes the world more coherent, makes the liver more alert and more generous. Stories cause people to reflect on their circumstances, motivating them to change whatever might jeopardize their living well. That's why literacy—which enables the making and reading of stories in the first place—matters so much.

When teachers tell their stories, produce their own classroom research, similar benefits accrue, initially to themselves, eventually to their students, other teachers, and the rest of us. First, they enact their own reflectiveness about the conditions of their life-world; as Ann Berthoff has repeatedly argued, they come to "know their knowledge." Stories are, among other things, comments upon actions: stories give actions a philosophical dimension, provided that they are both composed and read with the right kind of attentiveness. The habit of reflection that teachers can derive from their inquiries will make their teaching practices more thoughtful, more responsive to students' needs, more deliberately (as opposed to casually) flexible in the face of variable circumstances. As teachers read each other's stories, their sense of shared context and practice, of mutual aspiration, grows, along with an awareness of what needs to be changed—in order to enhance the quality of their own teaching lives and the quality of their collective social reality. At this point, teacher research truly becomes, and truly deserves to become, "an agency for change," as Goswami and others have insisted (*Reclaiming the Classroom*). One of the generative maxims Ann Berthoff offers at the start of *The Making of Meaning*, an observation from Paulo Freire, eloquently sums up this case for teacher inquiry: "The educator is a knowing subject, face to face with other knowing subjects. He can never be a mere memorizer, but a person constantly readjusting his knowledge, who calls forth knowledge from his students. For him, education is a pedagogy of knowing" (15). The teacher as knower, as learner, as agent for change exhibits a social power that many will fear, many legislators, school officials, and university researchers, because their own positions of authority and prestige stand to be challenged as such an ideal is realized. The docile teacher is a comfortable instrument for the designs of others. But students, and through them most of the rest of us, can only profit from critically conscious, informed, and self-directed teachers whose knowledge of the making of knowledge lies at the heart of learning and therefore the heart of our growth as a literate society.

Note

1. Arthur Applebee, current editor of *Research in the Teaching of English*, has recently published an editorial statement about teacher inquiry in education ("Musings . . . Teachers and the Process of Research," *RTE*, 21 (Feb., 1987): 5–7). The statement makes explicit a self-image in the research establishment that has long been dominant but seldom so directly asserted. While not denying the value of teacher knowledge, Applebee is intent upon showing the "different professional expertise" of the "researcher," specifically the "disciplinary rigor" that characterizes research. The teacher, he says, "is inevitably an imperfect researcher," because she or he lacks both a "detached, observational stance" and the requisite "methodological and disciplinary skills." Although Applebee's argument does not set out to belittle teachers, it clearly proceeds from the *topos* of "separate but equal," a tactic which is most likely to be applied whenever the more equal are addressing the less equal. Intellectually, the argument presumes clear-cut distinctions between teacher knowledge and researcher knowledge which cannot withstand scrutiny, while also relying on concepts of "detached observation" and "methodological skill" which belong at least as much to the self-serving rhetoric of educational research as to its practice. The political motivation of the Applebee statement seems apparent to us. Its power is apparent as well, given Applebee's authority and the prestige of his journal.

Works Cited

Berthoff, Ann E. *The Making of Meaning*. Portsmouth, NH: Boynton/Cook, 1981.

Eddington, Sir Arthur. *Nature of the Physical World*. Ann Arbor: U of Michigan P, 1958.

Geertz, Clifford. *The Interpretation of Cultures*. New York: Basic, 1973.

Goswami, Dixie and Peter Stillman, Eds. *Reclaiming the Classroom*. Portsmouth, NH: Boynton/Cook, 1986.

Gould, Stephen Jay. *The Mismeasure of Man*. New York: Norton, 1981.
Heisenberg, Werner. *Physics and Philosophy: The Revolution in Modern Science*. New York: Harper, 1958.
Mishler, Elliot G. "Meaning in Context: Is There Any Other Kind?" *Harvard Educational Review* 49 (1979): 1–19.
Planck, Max. *The Philosophy of Physics*. New York: Norton, 1936.

3

Burke
and the Tradition
of Democratic Schooling

JOHN CLIFFORD

University of North Carolina, Wilmington

What avail is it to win . . . ability to read and write, if in the process the individual loses his own soul.

John Dewey, *Experience and Education*

Pedagogy always echoes epistemology: the way we teach reflects the conception we have of what knowledge is and does.

Ann Berthoff, *The Making of Meaning*

"Correctness" of form depends on ideology.

Kenneth Burke, *Counter-Statement*

The inescapable molding influence of the culture into which we are born is an extremely important concept.

Louise Rosenblatt, *Literature As Exploration*

As Gerald Graff's *Professing Literature* relentlessly demonstrates, the dominant conversation in English Studies has been largely influenced by traditional voices urging us to prepare students for a seamless transition from the university's life of the mind to the values of competition and efficiency that inhere in our capitalist economy. Fifty years ago John Dewey characterized this kind of conventional education as concerned with "bodies of information and of skills that have been worked out in the past; therefore, the chief business of the school is to transmit them to the new generation" (17). Dewey reveals the hidden consequences of this strategy

29

by perceptively noting that "since the subject matter as well as standards of proper conduct are handed down from the past, the attitude of pupils must, upon the whole, be one of docility, receptivity, and obedience" (18). Anticipating what could still be said about most instruction in reading and writing, Dewey criticizes this traditional view of knowledge as "essentially static. It is taught as a finished product, with little regard either to the ways in which it was originally built up or to changes that will surely occur in the future" (19).

Especially in English Studies the positivist implications of this abstract theme are made concrete by teachers who conceive of language as a neutral vehicle for presenting a world which is objectively out there, beyond our confounding subjectivities. This suggests that in reading literature they believe meaning is located within texts, in the unresolved tensions and ambiguities of syntax, image and trope, unmediated through the hearts and minds of socially situated readers. In traditional writing classes structures are thought to pre-exist unproblematically, suggesting that form is a neutral container into which meaning can be poured. Writing, one's own disciplinary discourse and the writing of students, is in this formulation also thought to be uncontaminated by the unnerving political winds swirling "outside" the university's walls.

As philosophically grim as all this appears, Diane Macdonell points out in her study of ideology and discourse that there are always contradictions in the dominant conversation, always opposing voices, redirecting our attention away from hegemonic accommodation. It must be fought for and sustained, but there is always a space for voices of struggle and resistance. One of the earliest and most lucid is clearly John Dewey's, whose validation of personal experience as an instructional resource affirmed diversity while also uncovering the crucial connection between school and society. His attempt to deconstruct the walls written around the university has been an important move for educators hoping to make "society a function of education," hoping to produce individuals capable of critical consciousness. To deepen the notion that one's experiences are intellectually and politically empowering, Dewey also urged the "participation of the learner in the formation of the purposes which direct his activities in the learning process" (67), a collaborative strategy that has been a linchpin in progressive thinking ever since.

But Dewey went only so far, limiting his reformist vision to a general educational philosophy. Henry Giroux notes that "Dewey's struggle for democracy was primarily pedagogical" (238), while Frank Lentricchia, who sees Dewey mainly as a pragmatist with a healthy distrust for repressive structures, finds his underwriting of the "capitalist spirit" troublesome (3). It remained for other thinkers, Kenneth Burke, for example, to deepen Dewey's limited social perspective by making more explicit the connections among education, discourse, and politics. And in the same progressive tradition Louise Rosenblatt created a pragmatic perspective on reception theory that affirmed, within the parameters of acceptable classroom strategy, the value of the active, engaged and socially conscious reader. In writing theory Ann Berthoff has also extended this tradition by stressing a Freirean pedagogy of knowing that urges us to be scrupulously reflexive in understanding our understandings, that privileges context and perspective as interpretive tools, that sees language not as a mirror or objective instrument but as a rich heuristic. These three theorists have for several generations been directly and indirectly conversing with Dewey's texts, perhaps arguing with his political timidity here, agreeing with his distrust of custom and authority there, but always incrementally helping us to move between the speculative power of abstraction and the instructional specifics of the struggle within schools for an empowering pedagogy that might create a truly democratic society.

Although it is often assumed that a heightened socio-political awareness in English Studies began to surface around 1968 and, after five years or so, went into a period of dormancy, to be resuscitated during the liberal backlash against Reagan's conservative agenda, now, as Patricia Bizzell notes, "social" is a central concept, "the key word" at the 1985 CCCC. But for decades there has been Kenneth Burke, whose work is permeated with a keenly contemporary socio-political perspective of how reading and writing are always more than they seem, always tossed by political winds. The difficulty the profession has always had with Burke and his politics stems from our formalist theories of reading, especially the tendencies to look for propositions that are clearly supported for textual continuity and coherence, for unity and clarity. But that is not his way.

In fact, Kenneth Burke gives us a surprisingly contemporary perspective on reading and, consequently, apt advice on how best to approach his seemingly enigmatic texts. In *Counter-Statement*, for example, Burke notes that "any reader surrounds each word and each act in a work . . . with a unique set of his own previous experiences (and therefore a unique set of imponderable emotional responses)" (78). This approach allows us to read him, as he himself urges, according to our own appetites. Meaning will occur, he suggests, in the "margin of overlap" between reader and text, in the interaction between the assumptions and values that are invariably brought *to* the reading experience. This sounds remarkably like the response theories of Louise Rosenblatt, most recently given a post-structualist twist by Kathleen McCormick in *College English* when she claims that not only does meaning result from a matching of literary and ideological repertoires, but that texts are "always already driven by particular theoretical assumptions"; consequently, responses to these texts must always be interested (849).

This perspective goes a long way toward explaining why there are so many varied readings of Burke. The dynamics of C. S. Peirce's triadicity tells us why Wayne Booth finds Burke a model for pluralistic criticism, why Frank Lentricchia's socialist inclinations permit him to read Burke as a model of the engaged critical intellectual trying both to interpret and to transform a flawed, unreasonable social order, and why Ross Winterowd sees in Burke countless examples of the appositional style: replete with representative anecdotes, organizational flexibility, foregrounded style and great presence—qualities Winterowd personally admires and often tries for in his own work. Since Burke encourages our multiplicity, it should not be unusual for those of us interested in a rhetoric with a sociopolitical dimension to see in him traces of ideologically focused thinking. His sophisticated view of language and his emphasis on the social and political context of discourse seem especially compatible with current political and theoretical concerns in English studies.

This is a somewhat different critical tactic than the usual positivist gambit of claiming that previous commentators misread what is clearly in Burke's texts. With a resurgence of interest in the social context of reading and writing, it is simply that the cultural and intellectual context for re-reading Burke has changed; hence, we now see differently. For now I am most interested in the ways our "re-discovery" of the radical Burke extends the progressive ideas of John Dewey while also anticipating the political insights of Michel Foucault and Antonio Gramsci.

It is obvious, however, that this politically radical dimension of Burke's work has been generally ignored or repressed, especially in composition studies. The Burke that survives in our rhetorics has been truncated and neutralized beyond recognition, his comprehensive view of motivation reduced to the pentad, presented merely as a heuristic for exploring topics. Perhaps the politically marginal position of composition theorists within English departments guarantees that only the most utilitarian aspect of his work would enter the mainstream conversation.

It must be admitted, however, that as a theorist Burke's rhetorical ideas do not easily translate into pragmatic solutions for our writing or literature classes. For that we have to turn to Berthoff and Rosenblatt and others able to develop classroom methods capable of blending sophisticated theory with practice. But he does have relevant things to say if we take a wider view of our profession, if you will, a dramatistic perspective, with an emphasis on scene, on the socio-political context of teaching writing within universities situated in an ideologically saturated culture.

A recurring theme in contemporary theory is the pervasive force of ideology, variously defined as false consciousness, an aggregate of one's beliefs, the unconscious ways we represent our existence to ourselves or Clifford Geertz's "maps of problematic social reality and matrices for the creation of collective conscience" (64). It is, incidentally, ironic that Frederic Jameson in a critique of Burke, a decade ago in *Critical Inquiry*, would accuse him of repressing the power of ideology in his writing. In a deeply detailed reply Burke cites numerous references to the term *ideology* and to discussions of its implications, demonstrating not only his awareness of but also his commitment to socialist principles. In his early work and later in his comments on that work it seems clear that Burke anticipated what is now, after Foucault, a commonplace in our thinking about discourse: that however disinterested and apolitical the form and substance of our language appears on the surface, it is nevertheless thoroughly ideological, that is, imbued with assumptions, biases, constraints, and variable judgments of a specific intellectual community composed of people with their own social and political allegiances. Discourse is thereby always ideologically situated in a community already in existence, already value-laden.

From this perspective there is no objective academic discourse. Burke knew this as far back as his 1931 *Counter-Statement* where he stresses the interrelatedness of form, rhetoric and power. Rhetoric, for Burke, does not exist in isolation from the larger social world. That is what previous commentators on Burke, and on rhetoric in general, did not, perhaps could not, fully confront: the illusion that there is a clear distinction between the inside and the outside, between the socio-political struggles of the "real" world and the work of university humanists. Anticipating both Foucault and Althusser, Burke knew that discourse tends to underwrite the "political and ethical values of the state" (Eagleton 103), because, finally, behind all writing in Burke's terms, "the mind is a social product" (173). It is difficult to find any reference to this aspect of Burke's rhetoric in composition studies, perhaps because the usual humanist version of the cultural conversation focuses mainly on the value of uncontexualized ideas. Kenneth Burke did not. In this regard Burke goes beyond Dewey and is more compatible with Frank Lentricchia's notion that this "conversation has been propelled and constrained mainly by collective voices, socio-historical subjects, not by private ones, not by 'autonomous' intellectuals" (16). Along with many of today's progressive educational critics like Henry

Giroux and Michael Apple, Burke believes that as teachers within cultural institutions we cannot hold disinterested positions, somehow standing on neutral ground, outside power. Some, like Foucault, view this complicity as dark indeed and see little space for reform. For Foucault, the ability of subjects to resist the unifying, controlling urge of modern institutions is limited. While some would agree that our institutions are an Orwellian nightmare, with institutional discourse a prison of ideological hegemony, Burke and those in concert with his ideas are clearly not as pessimistic as this. Burke is not a messenger of despair or cynical resignation. On the contrary, his political insights allow for, even call for, oppositional thinking, or what some Marxists call disidentification. Burke, who believes with Dewey that the function of education is to reform a limiting, unjust society, is also sanguine about the ability of teachers to intervene in the dominant discourse to alter its direction for the better.

As a first step toward that transformation, Burke wants us to understand that because knowledge is a social construct "ideas not only have material effects; they have material circumstances as well" (Lentricchia 5). That suggests that we first have to identify ourselves as intellectuals working within an interested web of socio-political values. An awareness of how we are culturally situated is crucial if we are to move toward a praxis that conceives of writing, ours and our students', as cultural work with political consequences. According to Lentricchia's meditation on Burke, the most effective site to fight against the socializing implications of traditional educational philosophy is where we work, doing what we do—professing reading and writing. This is, in fact, a logical move if the usual oppositions between the classroom and the real word are deconstructed. Our resistance to giving up our traditional academic notions of autonomy is, Lentricchia suggests, a double deception, since it also permits us to deceive students as well. "Thus," he argues, "do humanists help to fashion the hegemony that will keep us and themselves in the dark" (151).

Burke's goal as a critical rhetor, then, is to shed light on the ways in which we can, through the writing and teaching of discourse, be responsible to the larger social whole. In *A Rhetoric of Motives* he writes:

> Any specialized activity participates in a larger unit of action. Identification is a word for the autonomous activity's place in this wider context, a place with which the agent may be unconcerned. The shepherd, *qua* shepherd, acts for the good of the sheep, to protect them from discomfiture and harm. But he may be "identified" with a project that is raising the sheep for market. (27)

It is not hard to interpret this passage as a comment on our service role as writing teachers, training students who might write well technically and are therefore employable, but who lack a critical rhetorical perspective and are therefore unlikely to be agents of change. To raise our political consciousness, then, Burke would have us interrogate our received ideas about rhetoric, problematizing such notions as form, intention, and identification. Form, for example, still appears in our rhetorics and handbooks as merely a problem in organizing our thinking. We are still inheritors of the formalist attempt to objectify structure by decontextualizing it, removing it from an historically situated writer and an ideologically interested audience. For Burke, form is far more problematic. For him it is the embodiment of the writer's attitude toward reality and toward an audience. As such, it helps to create a certain relationship between a text and its reception. Form is rhetorical power, a way to shape reality and manipulate audiences. The forms we inherit from our rhetorical past gather an aura of tradition around them, making them seem natural, commonsensical. That is, according to Catherine Belsey, exactly what ideology achieves—making one possibility seem like the only option. But no form can develop in a vacuum. Forms are created to meet and express certain human needs and perceptions. When Burke claimed that form was the creating and the satisfying of an appetite in the mind of a reader, he was also implying that a particular form might *not* satisfy. Forms can help us see clearly, but they can also obfuscate; they can liberate or subjugate. In context they are never neutral. This linking of form and ideology, for example, is one of the reasons our teaching can never be disinterested.

It is, however, characteristic of discourse to allow space for resistance to these dominant forms. As Macdonell notes, within disciplines there are always theoretical struggles and contradictions that are reflected at the level of discourse. Burke anticipated this Foucauldian insight by claiming that form is a strategy writers use so that a self can exist in a certain relation to reality. And within the university community there are alternative stances to take toward reality other than the dominant one. This discursive struggle for acceptance of variant forms is on-going. Dissenters feel, along with Foucault, that a kind of intellectual tyranny is at work if the self is made to conform to a rigid discursive formation. For example, the conventions of the typical academic, deductive essay as it appears in countless handbooks can be seen, from Burke's perspective, as ideologically committed: the confident thesis statement and the logical arrangement of concrete evidence is, in fact, a specific way of asserting that the world is best understood in this way, that knowledge can be demonstrated in this unproblematic form, that the self can be authentic within these set confines. If the ideology of certain readers is troubled by a particular form, however, appetites will neither be aroused nor satisfied. The secular appetite, for example, is hardly satisfied by fundamentalist rhetoric, and the dominant academic essay is not geared to please those who stand on the margins, those who, like feminists and Marxists, often feel alienated and displaced by the academy's "normal" discourse.

For example, the post-structuralist affirmation of multiplicity and the deconstructive resistance to logocentric thinking has created a favorable climate for a Burkean critique of what some feminist theorists see as a discourse that is patriarchal and phallocentric and therefore one that is repressive to women.[1] Hélène Cixous, for example, along with Luce Irigaray, has repeatedly called into question the objectivity of Western discourse, arguing that it primarily reflects male values, such as the need for clarity and certainty, freedom from contradiction and ambiguity, and an assertive commitment to logic and order. They simply do not find their version of reality mirrored in the dominant discourse. Like Burke, Cixous wants to stress the political seriousness of this exclusion by claiming "that writing is precisely the very possibility of change, the space that can serve as a springboard for subversive thought, the precursory movement of a transformation of social and cultural structures" (879). On a smaller, syntactic scale, the Marxist critic Richard Ohmann criticized Christensen's cumulative sentence because it avoids critical thinking, by merely adding concrete detail to an unexamined base clause. The Burkean point here is that ideology seeps into discourse in many ways, not just in the most obvious dimension of ideas. And this socio-political element is not something added on to discourse but rather inextricably part of the very essence of rhetorical form.

If we follow Burke's advice and confront our complicity in this ideological discursive socialization, there are several options: first, simply to identify with all the values of the dominant discourse; second, to deny its validity and try to begin anew; or, third, and this I believe is Burke's position, to work within the constraints of our discourse, modifying and transforming its limitations. I think Burke clearly rejects the first and would probably agree with the impulse but not the finality of the second option.

The refusal of some feminists philosophically to accept conventional academic discourse does have political significance, however, as it highlights how language can be seen to constitute, not merely to reflect, reality. Cixous' strategy is to undermine masculine discourse through open-ended textuality, through a call for women to "write yourself. Your body must be heard. Only then will the immense resources of the unconscious spring forth" (880).

This commitment to writing the body is a more political, more mystical, yet more urgent variation of the call in composition theory to speak in one's own voice. In her provocative essay, "The Laugh of the Medusa," Cixous wants to focus on what women's writing will do in the world. When she says that women have been driven from their bodies in the same way they have been driven from authentic writing, she implicates the power alignment in the academy and clearly wants women to struggle against this male hierarchy by inscribing themselves in history. "Write," she urges. "Let no one hold you back . . ." (877). Cixous urges women to invent an "impregnable language" that will break down "class barriers, laws, regulations and rhetorics." She reasons that if woman has always functioned "within" the discourse of man, "it is time for her to dislocate this 'within,' to explode it, turn it around, and seize it; to make it hers . . . to invent for herself a language to get inside of" (886). Stressing the marginality of woman's language, Julia Kristeva and Irigaray also transgress established discourse by advocating tactics that parody, subvert, or disturb patriarchal logic (Moi 139; 163).

Burke would want to agree with this ethic of subversion and probably would applaud their search for a discourse capable of inscribing previously suspect ways of dealing with reality. But a fluid and plural semiotic discourse of creative excess will sound utopian indeed in the context of the American university. Burke is, in fact, quite explicit about the need to work within, not outside, established discourse conventions, especially if we are hoping for change. This position was, in fact, the reason for much of the criticism Burke received from traditional Marxists in the thirties for recommending that reformers adapt their rhetoric to the values of the American people, that is, to identify with their ideology. As Lentricchia notes, if one is working for a change in consciousness, "one must be careful not to rupture oneself from the historico-rhetorical mainstream of American social and political values" (33). Burke agrees; he does not hope to transcend what some might view as a regimented discourse. Instead he wants to unmask the neutrality of rhetoric, to alert us and our students to the need to be active, critical rhetors, conscious that the struggle that inheres in academic discourse is not merely over neutral academic conventions, but for power, the power to make meaning and interpret experience.

Armed with an awareness of the multiple and rather arbitrary ways different discourses privilege certain rhetorical strategies against others, writers can decide more knowingly which of these conflicting discourses to align themselves with. If these writers are students, they should be aware that acceptance into interpretive communities depends largely on one's ability first to master the conventions of that discourse. And those conventions are more complex than writing clearly: as David Bartholomae suggests, they are composed of "commonplaces, set phrases, rituals, gestures, habits of mind, tricks of persuasion, obligatory conclusions and necessary connections that determine the 'what might be said' and constitute knowledge within the university" (11). To see academic writing in this way, as a kind of anthropological behavior, is both to demystify and make more accessible our discursive formations. This is becoming an increasingly popular position in English Studies. Gerald Graff has recently made the same point in reference to literature: the need for our theoretical assumptions to be interrogated and made explicit, especially for students. It is a very Burkean notion that as educators our task cannot simply be to prepare students for tasks they have no historical or political sophistication about. Those students who lack a theoretical consciousness about the power of discourse cannot re-read culture, and they therefore risk becoming victims. This ability to see the contextuality of writing is part of Burke's rhetorical equipment for living the examined life.

Burke's much quoted and variously interpreted fable of history as a conversation is an interesting representative anecdote for his cogent historico-political vision. As you remember, a heated discussion is always already in progress when we arrive. We listen for a while and then without a full sense of all the previous discursive twists and turns, we begin to take sides, arguing and forming alliances. Eventually, of course, we must leave with the discussion "still vigorously in progress." As in Foucault's archeologies, we are here as teachers of reading and writing caught in a particular historical moment, enmeshed in a constraining discourse we did not choose. We are, in part, burdened and belated voices. But against Foucault, in Burke's scenario we are not helpless. As Lentricchia notes, "history is a masterful, powerful process: it 'makes' us, and yet, at the same time, at any moment in the process, our active willing 'makes' the conversation, gives it the propulsive energy that forces it on" (161).

As Burke's fable suggests, there is no conclusion to this conversation; it is an on-going struggle, a continuous remaking of rhetorical and literary tradition. This conversation began before our historical moment and will continue with or without us. The oppositional voice of Dewey has been powerfully and dynamically augmented by Burke, Berthoff, Rosenblatt, and many others. But it is only our intervention that can sustain and build on their counter-hegemonic themes. Only our active voices can inscribe democratic values on the evolving text of English Studies. That struggle offers to all of us who decide to put in our "oar" the possibility to re-Joyce in our ability to affect the consciousness of our profession and our society.

Note

1. My use of the French feminists as examples of oppositional voices was taken from a paper on discourse and gender I wrote with Linnea Aycock of California State, Fresno, for the Penn State Conference on Rhetoric and Composition, 1986. We also revised a version for SAMLA, Atlanta, 1986. Many of the ideas are hers and I am indebted to her, in many ways.

Works Cited

Apple, Michael. *Education and Power*. Boston: Routledge, 1982.

Bartholomae, David. "Inventing the University." *Journal of Basic Writing* 51 (1986):4–23.

Belsey, Catherine. *Critical Practice*. London: Methuen, 1980.

Berthoff, Ann E. *The Making of Meaning*. Portsmouth, NH: Boynton/Cook, 1981.

Bizzell, Patricia. "Foundationalism and Anti-Foundationalism in Composition Studies." *Pre/Text* 7 (1986):37–56.

Burke, Kenneth. *Counter-Statement*. 2nd ed. Los Altos: Hermes, 1953.

———. *The Philosophy of Literary Form*. New York: Vintage, 1957.

———. *A Rhetoric of Motives*. Berkeley: U of California P, 1963.

———. *A Grammar of Motives*. Berkeley: U of California P, 1969.

Cixous, Hélène. "The Laugh of the Medusa." *Signs* 1 (1976):875–93.

Dewey, John. *Experience and Education*. 1938. New York: Collier, 1963.

———. *Education and Democracy*. New York: The Free Press, 1966.

Eagleton, Terry. *Literary Theory*. Minneapolis: U of Minnesota P, 1983.

Geertz, Clifford. "Ideology as a Cultural System." *The Interpretation of Cultures*. New York: Basic Books, 1973.

Giroux, Henry and Peter McLaren. "Teacher Education and the Politics of Engagement: The Case for Democratic Schooling." *Harvard Education Review*. 56 (1986):213–38.

Graff, Gerald. *Professing Literature*. Chicago: U of Chicago P, 1987.

Irigaray, Luce. "When Our Lips Speak Together." *Signs* 6 (1980):69–79.

Jameson, Frederic. "The Symbolic Inference; or Kenneth Burke and Ideological Analysis." *Critical Inquiry* 4 (1978):507–23. Burke's reply appeared in Winter, 1978.

Kristeva, Julia. "Women's Time." *Signs* 7 (1981):13–35.

Lentricchia, Frank. *Criticism and Social Change*. Chicago: U of Chicago P, 1983.

Macdonell, Diane. *Theories of Discourse*. Oxford: Basil Blackwell, 1986.

McCormick, Kathleen. "Theory in the Reader: Bleich, Holland, and Beyond." *College English* 47 (1985):836–50.

Moi, Toril. *Sexual/Textual Politics*. London: Methuen, 1985.

Ohmann, Richard. "Use Definite, Specific, Concrete Language." *College English* 41 (1979):390–97.

Rosenblatt, Louise. *The Reader, the Text, the Poem*. Carbondale: Southern Illinois UP, 1978.

Winterowd, Ross W. *Composition/Rhetoric: A Synthesis*. Carbondale: Southern Illinois UP, 1986.

4

Composition and English Departments, 1900–1925

JOHN BRERETON

University of Massachusetts, Boston

In 1936 I. A. Richards described "the present state of Rhetoric" as "the dreariest and least profitable part of the waste that the unfortunate travel through in Freshman English" (3). Richards did not pause to look more closely at the deplorable state of college composition; he assumed, rightly I think, that his readers would instantly assent to his judgment. Indeed, in the first third of this century it is very hard to find *anyone* claiming that freshman English is or ever could be a lively course, brimming with intellectual excitement. At best freshman English seems to have been regarded as a grim necessity, a "problem" to be solved by teachers and administrators or a hurdle to be surmounted by students. A closer look at college writing instruction in the early part of this century might help us judge the accuracy as well as the causes of Richards' bleak characterization.

The early part of the century was, of course, a time of burgeoning college enrollments and the spectacular growth of the literature curriculum, both in the undergraduate college and at the relatively new graduate level. It is tempting to assume that, in their eagerness to devote themselves to literature, major thinkers in English Studies simply abandoned composition. Such an assumption is quite wrong. For the first quarter of the century, at least, some of the most prominent scholars devoted a great

deal of their attention to freshman writing: James Morgan Hart, George
Lyman Kittredge, John Matthews Manly, Fred Newton Scott, and Karl
Young, all presidents of the Modern Language Association, wrote composition textbooks, either alone or with collaborators. And between 1900
and 1925 many other well-known figures published on the subject of
student writing: Lane Cooper, Norman Foerster, Thomas Lounsbury,
Brander Matthews, William Allen Neilson, Bliss Perry, William Lyon
Phelps, Hyder Rollins, Stith Thompson, among many others. If the
subject of freshman composition was "a waste," a large part of the responsibility must be placed on the leading members of the profession,
who far from abandoning the subject, contributed mightily to it with
their articles and their textbooks.

As recent studies of this era by Berlin, Connors, Douglas, and Stewart
have demonstrated, rhetoric was rapidly being reduced to a close study
of style, and style was being reduced to a series of admonitions about
grammatical and mechanical propriety.[1] What was left of rhetoric appeared as the modes of discourse (description, narration, definition, and
argumentation) which, as popularized by Alexander Bain, dominated
writing instruction from the 1870s until well into this century. It is this
dreary sameness that, no doubt, gave rise to Richards' grim
characterization.

Yet despite the dull routine that dominated composition instruction,
it is possible to discern some distinctly different approaches to the subject.
I want to look closely at two prominent English professors whose conceptions of a college writing course seem to stand out from the herd. I
will term the first approach the democratic, which was dominated by a
simplification of the subject of writing in order to make it accessible to
more students. Its prime exponent was John Matthews Manly (1866–
1940), who taught at Brown and, most prominently, at the University
of Chicago. He was president of the MLA in 1920, and with his collaborator Edith Rickert edited the mammoth eight-volume Chicago edition
of the texts of the *Canterbury Tales*. The second approach I will call the
natural aristocratic, since it attempted to combine high standards of
culture with the realities of mass higher education. Its prime exponent
was Norman Foerster (1887–1956), an educational conservative who drew
his beliefs in natural aristocracy from Jefferson. Foerster was the most
prominent of the second generation of New Humanists, following the
lead of Irving Babbitt (his teacher at Harvard) and Paul Elmer More. He
was a vigorous, controversial writer on literary criticism and higher education and served as faculty member at North Carolina and later as a
dean at Iowa. Both Foerster and Manly were men of extraordinary accom-

plishment who were known to all English scholars in the first third of this century and still, I think, are familiar to many today.[2]

As English professor at the University of Chicago, John Matthews Manly wrote an impressive number of textbooks: *A Manual for Writers*, 1913; *The Writing of English*, 1919 and 1923 (these two are the ones I will concentrate upon; his collaborator in both was his fellow medievalist Edith Rickert [1871–1938]); *Better Advertising*, 1921; *Better Business English*, 1921 and 1925; *Better Business Letters*, 1921; and *The Writer's Index of Good Form and Good English*, 1923. Each embodies its democratic notion of writing in a tone that seems closely connected with the gospel of self-help; Manly brings to writing instruction the attitude of Horatio Alger and Dale Carnegie. Running through all his books is an exhortation to success: ambition can be rewarded if only the writing student will follow a simple, straightforward method.

Here is Manly in his fullest form, from the opening of *The Writing of English*, 3rd edition, 1923:

> The man who would succeed today must be able to use his native tongue. If he can speak or write so that his words will have upon those who listen or read the effect that he desires, he is master of one of the great sources of power. To realize this fact is to see that the art of expression is not an ornament for the few, but a tool without which no ambitious man can be properly equipped for life. (3)

In this one paragraph we can find all the major strands of Manly's democratic attitude toward writing: good English is a key to success; it connects inevitably with terms like "succeed," "master," "power," and "ambitious." And English is not to be regarded as something special "for the few." Writing is merely a simple "tool" available to everyone who wishes to be "properly equipped for life."

Manly goes on to demonstrate that success is available to all:

> The theory that good writing depends upon a special talent has been exploded. This theory grew out of confusing genius with workmanship. A genius is a being of marked originality, whose self-expression may be helped or hindered by special training. But any intelligent person can be trained to become a successful workman in the art of shaping language to thought. His degree of success will depend largely upon a single factor—the active interest that he brings to bear upon the process of learning. (3–4)

Manly is careful to distinguish his kind of writing from old fashioned rhetoric on one hand and "art" on the other:

> Many individuals . . . are seriously hampered in their efforts to write by the feeling that writing, especially writing for the public, should be something superfine, should be artificially, or at least artfully, decorated, that over the original form of their thought should be draped a beautiful garment called style. This is, of course, a thoroughly pernicious idea; it has not only prevented many from writing who might have written simply and agreeably, but, worse than that, has burdened the world with thousands of pages of that useless and bad product known as "fine writing." (*Manual*, 5–6)

He proceeds to illustrate success in the field of contemporary letters, invoking the names of well-known English writers who looked about them and wrote of their own experiences: Conrad, Masefield, Blackwood, Wells, and Bennett, all men of humble origins who achieved fame. (Presumably the American writers who might serve as examples for emulation—Twain, Dreiser, Crane, Norris—were still too raw and unpolished compared to their British counterparts.) Manly's message is refreshingly simple: experience close at hand may be transformed into material for writing; one does not need to start with a particularly refined imagination or any aids to invention; ideas are immediately accessible.

There is something characteristically American here: naive, optimistic, yet somehow admirable. Manly's attitude matches the openness to the city and the widening of educational opportunity then characteristic of the University of Chicago. (All this would soon disappear, along with championship football, after Robert Maynard Hutchins took command at the end of the 1920s.)

Manly's optimism appears at its most appealing when he celebrates the success of his basic writing students: "To see the stirring of interesting and original lines of thought in students supposedly dull or indifferent was no less gratifying than to read almost faultless English written by Russians, Poles, Lithuanians, Chinese, Japanese, and young people of many other nationalities, whose work in the beginning was almost unintelligible" (vi). This is one of the only times a major English scholar of the 1920s affirms the success of college remedial programs. Early twentieth-century English faculty were strangely silent about the massive influx of new students during this era, and almost never mention the amazing achievements of immigrant children. Sadly, we must note that Manly's price for success is wholesale acculturation to the traditional norms of good writing as preached by hundreds of textbook writers. As we shall see, Manly, like some writers of remedial texts in the 1970s, essentially repackages the same old material in a new, more appealing guise.

Success to Manly is a matter of following rules, and his books erect a standard of propriety in writing that reads like Emily Post's 1922 best-seller on etiquette:

> Some linguistic errors are analogous to the wearing of a skirt by a man; others to attending an evening party without a coat or a collar; others to wearing a gaudy waistcoat. . . . To use slang or undignified collo-quialism on an occasion calling for seriousness and dignity is like wearing a pair of overalls at a formal dinner; to use superfine poetic terms in buying a railway ticket or in ordering the family groceries is like wearing evening dress to a baseball game. (43)

The extent of Manly's concern is indicated by his naming an entire chapter "Good Form": "Good form in writing is not a trifle. It belongs in the same class with good table manners and social ease. There are people who do not think any of these worth while; but such people as a rule do not go to college" (36).

Bad form has such innumerable ways of showing itself that one has to be on constant guard. In writing letters one has to watch for:

> cheap and showy writing materials; cheap paper; lined paper (which suggests that you cannot write straight); gilt-edged paper; paper stamped with a gilt initial or other ornament; perfumed paper (which suggests ill breeding); tinted paper (except grey); cheap ink; colored ink; diluted ink; torn half-sheets of paper; envelopes that do not match the paper (which suggest a rigid economy); and so on. (36)

Later we hear of bad form in handwriting, in numbering of pages, in folding the letter, and a whole paragraph on "failure to follow post office regulations with regard to envelopes" (36–37).[3] Good form, it seems, is like some versions of genius: an infinite capacity to take pains.

Manly's focus on minutiae seems particularly obsessive when one compares how much space he devotes to larger, more demanding issues. Under "What to Write About" Manly provides a one-paragraph subsection entitled "Procuring Special Knowledge" which blandly states, "If you need to consult books, bibliographies may be of assistance" (15). That's all the research help he gives in the whole book! And in his brief section on how to develop ideas, Manly provides half a page of very general directions and then moves on to the specific:

> The ideas suggested may arise very disconnectedly and in very crude form. The first thing to make sure of is that you catch and fix them

all. No better way has yet been discovered to do this than to jot them down as they occur, on small cards or slips of paper. Manila cards are better than paper, unless it is thick and stiff, because they are more easily handled. Three by five inches is a good size, though some writers prefer them larger, and some smaller. (*Manual*, 13)

This kind of movement from large, hopelessly vague generality to incredibly specific detail in less than two paragraphs reveals an author much more at home with the concrete particulars, perhaps a good thing in a textual scholar or a code expert (Manly's military specialty in World War I), but not especially useful in a writing teacher or a maker of meaning. At the same time, Manly's focus on such fine points might just bring an odd kind of comfort, the incredible detail serving as a confidence builder. The implicit message is that Manly has thought of *everything*, so the student need only follow his lead for things to turn out all right. (In this curious way the even greater obsession with detail in Wooley's best-selling *Handbook* reveals a similar democratic tendency.)

No self-help book is complete without exhortations, and *Writing* does not disappoint. In the preface Manly testifies that the student was "shown how errors in form can be eliminated; and if, after fair trial, he did not begin to take an active part in his own salvation in this respect, his work was ruthlessly rejected on this basis alone" (vi). To frame the issue in terms of salvation carries more than faint overtones of missionary exhortation. And sure enough, when Manly gets to grammar he describes improvement in terms of a growing self-awareness of sin: the student "must realize, in the first place, that he does express himself incorrectly; and in the second place, that in an understanding of grammar lies his help" (41). This first step, the admission of inadequacy (to be adopted later by Carnegie and Alcoholics Anonymous), has its roots in Christian conversion, as does the confessional approach embodied in Chapter V's only assignment: "Discuss in class the best ways of overcoming your individual defects in matters of form" (44). Descended from a long line of Southern Baptist preachers, Manly draws on his heritage when he exhorts his students to reach their goals.

The democratic tendencies in Manly's approach cannot hide the fact that at the core his books are filled with the same old rules and admonitions, newly garbed in the language of success. Though Manly in his prefaces testified about "the stirring of interesting and original lines of thought," the books seem much more concerned with producing "almost faultless English." A student who follows Manly's exhortations must purchase the proffered "success" at a high cost, through adherence to the etiquette of old, tired rules rather than through real engagement with writing itself.

In his *The American State University* (1937), Norman Foerster admiringly describes Jefferson's ideal of a natural aristocracy that can be produced through widespread public education, with a continual weeding-out process so that, as Jefferson put it, "the best geniuses will be raked from the rubbish" (19). Unfortunately, Foerster claimed, populist, Jacksonian ideals of democracy prevailed, preventing the natural aristocrats from rising to the top. Still, Foerster saw in public education a genuine chance to develop excellence, and he viewed the unbridled expansion of state universities with alarm: "In the American state university of today, no important steps are being taken to secure the best students and to give them a substantial education, but much is being done to secure the less able and least able and to keep them in college as long as possible by giving them a superficial education" (177).

Foerster, then, was a strong advocate of "substantial," demanding education. He believed in a classics-centered core curriculum, and would become a natural ally of Meikeljohn's experiments in general education at Wisconsin and Hutchins' new curriculum at Chicago. (And of course he would have had no sympathy at all for Manly's remedial students.) Examined in light of the intellectual climate of the first quarter of the twentieth century, Foerster's composition work provides a glimpse of something rare for the time, a genuine *system* of writing instruction, an attempt at a coherent approach to a liberal education that once exerted great influence and still, I suspect, remains attractive to some today.

Early in his career Foerster compiled two anthologies, *Essays for College Men*, first and second series (Holt, 1913 and 1915; both with Frederick Manchester and Karl Young as collaborators) and accompanied them with *Outlines and Summaries: A Handbook for the Analysis of Expository Essays* (Holt, 1915). These three books, taken together, seem to represent an educational philosophy. The two series of *Essays* linked their readings by a common theme: the aims of a liberal education. Writers included Woodrow Wilson, Newman, Huxley, Tyndall, Paul Elmer More, Matthew Arnold, William James, and Emerson. (These were not uncommon authors to select in 1913; it was unusual to organize them around such a sharply pointed theme, though Lane Cooper's 1907 *Theories of Writing* had linked all its essays to style.) Each anthology simply presented the essays without introductions or "apparatus." *Outlines*, their companion book, demonstrates some of the principles behind the selections in *Essays* and also reveals Foerster's attitude toward the integration of writing and reading in a college composition course.

In his preface to *Outlines and Summaries* Foerster suggests that the only essays worth teaching are those containing carefully worked out thought, organized logically, with the inductive or deductive operations clearly visible. Lamb and Stevenson he singles out as too personal; their prose was not structured enough to illustrate reasoning powers on the page. It is noteworthy that almost all the selections in *Essays*, linked as they are by their subject matter rather than by rhetorical mode or style, originally appeared as addresses or manifestos, and all share a high Victorian sensibility and culture.

The opening chapter of *Outlines* uses Woodrow Wilson's "The Spirit of Learning" (from *Essays*, first series) as a demonstration of how to outline. Foerster's approach is to transmit Wilson's ideas *as* ideas, so he insists that students understand the propositional content of Wilson's speech. This proves to be a formidable task; Foerster expects an effective outline to take three or four pages and to reproduce the original's ideas in what now seems like painful detail.

The book includes a suggested syllabus. Each essay should get five class days:

- Day 1: Summary Sentences
- Day 2: Outline of Theme Due
- Day 3: Group Sentences
- Day 4: Theme (500–600 words)
- Day 5: Outline of Essay (104)

Class hours will "be given to a careful reading of all or parts of the essay" (104). For topics of Day 4's 500–600 word theme, Foerster provides a choice:

1. The Spirit of Learning in My College
2. The Relation of Learning and Athletics in My College
3. The Relation of the Spirit of Learning to "College Spirit"
4. College Conversation
5. Types of College Students

These topics, it seems, are not meant to generate original thought so much as to allow students to apply Wilson's attitudes to new settings. One wonders how Foerster would have treated vigorous dissent from Wilson's highly elitist conception of college learning.

Many of the same attitudes toward thinking embodied in *Outlines and Summaries* were carried over to Foerster's next and most successful text,

Sentences and Thinking (Holt, 1919), which he published with John Marcellus Steadman, Jr. (1889–1945), his teaching fellow at North Carolina and later a professor at Emory. This book concentrates on style within the sentence, since "the sentence is, as everybody recognizes, the crux of the problem of sound writing" (iii).[4]

Foerster's book embodies a Romantic conception of thought that he terms "organic": thought and expression, or content and form, are inseparable:

> The words required for the expression of the thought or feeling are the words inherent in the thought or feeling itself. They are not cunningly devised by the writer, invented and arranged by him with a view to impressing the reader; he does nothing but find them. They were there in his mind the moment that he experienced the thought; and his task is merely to hold the thought firm before his mind's eye till the words spontaneously flash into being. When the words thus reveal themselves, he says, "That's what I mean," and writes it. (1–2)

Such a view had appeared before, notably in Emerson and Newman. Foerster attributes it to Coleridge, invoking the famous distinction between organic and mechanic form in the *Biographia Literaria*.

Given such a conception of the composing process (which obviously foreshadows many ideas of the New Critics), what kind of pedagogy results? Clearly, everything derives from the thought, just as, to use Foerster's example, an oak derives from the acorn. Thus the teaching has to *assume* worthwhile thoughts, and adjust the sentences accordingly. There is some sleight of hand involved, to be sure, since certain oaks are obviously more worthwhile than most acorns. Despite his claim of an indissoluble link between thought and expression, Foerster privileges thought over language: "To write expressive sentences, therefore, we are to lean on the thought, deriving from it the power of utterance. The sentence is an organism, of which the soul is the thought, and the body is the words. It is an embedded thought" (7). Like Manly, Foerster virtually ignores the question of how one gets the thought in the first place. Instead he relies on a series of quotations that make his approach seem natural and hallowed by time:

> Lay hold of the subject, and the words will follow.
>
> > Cato

> The style of an author is the true image of his mind. He who would write clearly ought first to think clearly, and whoever would have a grand style must first have a grand character.
>
> > Goethe

As soon as a thought has reached its full perfection, the word springs
into being, offers itself, and clothes the thought.

Joubert (1)

This being a textbook, such assertions are delivered crisply, with little
explanation or backup; the authority of such famous writers is, one sup-
poses, warrant enough.

Foerster situates the writer in a world in which the primacy of the
individual thoughts meets the impersonal rules and laws imposed by
language:

While it is true that the thought determines the expression, that *my*
thought requires *my* expression, it is also true, happily, that in the
main all men think alike. Style . . . is the man; but style is also Man.
We are all individuals, but individuals of the same species. Broadly
speaking, our thoughts are those of all other men; if they were not,
other men could not understand us. Even more, no doubt, our *ways*
of thinking, the logical modes in which our minds work, are human
rather than personal. And while the personal element in expression
may safely be trusted to take care of itself, this impersonal element
requires of us a severe discipline. (7)

This transition allows Foerster to switch from thought to language, but
doesn't allow him easy access from language back to thought. Revision
is a rigorous process of clarifying the thought or of adjusting the thought
to the rules of language, rather than a spur to further, deeper thought.

Foerster makes some passing references to rhetoric, but in doing so
reveals a basic conflict: invention and arrangement to him is practically a
single, quasi-magic process, stemming from the soul or the character; on
the other hand, traditional rhetoric is supposed to help develop the
thought in the first place, as well as help give it shape. So Foerster virtually
ignores traditional rhetoric, explicitly rejecting the classical rhetorician's
terms of invention and arrangement (1–2) and practically bypassing the
modes of discourse. His rhetoric is sentence rhetoric, which means grammar and intense concentration on style as it reflects thinking. Consequently,
throughout the book Foerster constantly connects the expression—the
words of the sentences—to the initiating principle, the original thought.
He emphatically exhorts, "If we will but resolutely endeavor to say what
is in our minds, our words will be fresh and vital and not trite and lifeless"
(32). Such a statement assumes more than a one-to-one relationship between word and idea; it also assumes that what is in the mind is easily
accessible, and that there are no interesting changes to be produced by
putting thought into words.

Foerster tries to adapt an imperfectly sketched out, essentially Romantic, inspirational theory of composing to the rigors of the rules of language usage and sentence grammar. What distinguishes his book is its demanding conception, its thesis, its rigorous, single-minded devotion to a theory of composing and language that stands out from its contemporaries. Unfortunately, the actual working out of that theory remains quite familiar. Foerster devotes 96 pages to Book I, "Principles of Construction," while Book II, "Principles of Revision," which does not differ very much from previous books on sentence style, gets 220.[5]

In 1930, Foerster became dean of the School of Letters at the University of Iowa, where he attempted to put his combination of natural aristocracy and general education into practice. Breaking down barriers between departments, he created a new major, American Civilization. To counter the German ideal of doctoral study he threw out the dissertation requirement for a Ph.D. and permitted students to put forward a shorter piece of "imaginative or critical writing," sometimes a collection of poems or a brief article embodying original research. The organic, unified approach apparent in *Sentences and Thinking* enabled him to regard all writing— student, creative, and critical—as part of a single continuum, rather than in the isolated, watertight categories that marked almost all his contemporaries' thinking. Under Foerster's tenure Iowa instituted the famous Writer's Workshop, and thus his long educational career supplies some nice connections between composition and creative writing, connections which remain to be explored more fully.

What conclusions can we draw from these different attitudes towards composition instruction? The first may be that paradoxes abound. Manly, the more openly democratic, was the scholar trained in the old school, a product of what Irving Babbitt called the Harvard "Philological Syndrome." His scholarly work was exacting, minute, scientific in the extreme. On the other hand, his writings on composition were the most accessible and at the same time the least thoughtful. His books seem almost mindless in their simplicity, and mind-boggling in their stress on inessentials. What rigor we might associate with being a scholar appears in the details, not in the thinking or the framing of assignments, which are pedestrian in the extreme. The appealing message in his books is that writing is easy, a craft rather than a remote art; the sad part is that meaning for Manly lies in the meeting of social expectations, not in the educated imagination.

On the other hand, Foerster's unified theory treated all writing, creative and expository alike, as the embodiment of a certain kind of thinking, the working through of moral issues in the imagination. Since that was the only way Foerster could understand or judge writing, his ability to teach composition was necessarily limited, for he had no theory of how language works and, like Manly, fell back on the familiar handbook admonitions. Nonetheless, there is a kind of integrity in Foerster's approach, limited though it no doubt was.

A second conclusion is that, despite the great differences that separate them, Manly and Foerster are alike in key ways, and share a great deal in common with their contemporaries. Both uphold the dominion of the traditional expository essay, even though Manly is willing to allow for a good deal more personal expression. Both regard the rules of language as givens, as rigorous standards students must live up to. And both argue for a vision of writing as the embodiment of thought pure and simple. They are also very earnest; the word "fun" does not appear in their vocabularies, and students are never invited to experiment for their own enjoyment, nor asked to depart from the straight and narrow path of practicality. Both regard the instructor solely as an examiner and grader, and neither draws in the slightest on the exciting, controversial work being done in the schools at exactly this time.

A third and final conclusion about Manly and Foerster (one that also applies to all early writers on composition) is their confidence about their subject, the easy familiarity they display about how students can best learn to write. Granted, textbooks are not the places for uncertainties, but it is still startling to watch eminent scholars and critics discourse upon such a knotty subject with so little hesitancy and humility. Few English scholars displayed much regard for composition as an *intellectual* problem to be wrestled with, and few hesitated to make pronouncements without first making a serious study of their subject, as they certainly would have done in their scholarly specialties. Rarely does one find an inkling that this is a field well worth investigation by the best minds. (Books and articles by Fred Newton Scott and Sterling Andrus Leonard are two of the rare exceptions I know.) Ultimately, the failure Richards pointed to resulted not from the best minds' avoiding composition studies; on the contrary, eminent scholars plunged into the subject without enough respect for its complexities, and without posing the interesting questions that Richards was to ask in 1936 and which now appear so obvious to rhetoricians and composition theorists alike.

Manly and Foerster represent unique ways of approaching composition, but like their more traditional contemporaries they still represent the Old Criticism, the kind of understanding of writing that a whole new generation of thinkers revolted against. In 1930 Foerster edited a collection,

Humanism and America, with essays by Babbitt, More, T.S. Eliot, and others enlisted for the moment under the New Humanist banner. The book was answered immediately by *The Critique of Humanism* with essays by some younger critics: Edmund Wilson, Malcolm Cowley, Allen Tate, Kenneth Burke, R. P. Blackmur, Yvor Winters, and Lewis Mumford. The sweeping change brought about by these and other figures would usher in a new era of criticism. The leading literary critics of the new generation, especially I.A. Richards and Kenneth Burke, would be primarily rhetoricians; it would be *their* ideas that would slowly transform thinking about composition and relegate Manly and Foerster to the past.

Notes

1. The current, quite tentative explanation for this shift in rhetoric's importance is that rhetoric was undone by the Harvard elective system, which leveled the curriculum and reduced freshman English to a dull focus on mechanical correctness.

2. Another significant category of the time would be the elitist, which attempted to relegate required composition entirely to the secondary schools. Quite naturally, the elitists produced few freshman composition textbooks, since they didn't believe the subject belonged in college.

3. Manly is not alone in this obsession with rules; the 1907 edition of Wooley's famous *Handbook of Composition* devoted four full pages to rules on folding writing paper (137–41).

4. Later editions of this book would expand the subject to include more than just sentences, but the basic approach would remain the same, although the 1931, 1941, and 1952 editions were called *Writing and Thinking*.

5. Another version of the natural aristocrat position can be found in the books that combine literature and composition. Greenough and Hersey's *English Composition* (1921), for example, mixes standard textbook information with excerpts from canonical writers. When students are assigned a descriptive essay, they first read Henry James on Chartres Cathedral or Hardy on Egdon Heath (complete with sepia illustrations). Such a models approach sets out to teach elementary methods of organization by means of extraordinarily high standards of achievement and presumes to judge students by how successfully they ape literary masters. See also Gardiner, Kittredge, and Arnold's *Manual of Composition and Rhetoric* (1907) for an even more thoroughgoing approach employing literary models.

Works Cited

Berlin, James A. *Writing Instruction in Nineteenth-Century American Colleges*. Carbondale: Southern Illinois UP, 1984.

Connors, Robert J. "The Rise and Fall of the Modes of Discourse." *College Composition and Communication* 32 (1981): 444–55.

Connors, Robert J., Lisa Ede, and Andrea Lunsford. "The Revival of Rhetoric in America." *Essays on Classical Rhetoric and Modern Discourse*. Eds. Robert J. Connors, Lisa Ede, and Andrea Lunsford. Carbondale: Southern Illinois UP, 1984. 1–13.

Douglas, Wallace. "Rhetoric for the Meritocracy." Ed. Richard Ohmann, *English in America*. New York: Oxford UP, 1976. 97–132.

———. "Barrett Wendell." *Traditions of Inquiry*. Ed. John Brereton. New York: Oxford UP, 1985. 3–25.

———. "Accidental Institution: On the Origin of Modern Language Study." *Criticism in the University*. Eds. Gerald Graff and Reginald Gibbons. Evanston: Northwestern UP, 1985. 35–61.

Foerster, Norman. *The American State University*. Chapel Hill: U of North Carolina P, 1937.

———. *Humanism in America*. Boston: Houghton Mifflin, 1930.

———. *Outlines and Summaries: A Handbook for the Analysis of Expository Essays*. New York: Henry Holt, 1915.

Foerster, Norman, Frederick Manchester, and Karl Young. *Essays for College Men*. First series. New York: Henry Holt, 1913.

———. *Essays for College Men*. Second series. New York: Henry Holt, 1915.

Foerster, Norman, and J. M. Steadman, Jr. *Sentences and Thinking: A Practice Book in Sentence Making*. Boston: Houghton Mifflin, 1919. 2nd ed., 1923. 3rd ed., 1931 (Title changed to *Writing and Thinking*). 4th ed., 1941. 5th ed. (Revised by James B. McMillan), 1952.

Gardiner, John Hays, George Lyman Kittredge, and Sarah Louise Arnold. *Manual of Composition and Rhetoric*. Boston: Ginn, 1907.

Grattan, C. Hartley. *The Critique of Humanism: A Symposium*. New York: Brewer and Warren, 1930.

Greenough, Chester Noyes, and Frank Wilson Cheney Hersey. *English Composition*. New York: Macmillan, 1921.

Manly, John Matthews and John A. Powell. *A Manual for Writers*. Chicago: U of Chicago P, 1913.

Manly, John Matthews, and Edith Rickert. *The Writing of English*. New York: Henry Holt, 1919. 2nd ed., 1920; 3rd ed., 1923.

———. *The Writer's Index of Good Form and Good English*. New York: Henry Holt, 1923.

Richards, I. A. *The Philosophy of Rhetoric*. New York: Oxford UP, 1936.

Stewart, Donald. "Some Facts Worth Knowing about the Origins of Freshman Composition." *CEA Critic*, May, 1982. 2–11.

———. "Two Model Teachers and the Harvardization of English Departments." Ed. James J. Murphy. *The Rhetorical Tradition and Modern Writing*. New York: MLA, 1982. 118–29.

Wooley, Edwin C. *Handbook of Composition*. Boston: D.C. Heath, 1907.

5

The Reading of Reading
I. A. Richards and
M. J. Adler

DAVID BARTHOLOMAE
University of Pittsburgh

After that first year of teaching, I had few illusions left about my literacy. Since then, I have been teaching students how to read books, six years at Columbia with Mark Van Doren and for the last ten years at the University of Chicago with President Robert M. Hutchins. In the course of years, I think I have gradually learned to read a little better.

Mortimer Adler, *How To Read a Book*

[*How To Read a Page*] went down . . . perhaps where the ground was prepared . . . with the teachers who at that time were feeling, as I was—many of us were—feeling really swamped by the Chicago sort of thing. And all of our effort had been, you know, in the opposite direction. There were so many badly conceived courses that just grabbed Great Authors right and left, and threw them in.

Reuben Brower,
in an interview with I. A. Richards,
I. A. Richards: Essays in His Honor

Since many of us are once again feeling swamped by the Chicago sort of thing, it is instructive to consider its 1940 manifestation, Mortimer Adler's *How To Read a Book* and I. A. Richards' peculiar response, *How to Read a Page*.

Adler tells his story this way: "I did not discover I could not read until after I had left college" (6). He looked—and I think it is fair to say he looked bravely and acutely—at what he *didn't* know about the books he had read as a student, saw in his ignorance a sign of a general failure in our educational system—one confirmed by his recent experience as a teacher of undergraduates, by professional studies (including Richards' *Practical Criticism*), by academic conferences, and by a recent Carnegie Report—and set about to devise a pedagogy for teaching young adults to read great books with understanding.

Richards had already established his concern for the problems of reading and education, most recently in *The Philosophy of Rhetoric* (1936) and *Interpretation in Teaching* (1938). Of his next book, he said:

> I had admired Mortimer Adler immensely but I somehow got irritated by *How to Read a Book*. So I wrote a counter-blast: *How To Read a Page*. Instead of a hundred *books*, chosen regardless of what translation, version or anything, I wanted to take just a hundred *words* and then I revolted again and made it a hundred and three. And it so happens that the Great Books are now a hundred and three. It was partly a bit of fun. But it was a very serious book, unusable, I know now, for the populations I hoped I was addressing. . . . It didn't go down where it was hoped it would go down. One has to be used to that. (Brower, Vendler and Hollander 36)

Adler's book was at the top of the best-seller list for over a year; Richards' is long out of print and seldom read.

I would like to talk about *How To Read a Book* and *How To Read a Page* as blast and counterblast, the "Chicago thing" in one corner and poised against it something else altogether. As I reproduce passages from these books, you will find yourself in familiar territory. Almost fifty years later, teachers are fighting the same battles, in the same terms, while standing on the same turf.

I

I need to begin, then, by establishing a place called "Chicago," a place where they have powerful and distinct ways of speaking about reading, writing and teaching. (Mortimer Adler is there, but also Alan Bloom, Wayne Booth and—at least in my Chicago—E.D. Hirsch.) None of these people in Chicago quite agrees with the others, but this Chicago I'm talking about is big enough to contain competing voices and still remain the same place. There are disagreements about this exercise or that text, but the talk all issues from the same source. Here, for example, is someone from Chicago talking to students about reading and writing. It is not Adler speaking, but in its tone and language it sounds remarkably familiar to anyone who has recently read *How To Read a Book*. It is, in other words, a fine example of the Chicago sort of thing:

> Just as exercise, study, and discipline can improve our health, they can also improve our "verbal health"—our power to use and respond to language. People often act as if being able to read a newspaper or ask for directions proves that they are fluent in their native tongue. But in fact most of us perform even these basic language tasks less well than we could. People who think they "know how to read" often misread even the simplest news accounts, as all newspaper editors and reporters learn to their sorrow. And we all have had the experience of finding ourselves on the wrong side of town because we either asked for directions unclearly or received unclear directions from someone else. The number of our confusions, misunderstandings, and misspeakings can be decreased if we only know how, but not without work, not without the exercise, study, and discipline that strengthened our performance. The main objective of this course is to provide such systematic exercise in reading and writing. (Booth and Gregory 3–4)

This is an introduction to a textbook, Wayne Booth and Marshall Gregory's *The Harper and Row Reader*. It sets up the terms through which students, and their teachers, can begin to imagine the work of the course— reading and writing. My guess is that the course description will read as a familiar document to any English teacher: its language seems inevitable, seamless, natural, right. And depending on where you stand, of course, it is. Reading and writing are good for you; they make you healthy (or healthier); they require discipline and exercise; the goal is to reduce misunderstanding and improve communication.

Perhaps the best way to get a purchase on this excerpt is to imagine what it excludes, to imagine what can't be said (or asked) in Chicago, not necessarily because of taboo but because, to this way of speaking, such statements or questions simply aren't there.

We have all, it is true, phrased questions poorly or received unclear directions. There are other ways, however, of imagining the difficulty of language use, particularly in a class where, as I look at the table of contents in Booth's reader, students are going to read essays by Freud, Marx and Adrienne Rich. There are, that is, problems of understanding that are rooted in problems of interpretation, problems that require critical methods (ways of asking questions that don't come naturally, for example), problems that follow when competing ideologies or irreconcilable ways of thinking are brought into the scene, and these problems are of a different order than problems of misspeaking on the street or misunderstanding directions. If you look in on this from the outside, it is possible to imagine problems with Freud or Rich that require a method, and not just discipline and exercise.

It is possible to imagine a course in reading and writing that is a course in method ("method," that is, as Berthoff defines it: the critical tool enabling us to interpret our interpretations, to think about thinking, to understand not only what our ideas are but "how they are working for us—or against us"), but it is impossible to imagine such a course in a setting where Booth's words are the inevitable language of instruction (Berthoff 4).

The trivial example (bad directions) and the obvious evasion (the absence of any reference to the essays that make up this "reader") are not, as I am reading the passage, a slip or a strategic mistake but the inevitable result of a way of speaking about reading and writing that cannot refer to certain kinds of reading and writing—where a student, for example, tries to make sense out of or do something with Adrienne Rich.

And, in fact, if you turn to the writing assignments in the Booth reader, you will see the presence of this absence in classroom practice. The Rich essay in the textbook is "The Kingdom of the Fathers" (from *Of Woman Born*), a selection that asks students to think about the situation of women by thinking about patriarchal structures of oppression. The writing assignment that follows the selection asks students to describe a member of the opposite sex, "the kind of person you would consider marrying" and "the kind of relationship that you think would form a satisfying and stable union." Students are told to organize their essays according to three levels of expectations:

> first, the features (or traits) of character and behavior you think are essential in a mate; second, the features that you think are highly desirable but which might be negotiable; and, third, the features you would like to find in a partner, but which, like ice cream on your cake, are dispensable.
>
> Take care as you go to correct any mistaken notions you think members of the opposite sex hold about the needs and expectations of your sex. The point of your essay is to lay out the basis of a healthy relationship. (450)

One of the methods Richards developed for writers was a series of "specialized quotation marks" to indicate how a word should be taken. One of these was a superscript exclamation point, to indicate "Good Heavens!

What a way to talk!" Such marks seem entirely appropriate to Booth's use of "opposite sex" or "healthy" or "marriage" as innocent or unproblematic terms for a discussion of Rich's essay.

Booth's writing assignment makes Rich's essay, and the reading of it, disappear; in a sense, it says put away (as in erase) what you have, now that you have read this essay, and write as though there were nothing inappropriate in using Rich as an occasion to talk about marriage and choice in your usual way of speaking (where it is simply a matter of taste or desire: "I've always loved a great pair of legs"), or in speaking about choosing a mate as necessarily a matter of choosing from the opposite sex, or in assuming that the issue is simply one of "mistaken notions" about sex roles (as though we just don't speak clearly when we talk to each other on the street), or in implying that this conflict between men and women (the unhealthiness in our relations) could be resolved if students would just "take care" in a weekly essay.

II

The point of the preceding exercise was to highlight a way of speaking and to characterize the scene it creates, where students (writers/readers) are situated in a necessary relationship to books and teachers, reading and writing (as activities), and to the values of a culture and an institution. Whatever the instruments of education (great books, pre-reading exercises, question-asking procedures), those instruments are used, particularly by novices, only as they can be imagined to be used. You give a student a book, particularly one that she has reason to believe she *cannot* read, and she will imagine a way of beginning with that book according to the available terms to define reading—terms, that is, that define what a person might do with such a book.

This, anyway, is the guiding assumption of both Richards' and Adler's pedagogies. Both assume that they are addressing an audience who knows how to read—an audience, that is, who knows how to read sentences, who feels confident with common material, like the newspaper. Both assume that these readers have a problem reading, and that the first step in addressing that problem is to re-imagine what reading is and what a reader does—for both, the first step is to "read" or "re-read" reading. One sign of this is that Adler writes 116 pages of introduction, playing at length with the implications of a statement like "reading is learning," before he gets down to the "rules" for how to read a book. And, although Richards subtitles his book, "A Course in Efficient Reading," those looking for a self-help manual may well complain that he never gets around to talking about how to read a page at all.

For Adler, the "problem" of reading resides in certain kinds of books, books that are "great" and (the equation goes) hard and, therefore, resist the "average" reader. And, he says, the problem resides in the average reader's ignorance of (or misapplication of) techniques for handling a book as a medium of presentation. In the second case at least, problems of understanding are procedural. Adler tells the story of students who could not, at Mr. Hutchins' request, summarize the argument of Lucretius' *The Nature of Things*:

> I repeat, we did not have to teach them logic or explain in detail what the argument was. . . . But they could not find arguments in a book because they had not yet learned to read *actively*, to disengage the important sentences from all the rest, and to observe the connections the author made. Reading Lucretius as they read the newspaper, they naturally did not make such discriminations. (222)

When Adler begins to offer lessons in how to read, he offers procedures for "finding arguments in books," and they include disengaging key terms and sentences and charting the connections between them (characteristically referred to in Adler's pedagogy as the connections "an author made").

Adler has a three-part system (which I will not summarize) for dealing with the difficulties of a long and complex text and for countering the unproductive habits of "novice" readers. Here are some of the guidelines: you need to preview a book before you read it, begin with a sense of the subject area and the problems the writer wants to solve; you need to make connections between what you are reading and other books you have read, other courses you have taken or with your own experience; you need to look for the key terms in a discussion and distinguish between an author's use of them and common usage; readers should withhold judgment, ask questions while they are reading and not later, and put complex passages in their own words; readers should learn to write in the margins and develop the ability to talk back to a writer.

I have spent a good bit of time in my career reviewing the kind of research on reading that is conducted by reading "specialists," and I have read much on reading instruction. I can't recall a book that offers more good advice on how to handle a long and complex text than Adler's, and I would say that fifty years of reading research has offered no improvement on the suggestions he makes to adult readers. Adler certainly has more good advice to offer than Richards, who actually offers little that could be called advice at all. In all of this, however, Adler is not talking about reading, as reading involves interpretation or decisions about meaning. He is talking, rather, about how to handle or manage a book—how to work with this strange form of verbal communication. The problems generally come down to problems in "finding" things in a book or managing the complicated flow of information. The meaning is taken to be fixed, something inside the book if one only has the proper techniques for getting to it or getting it out.

Books, then, represent an unusual system for communication whose buried logic and strategies need to be unearthed for students. Once they know how the system works, the argument goes, they'll know how to move around in it.

This is one problem of reading. The other is represented by the gap between a "great" book and an "average" reader. And this problem is represented in familiar terms of precedence and authority:

> The writer must be superior to the reader, and his book must convey in readable form the insights he possesses and his potential readers lack. . . . The reader must be able to overcome this inequality in some degree, seldom perhaps fully, but always approaching equality with the writer. To the extent that equality is approached, the communication is perfectly consummated.
>
> In short, we can learn only from our betters. We must know who they are and how to learn from them. The man who has this sort of knowledge possesses the art of reading in the sense with which I am especially concerned. (32)

And, as one might suspect in Chicago, the triumph of this knowledge (which is both a knowledge of what one might do and where one stands) is "democracy" (also called "freedom," "the good life," and "happiness").[1] The fruit of this knowledge is "the good life," and the good life is defined as a place of constant intelligent conversation, which comes to mean, as Adler extends the scene, the occupation of a space totally free from the language of daily life (or, perhaps more practically, the periodic withdrawal to a place free from the language of daily life):

> Reading . . . is a basic tool. Those who can use it to learn from books, as well as be amused by them, have access to stores of knowledge. They can furnish their minds so that the prospect of hours spent alone is less bleak. Nor, in the hours they spend with others, need they fear that hollow sound of empty conversation. (vii)

It is also a place of peaceful conversation, free from competing voices or
nay-sayers.

The crude representation of Adler's argument goes something like this:
if you have the right technique, you can get what an author said ("Your
success in reading is determined by the extent to which you get all that
the writer intended to communicate" [26]), and if you get what an author
says, you can have a conversation with him. (Readers, Adler says, can
ask questions and "talk back.") The goal of reading is the achievement
of a community bound together by a shared language—which means a
common set of key terms and examples, a common background, a common
set of values, and so on. (Or, perhaps more properly, the goal of instruction
is to define a use of language to celebrate the values of such a commonality.)
I see no reason to dwell on the dark secrets of this community (the identity
and status of those who would be excluded—those, in the rubric, who
lack "normal" intelligence), except to point out how Adler's argument
provides a gloss to more recent, similar arguments about literacy and
community.

This democracy must be a place where disagreements are impossible—
"real" disagreements, that is, between "reasonable" men, since reasonable
men agree that an "argument is both empty and vicious unless it is
undertaken on the supposition that there is attainable truth which, when
attained by reason in the light of all the relevant evidence, resolves the
original issues" (248). It is a world, then, in which there is no interpretation, and differences are signs only of error, ignorance or viciousness.
"Yet to the extent that men are rational, these obstacles to their understanding one another can be overcome. The sort of disagreement which
is only apparent, resulting from misunderstanding, is certainly curable"
(247).

If this democracy comes to sound like an idealized college seminar,
perhaps it is because that was its founding vision. The Great Books
program began with John Erskine's memories of Columbia where "good
conversation had flourished and, more than that, there had been friendships
with respect to ideas as well as on the playing field or in the fraternities"
(356–57). In such a community, Erskine said, "democracy would be
safe."

For Adler, similarly, the power of reading is that books "form a community of friends who share a common world of ideas." If all of this
sounds a bit like fraternity rush, the echo apparently was not completely
lost to Adler, who confronts, at least momentarily, the exclusionary agenda
of this vision:

> Good conversation requires all those who engage in it to speak within the same frame of reference. Communication not only results in something common; it usually needs a common background to begin with. (356)

This is one way of explaining why it is impossible, in Chicago, to ask students to read, that is, enter into serious conversation with, Adrienne Rich. There is no way of establishing common ground:

> What I am saying may sound as if it had drastic implications. Not only do I want you to learn to read, but now I am asking you to change your friends! I fear there is some truth in that. Either you yourself will not change very much, or you must change your friends. I am only saying what everyone knows. . . . (356)

Change your friends (that is, remake them) or change your friends (that is, leave them); there is no possibility for community on other grounds: such terms define the either/or of a community bound together by this version of cultural literacy.

III

There is little to summarize or paraphrase in Richards' *How To Read a Page*, since the book provides more demonstration than exposition. It offers demonstrations of how one (but most often I.A. Richards) might read a page from Aristotle's *Posterior Analytics*, Collingwood's *Metaphysics*, Whitehead's *Modes of Thought*, Locke's *Of Human Understanding*, and Plato's *Republic*, and demonstrations of how one might "read" (that is, imagine the possible uses of) certain key words ("the words we should study most if through them we are to understand the others"): make, get, give, love, hate, seem, be, do, see, mind, thought, idea, knowledge, reason, purpose and work.

The purpose of Richards' demonstrations is to reflect on the process by which words come to be meaningful. If Adler is concerned with how books work (or how people might work on books), Richards is concerned with language, with how words work (or how people might work with words). Most chapters, then, establish a counterpoint between text and paraphrase, where Richards takes a line from his source (Aristotle, for example) and considers not only ways of reading the line but also the consequences of choosing one reading over another. (He is demonstrating, then, both the making of meaning and the audit of meaning.) For Richards, reading is not a conversation with great teachers from the past (Adler's metaphor) but that "internal drama in which what a word is to mean in a place is decided" (237). Words, phrases, sentences, pages— these things can be read in many ways

> because they touch us at points at which each one of us is himself many-minded. Understanding them is very much more than picking a possible reasonable interpretation, clarifying that, and sticking to it. Understanding them is seeing how the varied possible meanings hang together, which of them depend upon what else, how and why the meanings which matter most to us form a part of our worlds—seeing thereby more clearly what our world is and what we are who are building it to live in. (13)

Richards enacts the drama of reading for us, but the sources and passages he chooses also provide the occasion for reflection on what he calls the "archproblem" in the study of reading: "What should guide the reader's mind?" (240). If reading is a matter of choice and negotiation, who decides when decisions are forced? If reading is an internal drama, which of our many minds should take precedence when we must strike a line and move on, when we must do something *other* than spin out one possible reading after another? This thing that enables us to decide is variously called "will," "desire," "logic," "thought," "reason," and "power."

Richards is not naive about the violence of interpretation or the struggle for power and precedence in interpretive communities.[2] He begins with what he takes to be the most common, but most "dangerous" and "baffling" answer to the question of what should guide us—the belief that usage fixes meaning, the notion that "a word when rightly used carries one only meaning (or exceptionally two or three), and that reading is essentially collecting these right meanings and a sort of adding them together" (235–36). (The clumsy prose is Richards'; the attitude, while not attributed to Adler, could be.) Richards' answer to his question is that the reader should be guided not by words alone but by the relations between words, not by single meanings but multiple meanings, not by sticking to one reading but by examining one's motives in choosing one interpretation over another, or as he puts it, "Our awareness of interdependence, of how things hang together, which makes us able to give and audit an account of what may be meant in a discussion—that highest activity of REASON which Plato named 'Dialectic' " (240).

As Richards acknowledges, this appeal to dialectic does not really answer his question, "What should guide the reader's mind?" It is, rather, only the substitution of a borrowed (and favored) term, "dialectic," for other, less favored terms: "logic," "thought," "desire," "will," "reason," or "power." If one reading may not be said to be more "reasonable" or "logical" than another, and if the resolution of disputes (rival interpretations) is not to be a matter only of will and power, what is the alternative of "dialectic," particularly as Richards names it?

For Adler, the answer to the question, "What should guide a reader's mind?" is always "the text." The text should guide. To read means to overcome the problems of presentation in books and to get it right, to get what the author said. It is true, you and I may differ over what a book says. "After all, a book is something different to each reader." For Adler, however, this does *not* mean that "anything goes":

> Though readers be different, the book is the same, and there can be an objective check upon the accuracy and fidelity of the statements anyone makes about it. (171)

Richards is also unwilling to say "anything goes." For one thing, there are errors and misreadings that can be corrected through instruction and application. Readers can learn how to pay attention to a text and how to pay attention to the ways they pay attention. With what Richards calls a "method" for attending to words, a reader's reading becomes less automatic, less routine. Readers can learn to put aside their desire to make a text too stable ("the easiest way to control a meaning is to pin it"). But there is a point at which Richards becomes impatient with the implications of his own performance as a reader—that is, the implication that a text is open for endless, brilliant readings. A reader's skill, in other words, can also become his problem. The potential for every word to mean many things can make it impossible to get past the first sentence or to say anything at all.

> There are no simple acts anywhere in our lives. But we do well to forget this except when forgetting makes us unjust, dogmatic, or unimaginative toward our own or others' meanings. (183)

At the level of practice, this is Richards' dilemma. It also points to the problem of maintaining a community of readers who might share their knowledge. We need to make things simple unless doing so makes us unjust, unimaginative, or dogmatic, but doing so will always make us unjust, unimaginative, and dogmatic. How then can one choose and still "balance enough possibles"? The answer, again, is "dialectic": "The art of remembering [that there are no simple acts] . . . is that supreme art of knowing, Dialectic." Dialectic, then, is both a way of handling texts and a way of handling one's relations to others, a way of being present without erasing the presence of others.

Dialectic is a term Richards can use but not command. Behind it lies the unresolvable point and counterpoint of his project—the swing between freedom and restraint, between open and closed systems, between the balance of possibles and the necessity of choice. These remain opposites he cannot combine into a new term, and (perhaps as a consequence) they are the root of his playfulness—as when, for example, he announces a list of 100 key words and produces 103; or when he creates a set of specialized quotation marks (a wonderful conceit), but then *uses* them to fix his words and clutter the page, until the text becomes almost unreadable. He resists order and requires it. He is both radical educator and fussy schoolmaster. He wants to celebrate ambiguity but not be misunderstood.

At the end of *How to Read a Page*, at the very point at which he questions the possibility of dialectic (since there is forever warfare within "the sphere of intellectual desire"), he expresses both a fond and a desperate wish:

> Can we not—as a parallel to the possibilities of World Communication which Basic English holds out—make an attempt in education which would measure up to our need? Can we not contrive that the funda- mental *ideas* through which alone we can understand one another are studied in place of so much else which today leads us apart and into opposition? We might at least make the three or four books which best embody these ideas available in the most readable form. But this study must be by Dialectic not debate. Word-warfare on such great themes in this bomber-shrunk world is but incipient battle, prelude to oppres- sion or surrender, and we have, most of all, to reconceive discussion itself. (241)

Richards is trying to imagine a world culture centered on three or four books written in Basic English (that is, the English language reduced to 850 words). Of course Richards is serious. But at the same time, his own extended argument has shown how such a proposal is crazy. These three or four books, he has taught us to say, cannot really be books at all. One would have to call them something else, perhaps "Great Books"—that is, books with important ideas that everyone can read and discuss without misunderstanding. This is the intellectually serious alternative to Adler's vision of a community of common readers sitting in a lovely room looking out onto a lovely quad and talking about great books. Richards is trying to imagine a world community bound together by a common culture, but it remains a naive utopia given all that he has said about the nature of understanding and misunderstanding.

Richards desires a world guided by his own key words and ideas; the counterpoint to this is his claim that, most of all, we must "reconceive discussion itself" and replace debate with dialectic. This is the expansive Richards. Adler, you will recall, could tell us only to change friends if the discussion got tough or unseemly or out of hand. Richards would have us change the scene and the relations between the actors. This new way of speaking, if it can be achieved, is what he would like to call "dialectic." This is his hope for the future. And this, it seems to me, is where teachers are right now: wondering still, while faced with violence in the classroom and out, whether we need to change our friends or re-imagine what it means to talk together about books.[3]

Notes

1. Chicagoans, like members of any community, put restrictions on key terms—in this case terms like "freedom" or "democracy." "Docile," for example, must be synonymous with "active" in Chicago: "A person is wrongly thought to be docile if he is passive and pliable. On the contrary, docility is the extremely active virtue of being teachable. No one is really teachable who does not freely exercise his power of independent judgment. The most docile reader is, therefore, the most critical" (238–39).

2. I don't agree with Geoffrey Hartman, in other words, that Richards was compelled to evade a "meditation on authority" (Brower, Vendler and Hollander 162). The second half of *How To Read a Page* could be read as just such a meditation.

3. I am grateful to Matt Cooper and Christine Ross for their help as research assistants on this project.

Works Cited

Adler, Mortimer J. *How To Read a Book: The Art of Getting a Liberal Education.* New York: Simon and Schuster, 1940.

Berthoff, Ann E. *The Making of Meaning.* Portsmouth, NH: Boynton/Cook, 1981.

Booth, Wayne C. and Marshall W. Gregory. *The Harper and Row Reader.* New York: Harper & Row, 1984.

Brower, Reuben, Helen Vendler and John Hollander, eds. *I. A. Richards: Essays in His Honor.* New York: Oxford UP, 1973.

Richards, I. A. *How To Read a Page.* New York: W.W. Norton, 1942.

II

Levels

A stone fence holds the heat.
Close to it, the earth face opens:
a little eye
rimmed with dirt crumbs,
a nerve inside winks
alive with ants.
The yellow-shafted flicker
before it strikes inspects
the spot, drops
from the fence, calculates,
lifts the lid off.
Air fractures, and
inner alleys collapse, as
diamond-cutter the flicker
like a good writer starts
at the heart.
Its bill its tool,
it chisels toward the fault,
beaks at the crux of it, and
chambers of egg-cases
crack open. As the bird
eats, insects by hundreds
scatter in patterns carrying
clustered eggs, rushing
some to safety, later.

Ants leave me cold,
their bitty parts reflexive,
like cells of lung or muscle,

unprincipled, lacking
a visible body to serve—
oh, why qualify. Ant-mystery
drifts out of mind.
The bird is flicker;
its action exhibits it,
pinioned to a wheel which
the mind's eye axles,
the mind's eye spins.

MARIE PONSOT

6

Discovering the Forms of Academic Discourse

ROBERT M. HOLLAND, JR.

University of Akron

In nearly every scholarly discipline a teacher is expected to be also, in some sense, a teacher of writing—a teacher of the special composition techniques or discourse routines required of scholars working within that discipline. Contemporary school and university movements sometimes called "Writing in the Subject Areas" and "Writing across the Curriculum" express a long-standing, if not always stated, assumption: the way a teacher chooses to define the place of writing within an academic discipline profoundly affects not only the general literacy skills of students but also the ways students come to understand writing as a *necessary* constituent of the academic discipline itself—*as* "academic," and *as* "discipline."

What we believe academic discourse to be, how we believe it comes into being, and what we believe it is valuable for—these are questions that ought to shape the ways we invite new scholars to write *as* scholars, whatever their academic discipline. These questions ought to guide us in deciding how to help new scholars discover writing as intrinsic and essential to their "subject" or "field" or "major" as not merely "topic" or "specialty" or "area," but as academic discipline, a community enterprise which is defined by specific forms of discourse. What follows takes up these ideas in three ways. First I explain the sense in which I am using the term *form*. Then I offer a short narrative as exemplum. Finally, I summarize a sequence of writing assignments adaptable for teaching the forms of academic discourse in most of the conventional disciplines.

The term *form* is problematic. It is widely used to indicate a number of conceptions, three of which I need to discriminate here. In any discourse, we might say, there is *form*, there is *formula*, and there is *format*. That is, any discourse has a semantics (form), a syntactics (formula), and a syntagmatics (format). To put it another way, any discourse is a linguistic representation of someone's meaning-making (it is formed); this representation is recorded or expressed according to some linguistic community's code (it is formulated); and it is presented to others—assembled, arranged, ordered—within systematic conventions stipulated by that community (it is formatted). The assertion that a discourse "has" form, formula, and format is meant as an analytic premise; obviously, one *composes* with form, formula, and format jointly, or alternately, or simultaneously in mind—a composer may focus on any of these at a given moment, and attention to one may provoke or require attention to the others as one proceeds in composing or construing. The terms can be useful in discussing writing instruction, so long as we don't imagine them as a necessarily sequential set of concerns or topics.

By *academic* discourse I mean discourse which is primarily and necessarily "referential": that is, "exploratory," "scientific," or "informative." (Here I am using James Kinneavy's terms; cf. Chapter 3 of *A Theory of Discourse*. Of course, not every specimen of referential discourse need be exclusively exploratory, scientific, or informative. These terms are qualitative, not generic.) The form of referential discourse is always dialectic and didactic; all three kinds of referential discourse have in common a search for truth through questions and answers designed to rectify, using logic, the evidence of observed data with the assertions of theory. Academic discourse is, then, both Aristotelian and Platonic: Aristotelian in its empiricism and its appeal to logical relationships claimed between particular instances and general truths; Platonic in its commitment to an intersubjective search for truth through dialectic.

Plato has Socrates define the ideal of academic discourse in the *Phaedrus* (277–78): "true written rhetoric" must not be a creation of fantasy or something aimed merely at creating belief without any attempt at instruction by question and answer; it must be more than a record or mnemonic device; it is written by one who has knowledge of the truth he writes, who can defend what he has written by submitting to an interrogation on the subject, and who makes it evident as soon as he speaks how comparatively inferior are his writings. A scholar teaches what he knows; inquires, through dialectic, into what he does not know; and not only submits to but *seeks* the best interrogation, refutation, or criticism that may be developed by other scholars. Academic discourse, at its best, is both dialectic and didactic.

Such is the case with ideal academic discourse. In the world of school, however, from the earliest "sharing" of pre-school through doctoral dissertations, the academic writer may choose an *eidolon*, a "dream-image" of academic discourse; furthermore, he or she may be quite unaware of having made such a choice. Format and formula may become primary, for they often appear to be the observable determiners of esteem or success. Teachers, also, (whether aware of it or not) may invite either the idea or the eidolon of academic discourse by the way they design their writing assignments.

Let me illustrate this concept of eidolon with a story from my own early schooling. In September of 1955 our high school chemistry class went to the chemistry laboratory for the first time. We had been told that there was to be no talking while we were in the lab; we were to follow the written instructions on how to work with the material assembled at our stations and to submit a written report before leaving the lab. At each station were four numbered beakers containing clear liquid, two pads of litmus paper (blue, pink), and this assignment: "Use only the litmus paper to find out what you can about the contents of the beakers. Write a report of your findings and what you think those findings mean."

Of course, none of us was entirely in the dark at that point: we had had some experience with "chemistry sets," we "knew" the simple magic of litmus. We set to work, systematically dipping little strips of blue and pink litmus into the series of beakers. For me, as I recall, it went like this: with beaker #1, the pink litmus became blue and the blue litmus became merely damp; with beaker #2, the pink litmus became damp and the blue litmus became pink; with beaker #3, both the blue and the pink litmus paper became damp, neither of them changing color; with beaker #4, both the blue and the pink litmus paper turned white.

Now, I hadn't the slightest idea what was happening with beaker #4. I peeked about the lab to see how my classmates were doing and found them peeking about, too: we all had before us, from one or another of our beakers, pink and blue litmus paper strips which had both turned white. Since we had been prohibited from discussing our work, we each turned to the task of composing a written report.

Though puzzled by the whitened litmus, we did know something about writing reports. We each drew up a chart or table (columns for the beakers, rows for the litmus, that sort of thing) and wrote in our findings. We added an introduction, repeating the written instructions at our stations, and we made some sentences about how we had done what we had been told to do. But here is the curious part: *not one of us included the information about both the blue and the pink litmus strips turning white.* (I believe I wrote in my report of both blue and pink litmus for beaker #4: "No change." Others wrote, "Both became damp," or, "Nothing happened.")

The following day, the chemistry teacher began by asking each of us in turn what we had experienced with the litmus and the liquid in a particular beaker (he asked me, of course, about beaker #4). One after another we stated not what we had seen, but what we had written in our reports. The teacher then asked whether any of us had noticed litmus paper turning white. Well, we all had, and now we said so. But none of us, he pointed out, had reported that; how, he asked, did we account for this phenomenon of our concurrence in a fiction? Why had we all written what was untrue?

We replied as best we could, explaining that we had been afraid of being wrong and admitting a shared belief that every finding must be explained; since we had no idea of what was happening with the whitened litmus, we had chosen to describe that occurrence by redefining it. Our replies, taken all together, made clear to us that our reports were not academic discourse but an imitation of academic discourse. While none of us had pretended not to see the litmus paper turn white, we all had pretended so in our reports.

We had missed the point of the laboratory assignment, which had been designed to enable us to discover for ourselves the dialectic of chemistry, and we had chosen to substitute our eidolon of academic discourse. Having assumed that the true subject of our exercise was "Using Litmus Paper," we then formulated our "learning" to fit our expectations. We formatted our findings to fit the fantasy of our waking dream of science—*in spite of* our first-hand experience that called into question the very tool we imagined we had mastered. (Beaker #4, it turned out, contained commercial bleach, which subverted the dye system of the litmus paper itself.)

We had used format and formulation to excuse ourselves from the learning of form, creating an illusion of knowledge based on an absurd and unspoken premise: "What you do not understand, hide." In imitating scientists, we had behaved as no true scientist ever would. What made the exercise nonetheless useful for us, in spite of our failure, was that our reports were in writing: having created ignorance (or, more generously, having made a predictable student error), we had to confront, in the written testimony of our reports, the consequences of our creation. Written discourse made possible a scene for learning that would have been impossible through vocal discussion. By discovering ourselves as a community of *non*-scholars we were able to see what it might mean to become a community of scholars.

The lesson was not learned all at once, of course. In another year, doing physics, we went about the business of heating metal rods, viewing salt and other things in a flame, and rolling steel balls down troughs—and then looked up in handbooks the correct coefficient of expansion or wavelength of light or acceleration of gravity and worked our calculations backwards, leaving what we called a "margin of error." In biology we knew better than to try to draw precisely the protozoa we tracked through our microscopes; no, we traced perfect circles into our laboratory reports and drew within them adaptations of what our textbooks showed. If you were "seeing" a paramecium, it better have a fringe of cilia all around; if an amoeba, include one contractile vacuole.

And so it went in other school subjects: we told back history as it was told to us—never mentioning an open question or an unresolved doubt, and never imagining that it was all right *not* to know the significance of everything. We wrote school discourse, not academic discourse but an eidolon of academic discourse. We dealt in formulas and format, not in form, not in meaning-making dialectic. One might argue that school students need to master formats and formulas before they can understand form—*real* chemistry, *real* history, etc., could be learned later, in college. Still, to me, at any rate, the academic discourse of students at higher levels has not always been markedly different.

Perhaps the most disappointing of assignments in academic discourse, year after year, has been the so-called research paper, or library paper, or term paper. The barrenness of the term paper enterprise is in one way indicated by the commercial availability of literally thousands of complete term papers on every topic under the sun, in another way by a note I found left in the stacks of a university library:

Roger—
{Oedipus the King}—Socrates
if possible . . .
* * * critics view on this trajedy * * *
* anything I could get research from
*things on *plot/setting* of it
Actually—just abt anything

Thanks,
Amy

(I don't need the story though)

Many of us have ourselves been there, grinding out library papers, term papers, research papers on "just abt anything" according to this or that format, in terms of this or that documentation scheme. We have followed the steps laid down for us in handbooks and publication manuals as we composed encyclopedic surveys or protracted forensic free-for-alls in imitation of an idea of academic discourse. What may not always have been apparent to us (or to those who made our assignments) is that how one defines for oneself the heart of the enterprise of academic discourse is a matter of choice. What we may have avoided facing, through it all, was the consequences of such a choice.

The heart of the enterprise of writing a research paper can be located in format, in formula, or in form. One can focus primarily on the creation of the object (the documented paper which presents the "research"); one can focus primarily on the assembly and organization of the "source materials," or one can focus primarily on the research itself, the questions and answers, the defining of issues, the interpretation and assessment of data, the use of the bibliographic or data-gathering and data-processing procedures by which one arrives at what one claims as truth. It is this third focus that best enables a student to discover the dialectic and didactic form of academic discourse, and at this point I wish to turn to a sequence of writing assignments that attempted to exploit that potential.

Some years ago Richard Binder (a research librarian at Drexel University) and I designed a sequence of assignments that sought to place the primary focus squarely on scholarly research itself. Our aim was to help each student discover the forms of academic discourse (dialectic and didactic) within his or her academic discipline. Here is what we did.

We began by asking students to define themselves in relation to their specific academic disciplines by writing responses to these questions: "What is your academic field? In what sense is it 'academic'? In what sense is it a 'field'? In what sense is it 'yours'?" Their responses were used by the instructors to raise fundamental questions about definition and classification. (We were after the idea of an academic discipline as a syntactics and a syntagmemics for a particular kind of semantics, though we did not use those terms at the start.) In revising their papers, students had the chance to begin redefining what it meant for them to be scholars in their chosen fields.

Then, in lecture, we traced relations among an academic field's *data*, its *literature*, and its *bibliography*: there is that which a discipline isolates and collects as the phenomena to be studied (data); there is academic discourse that formulates and formats the data (literature); and there are the means of access to the literature (bibliography). The second writing assignment sent students to current literature (journals, yearbooks, research reviews) to report on a current issue in their field and to define that issue as a set of written questions. In guiding students through revisions of these reports we worked on stating research questions which could be addressed by locating extant data or literature.

The purpose of the remaining exercises was to find that data or literature and then to explain to a beginner in their field what that data or literature is and how it may be found. Their discourse was to be "informative." The writing assignments week by week built on one another, culminating in the creation of a reference work, a guide to the literature on *one* specific question on *one* current issue in *one* well-defined academic field. Each assignment required the student to focus on a question, to use some bibliographic means to address that question, and then to report in writing on the search and its result. At each step of the sequence of assignments the student was asked to address a written report to a double audience— the other members of the class, and future students beginning to study in a specific discipline.

Our aim was to avoid, *by making irrelevant*, the kind of paste-up encyclopedic narratives, serial book reports, or extended argumentative essays that often pass for academic discourse. By intentionally framing each assignment to require an encounter with some bibliographic tool or system, we meant to provide the student with a first-hand "known" experience which could become the ground for informative dialectic. By making the object of the work the creation of a useful document for other scholars, we meant to invite the student to a new definition of responsibility.

Early in the semester, each student produced a one-page guide to bibliography concerning a narrowed subject (following the format known as "Pathfinder," an Addison-Wesley copyrighted design for a single-page bibliography of research materials and primary sources organized from general to specific). When satisfactorily revised and corrected, this one-page guide was made available for the use of other students. The one-page guide also served as a means for the student to design and write the final piece of writing for the course, a "guide to the literature." This final piece of writing was to be mainly bibliographic; the student composed not an argumentative essay or an encyclopedic survey of a topic, but a reference work to be used by other scholars—a guide to the literature concerning one specific question on a current issue within one's academic discipline. In this final report, the student presented a modest review of literature and an explanation of the use of particular bibliographic tools that provide access to that literature. (It, too, became a permanent part of the university library's reference collection.)

By emphasizing report writing about the bibliographic research process itself, we intended to raise fundamental questions about the forms of academic discourse. To be a sociologist, or an historian, or a chemist, or a linguist, and so forth—to be an "academician"—is to take part in the dialectic of the field, and to take part responsibly, not merely as one who tells a story, expresses an attitude, or argues a point.

Students made frequent errors in this sequence of assignments, but these we viewed as necessary conditions for the kind of learning we sought. For example, they did not adequately define subjects or limit questions, they overlooked or undervalued especially useful resources, they misused the tools of bibliography, and, sometimes after the best of efforts and with the best of intentions, they misrepresented their findings and what they claimed to know based on them. Again, we saw these errors not as failures, but as prerequisite grounds for the dialectic of instruction. In academic discourse within the schools, how one gets it wrong, and how one understands that, is probably more instructive than simply getting it right.

We expected students regularly to miss the mark, and we welcomed these "errors." We were not entrapping students, setting them up to fail, any more than the point of beaker #4 was to imply that we were all fools. We did believe, however, that the experience of a certain kind of failure was necessary to what we saw as the primary aim of our course. For example, during the semester each student planned, executed, and reported on a computer-assisted search of a bibliographic data base. This assignment, perhaps more than any other, confronted students with the limitations of tools and the consequences of procedural errors. Few students were familiar with programming or Boolean searching; as they applied their "known" to this new system, they faced frustrations and "failures" which became ideal moments for interrogation and discovery. Whether the student had misused thesaurus terms, or taken an imprudent shortcut in a Boolean search, or committed himself to a massive and expensive on-line printout request, the experience had to be reported and explained *in writing*. The written report was essential for documenting one's coming to terms with the problem, the experience, the known, and the as-yet-unknown. By holding oneself accountable to others as a report writer, the writer was more likely to be able to hold himself accountable to himself as a scholar.

To summarize, the writing assignments were designed to confront the student with unfamiliar formats (abstracts, research reports, research reviews, citation indexing, etc.) in a way that subordinated the format and the formulation to the form. The focus of each assignment was to establish, through question and answer, some "known" and to determine its limits and implications. By requiring the student to state in writing how he or she came to know what is claimed, and by expecting the student to be able to explain, in writing, the constraints of systematic bibliography, we intended to maintain epistemology itself as the real subject of study.

Over a period of three years we taught this course several times to classes made up of students concentrating in most of the conventional humanities and social science disciplines. Guides and reviews on sixty-six topics were added to the university library's reference collection. Subjects included Discipline in Inner City Schools, Food Additives, Juvenile Gangs, The 1973 Soviet Constitution, The U.S. Social Security System, Black Suicide, Biometeorology, Music Therapy, Gerald Holton, Equal Rights for Women Within the Church.

Our students did not become experts in these subjects, nor were they expected to; what mattered was that they did not have to pretend to become experts. We believe that they did acquire a more significant kind of expertise by using the formats and formulations of the bibliography and literature of their field in such a way that they could discover their discipline *as* a discipline.

Teachers assigning writing at all levels and in all academic subjects could similarly focus on the dialectic and didactic form of academic discourse as fundamental to academic discipline. By declining to make format and formulation primary, by designing assignments that avoid the inference that format and formulation are primary, the instructor has a better chance of enabling students to become scholars. The world is full of eidolons of "schooled" people; by offering students the chance to discover the forms of academic discourse, we may increase the number of true lovers of wisdom.

Works Cited

Kinneavy, James. *A Theory of Discourse*. Englewood Cliffs, NJ: Prentice-Hall, 1971.

Plato. *Phaedrus and Letters VII & VIII*. Trans. Walter Hamilton. New York: Penguin, 1973.

7

Toward a Hermeneutics of Difficulty

MARIOLINA SALVATORI

University of Pittsburgh

And although we are aware how much of any interpretation must depend on a tacit form of knowledge acquired from institutional training, we tend to reserve our highest praise for those interpretations that seem most intuitive, most theory-free, seeming to proceed from some untrammeled divinatory impulse, having the gratuity, the fortuity of genius.

Frank Kermode, *The Genesis of Secrecy*

Having reminded us that hermeneutics developed as a way of codifying and controlling the interpretation of sacred texts, Frank Kermode, in *The Genesis of Secrecy*, identifies Jesus' parables as the "original, uncompromising, and disquieting" instance of hermeneutical theory and practice (2). He says that "[w]hen Jesus was asked to explain the purpose of his parables, he described them as stories *told from without*—to outsiders —with the express purpose of concealing a mystery that was to be understood only by insiders" (2). The power, the gift to understand the meaning of the stories, separated the insiders from the outsiders. To all outsiders, "lest they should turn again, and be forgiven," the parables (another word for them, he suggests, might be "riddles") were inaccessible. Kermode acknowledges that "the true sense of this theory of parable interpretation is much disputed" (3), but he stands firm in his conviction that in this tradition only the insiders can hope to achieve correct interpretation:

> To divine the truth, the latent sense, you need to be of the elect, of the institution. Outsiders must content themselves with the manifest, and pay a supreme penalty for doing so. Only those who already know the mysteries—what the stories really mean—can discover what the stories really mean. As a matter of fact, the teacher, on the very occasion when he pronounced this rule, showed himself irritated with his elect for seeking explanations of what they already, in principle, knew. And, if we are to believe Mark, they continued to be slow learners, prone to absurd error. (3)

Traces of this "exclusionary" view are discernible in the language many students use to describe the act of interpretation as well as in the interpretive performances and the accompanying attitudes that act out their perceptions of themselves as "outsiders" and of the texts they read as "riddles." These traces indicate that their training either has posited this view or has not systematically called it into question.

To profess in the classroom, however unconsciously, a preference for "those interpretations that seem most intuitive, most theory free . . . having the gratuity, the fortuity of genius," amounts to professing a version of Kermode's theory of parable interpretation. But when that theory is transferred from the religious to the secular context—when that theory can no longer rely on unteachable faith, the *sine qua non* for the believer's access to the eternal kingdom—that theory becomes a profession of *lack of faith* in students' intellectual capabilities, an act of pedagogical sterility.

If we are really concerned lest pedagogy become a strategy of exclusion, our pedagogical imperative should be consciously and consistently to make *manifest* the rules and practices of interpretation we have acquired from institutional training, and to teach all students—remedial as well as mainstream, undergraduate as well as graduate—the very methods we practice in the classroom and use to produce the texts that grant us professional status.[1]

In my experience as a teacher of literature and composition, the method that has proven to be the most appropriate to fostering and to sustaining students' critical understanding of the text they read combines two reciprocally monitoring techniques: a self-reflexive "hermeneutical" critique and a "deconstructive" one. The hermeneutical critique posits the necessity for the knower/reader to understand herself in the act of understanding: thus it demands that the reader reflect on the motives, prejudgements, and preunderstandings that can both foster and impede interpretation (Gad-

9). The deconstructive technique posits the necessity for a /thinker to expose a text's fissures which are to be examined and studied less as symptoms of "flaws and imperfections" in the theoretical system that has produced the text than as indications of "that system's possibility" (cf. Johnson).

In the congruence of these two critiques I see the possibility of enacting a process with which a reader can negotiate her autonomy as "knower" from the silencing influence of "uncritically" accepted authority (the text's/author's/teacher's authority or the authority of the prejudices that can blind her to the question a text, an author, a teacher is trying to raise)—an autonomy, however, which self-reflexively she must always keep in the making, subject to scrutiny and revision (cf. Salvatori).

Once a text is credited with high authority it is studied intensely; once it is so studied it acquires mystery or secrecy.
>   Kermode, *The Genesis of Secrecy*

For several years now, I have taught "Introduction to Critical Reading," a prerequisite for English literature majors.[2] In order to make the practice of the method I have just described possible, the course charts an in-depth, recursive reading of three classic (canonical) texts—*King Lear, Madame Bovary*, and "The Waste Land"—and a set of professional critics' readings of these texts.[3]

As students first read the literary text and try to negotiate their critical understanding of it, they are asked to identify in a short "position paper" some of the difficulties they have experienced in their interaction with the text. The writing of the position paper, with its focus on what may be initially perceived as a reader's "failure," represents a radical change for students because it entails a reflexive inquiry which they are not used to practice, and about whose usefulness they are openly skeptical. (The development of the critical mind is a project that, as Robert Pattison argues, requires a kind of training "not generally available in the American scheme of education" (176). But more importantly, the position paper radically changes the traditional configuration of the pedagogical scene by forcing the teacher to acknowledge and to appreciate *as an insider* the difficulties her students encounter, and to remember what years of learning and training might have made her forget, i.e., that reading is indeed "a highly sophisticated skill *acquired only with difficulty*" (Said 24; emphasis added; cf. Newkirk).

When inexperienced readers read complex texts, their "difficulties" consistently identify actual and venerable interpretive cruxes. This, I believe, is a fact worth reflecting on. When my students read *King Lear*, they invariably tend to focus on the perplexing nature of Lear's motivations, on Cordelia's "mute" love, the juxtaposition of plots, the vagueness of topography in the play. When they read *Madame Bovary*, they are disoriented by the narrative voice, the disappearance of the "we" in the first pages of the novel and its sliding off into a perplexing distance, the stifling abundance of detail. And when they read "The Waste Land," they cite as sources of difficulty its erudition, its fragmentariness, its gloomy, nightmarish atmosphere, its voices that speak but do not communicate. But whereas experienced readers tame a textual difficulty by constructing an interpretation that accommodates it or by naming it a "textual" flaw or an "intended" difficulty, less experienced readers hastily assign authority to the text or to the author by either accepting the responsibility for the flaw ("He/she must be saying something I just cannot understand") or with an iconoclastic gesture that may well be their only way of claiming autonomy by refusing to deal with it ("He/she/it does not make sense"). Whereas experienced readers see in a difficulty the "beginning" of a critical reading of a text, inexperienced readers see in it a form of entrapment (cf. Flynn; Bartholomae; Berthoff).

Their initial insights, unexamined though they be, nevertheless indicate that these readers are *in principle* critical readers, "insiders," and that their tendency to invalidate their productive beginnings needs to be referred, as I've suggested, to their training—both as past schooling and as cultural and historical conditioning—in reading/thinking. If this is so, then their difficulties *are* the appropriate beginning for their critical investigation to focus on; for, only after they have reclaimed their own beginnings from "intransitivity" can they begin to understand and to practice the complex, "institutional" and "cultural" ways in which experienced readers negotiate their interpretations. Thus, rather than as "canonical interpretations" which readers can only contemplate/imitate/emulate, the professional critics' readings selected for the course are studied, and critiqued, as examples of some of the strategies expert readers use to gain autonomy, to negotiate power away from a text's/writer's authority. Not to do so, to offer them instead as inscrutable, hermetic models, risks magnifying students' insecurity about their own critical abilities and producing yet more uncritical docility or uncritical rebellion.[4]

What follows is a teacher's reading of a student's description and emergent interpretation of the difficulties that threaten to entrap her as she reads "The Waste Land." What I have learned from teaching this course is that although students' texts (particularly texts that tell stories of difficult readings) are not usually credited with high authority, when they are studied intensely they acquire a mystery and a secrecy the investigation of which makes "the genesis" of their difficulty manifest: students' stories of reading tell authoritative stories about reading and how they have been taught to read.

The excerpts I will offer below as a text to be credited with high authority were written in three consecutive class periods during the last two weeks of "Introduction to Critical Reading." At this time in the term, counting on my students' ability and willingness to exercise their own autonomy as readers, I exert my authority as a teacher by deliberately withholding it (as much as I can). Because I do not want to influence their interpretations, I do not engage with them in class discussions. My only explicit interaction with them takes place on the first day after their first reading of the poem. On this day, all I ask of them is that they identify particular features of the poem that they thought were problematic. By now students know that this question is meant to slight neither them nor the text they are reading, and so they eagerly and aggressively provide lists of problems. They speak; I write on the chalkboard; and for every feature they identify, I ask them why it constitutes a difficulty for them; what kind of understanding they were constructing that this feature works against or disrupts; what they expected to be there instead. My questions are meant to show my students that they can solve some difficulties through a careful reading of the text; to solve other difficulties, however, they must rely on different ways of knowing, even on others' knowing. Although what they can explain on their own might be minimal, I consider this explanation worth much more, in terms of the "relative" autonomy, the "limited" critical dependence it can grant them, than any borrowed, "parroted," extensive and well-polished explanation.

After this first session, I ask them to re-read the poem and to prepare to write at length about the particular difficulty or difficulties they experienced in their reading. When they next come to class, they are impatient to begin writing. Nobody ever leaves before the time is over. Many stay longer. At the end of the period I do three things. I collect their writings (which I will read and return virtually unmarked—I want to establish my presence as an audience so that they produce texts that are intelligible to others, but at the same time, I want them to start asserting their authority and autonomy). I then ask them to read a set of "explanatory footnotes" as a supplement to and a way of discussing the nature of Eliot's fifty-two notes (in Wilkie) and a set of excerpts from Eliot's "Tradition and the Individual Talent" and "Hamlet and His Problems." Finally I ask them to read the poem in light of these additional readings and to take detailed notes on, in fact to chart, any change in their understandings. Once more I collect their writings (which again I will return unmarked), and I ask them to re-read the poem (this time in light of Helen Williams' and Elizabeth Drew's critical writings) so that they can write about their understanding of it a third time.

This recursive structure of reading and writing teaches a method of reading that inches its way through difficulties, a method of reading, that is, that does not blindly and passively accept somebody else's knowledge as the solution to the problem, does not substitute somebody else's reading for one's non-reading, but rather creates its own source of understanding and constitutes its own resource of knowledge.

When a student I'll call Jan, in her diagnostic exam on the first day of class, wrote a description of her response to Julio Cortazar's "The Night Face Up," she unambiguously expressed her dislike for authors/texts that trick and confuse their readers. During the term, however, she progressively and graciously learned to examine both the reasons for her dislike and the consequences of it for her reading. Baffled by her confused response to a confusing text, Jan nevertheless manages in the following texts to give an account of that confusion, which both assesses some of the text's crucial features and their effect on a reader, and begins to generate an interpretation. I'm interested in finding out how. At the same time, I want to explore what Jan's work reminds us of about reading, in particular the reading of "The Waste Land," that our understanding of the poem, an understanding constructed over a long period of time, through many readings of the poem and other texts, might blind us to.

Jan's text begins with four lines from "The Waste Land":

> Who is the third who walks beside you?
> When I count, there are only you and I together
> But when I look ahead up the white road
> There is always another one walking beside you.

I am drawn to this section and the several lines following it (and the two sections preceding it). It is mysterious and compelling in that it seems to entice me into a closer examination. Although the description is strange, confusing me as to whether "the third" is a specific someone who must be sought out in order to better understand the poem, there is in these lines a feeling of *deja vu*. There is something that feels recognizable, familiar. Is it the universal experience of having glimpsed or briefly attained an insight and, later, recalling only the sensation that the higher awareness had brought, but having lost sight of the "thing" itself? That is what this image awakens in me, the realization that something is missing when one's strongest sense is that it should be there.

In the footnotes we have been given, there is a fascinating story from which Eliot's image springs. He had read of an account of an Antarctic expedition during which "the party of explorers, at the extremity of their strength, had the constant delusion that there was one more member that could be counted" (Eliot). We are also told that in this section of "The Waste Land," "V. What the Thunder Said," Eliot is using the theme of the resurrected Christ's journey to Emmaus, during which he met his disciples, but they did not recognize him ("Who is the third . . . "). This is where I am stuck. I can feel the despair and the sense of betrayal that Christ, in this story, told in Luke 24:13–16, must have felt when his closest associates no longer knew him, the sense of alienation. And independent of the Christ theme, the stanza evokes confusion, difficulty of comprehension, again, the feeling that something should be there, but is not.

This stanza echoes the theme of illusion in the preceding one. There is the sense that, with the rocks, there should be water.

> If there were the sound of the water only
> . . .
> . . . sound of the water over a rock
> . . .
> But there is no water

The song of the hermit thrush imitates the sound of the water dripping. "Drip drop drip drop drop drop." But there is no water. This thwarted expectation reverberates. There should be another walking beside you, but "when I count there are only you and I together." In this early interaction with Eliot's "Wasteland," I derive a sense of disappointed expectations and an accompanying feeling of confusion and disorientation.

Where, in Jan's text, is the dividing line between her reflections about reading and about her reading of her poem? I don't think it is always possible to draw that line. And I don't think it matters. What does matter, however—what makes the difference between confused thinking and writing on the one hand and thinking and writing about confusion on the other—is Jan's instinctive sense that in order for her to find her bearings through this confusion, she needs a point of reference ("something"—the water, "the third" that should be there but is not; and more abstractly, the answer to the question the text asks but does not provide an answer for). That point of reference is her notion of what reading is or should be, at least for her. That notion centers, rather than de-centers, her writing.

I was at first surprised that Jan should choose a "difficulty" in the latter part of the poem. Given her sense of progression, I thought she might first want to come to terms with earlier difficulties. I wondered what "compelled" her to begin with this section. Perhaps it is the direct question, the riddle-like mini-narrative perennially awaiting an answer. Or perhaps it is the feeling of *deja vu* she reads in these lines—the something "recognizable, familiar" she seeks in a reading and she so much appreciates. Is the *deja vu* actual or does she invent it? Does she see in these lines, in other words, a reiteration, a *deja vu* of responses to "The Waste Land" from a prior part of the text or from other texts, other readings, other situations? Is her *deja vu* a perception she conjures up not so much to shape a sense of closure as a sense of beginning?

Jan's attempt to discern the lineaments of "the third" can be seen as an example of the tendency in readers, and thinkers, to reduce "fortuity" before even deciding "that there is a way of looking that provides a place for it" (Kermode 64)—a nearly instinctive need for security, for closure, that should neither be denied nor made light of (cf. Leenhardt). What is remarkable in Jan's performance, however, is that her yearning for fulfillment does not paralyze her beginning. In fact, Jan's text articulates her dialogue with herself as to why she began where she did and why she responded the way she did. In her writing, Jan records and enacts the model of teacher/student interaction that, in the beginning of the term, used to disorient her (and the other students) so much.

The first paragraph is a text generated by successive and successful acts of reflexivity. Each sentence is the answer to what I would argue is the most fundamental beginning critical question: Why am I thinking/saying what I am thinking/saying? The result of this questioning is that, mysterious as the text may be, it does not silence or distance her, but rather it compels and entices her to lend a voice to that mysteriousness. The dialogue Jan begins with the text of "The Waste Land" is triggered by and is about her confusion as a reader. As she voices her confusion, however, she delimits it so that she is in more control of than controlled by it. Writing gives her a way to orient herself through that confusion. In writing she claims and exerts an authority that reading seems to deprive her of. (It can be argued, of course, that that control is limiting, that it reduces the complexity of the reading process—which is true, but inevitable for Jan as well as for anybody who in writing is trying to account for the multifariousness of thought that he or she generates while reading and that only successive readings can reactivate.)

Jan suggests that a text should construct and provide its own explanations (" 'the third'. . . who must be sought after in order to better understand the poem") and that the reading a text should promote is a matter of nurturing but also fulfilling a reader's expectations (*who is* "the third"?); a reader must be allowed to make connections between parts of the text, between images, between signifiers and signifieds. Reading, Jan seems to argue, may well be a matter of exploring unfamiliar terrains, embarking on unfamiliar journeys, but at the end the unfamiliar should be allowed to be made familiar. If Jan's assumptions about what reading should be prevent her from praising Eliot's "masterpiece," her description of what the poem "does not do" is nevertheless an account of what the poem does and according to many readers and many critics does very successfully. What is it that allows Jan to write with considerable poise about a text that clearly she does not enjoy? What is it that prevents her from falling into the trap of submissiveness or shrill opposition? And to what extent is her granting it mysteriousness, her finding it enticing, a demonstration of her own blindness to the concealed "influence" of a text "credited with high power"? Let me suggest for now that the reason might have to do with her sense of what reading should be and of what a reader should do and be allowed to do, a notion that while giving her an advantage—a way to begin—locks her in that beginning.

The concluding sentence of her first writing is: "In this early interaction with Eliot's 'The Waste Land' I derive a sense of disappointed expectations *and* an accompanying feeling of confusion and disorientation" (emphasis added). The sentence is not very carefully structured. Given her accurate account of her first attempt at coming to terms with the question "Who is the third who walks beside you?" that sentence should syntactically reproduce the causal link between her thwarted expectations and her confusion and disorientation, a link that, instead, the coordinate construction weakens to the point of elision.

Jan's attempt at constructing logical connections between phases of her reading continues in her second writing on "The Waste Land." This time she had been asked to extend to a larger passage the understanding of the particular difficulty she had chosen to deal with. Jan's "understanding" (though she doesn't seem to see it as such) is her "not understanding." And it is, consistently, this "not understanding" that she extends to comment on the whole passage.

She begins by saying that the sense of confusion and disorientation evoked by the "Who is the third . . . ?" lines pervades the whole section. But, she thinks, toward the end of the section, a competing mood prevails; thus she is "inclined to split [Section V] into two parts," dividing it either at the cock's crow "Co co rico co co rico" (393) or at "Then spoke the thunder" (400). She acknowledges that "there is much that seems uglier," but she does not seem interested in reflecting on the reason why, then, she chose not to deal with any of these images or why instead she chose to begin her reading with "Who is the third . . . ?" Once more it is on "unfulfilled expectations" ("one would hope to find solitude in the mountains, but there are others, antagonistic others") that she focuses; once more, she tries to integrate images and sections according to a logic that the poem defies. She writes:

> In the transition from the sections in the mountains (rocks but no water) and the accompanying scenario of "the third" who is seen but cannot be counted, to the next part, there are a few images *I cannot incorporate into my reading*. One of these is that of the black-haired woman who fiddled "whisper-music" on the strings of her tightly drawn-out hair, and the "bats with baby faces in the violet light" (38). But maybe it is enough to be struck by their weirdness. (emphasis added)

For the first time, it seems, Jan senses and acknowledges that her reading method might not be appropriate for this type of text: "But maybe. . . . " As if commenting *sotto voce* on how much "weirdness" she can be exposed to, she reminds herself of the "creepy, crawly, spooky atmosphere, with its 'bats with baby faces,' 'blackened walls,' 'voices singing out of empty cisterns,' " and "more decay, graves, dry bones. . . . " Then, with a relief and an appreciation commensurate to the disappointment and the disorientation she has so far felt, she savors the enjoyment of her first fulfilled expectation:

> . . . it is in this part that I feel a break in the gloom and decay and disorientation:
>
> > Only a cock stood on the rooftree
> > Co co rico co co rico
> > In a flash of lightning. Then a damp gust
> > Bringing rain
>
> Ah, I can feel the damp gust. It is literally a breath of fresh air, which will pick up momentum through the end of "What the Thunder Said."

So far, clearly, Jan's response to "The Waste Land" is determined more by her ideal of what reading should be than by her critical understanding of the reading that this text posits. She seems to assume that a text should provide "explanations," rather than "instructions." And yet we cannot say that she is *not* sensitive to the language of the text. In fact, if she were not, she would not be disoriented, and she would construct connections, arbitrary ones, where none can be extended. What, then, prevents her from recognizing that her repeatedly unfulfilled expectations *are* an actualization of the poem? And what, on the other hand, prevents her, in a gesture of frustration that is the response of many students, from lashing out at the poet's erudition, at his assumptions about writing, reading, readership?

In her third writing she reiterates the central theme of her first and second essays:

> . . . the poem suggests more than loneliness or separation through much frightening and macabre imagery. . . . The unknown. Fear of the unknown, on and on and on. It's difficult to say which is worse, the imagery that conveys "lifeless existence," such as the "well now that's done" and "I am glad it's over" sexual encounter of the secretary and the carbuncular young man or the truly horrifying images of corpses planted in gardens, "bats with baby faces," "red sullen sneer and snarl."

She then cites the ways in which "experienced readers" (teachers, critics) helped her to understand the cause of her frustration. Although she confirms her belief in and preference for "clear, straight-forward communication," she remembers having learned (from one of her former teachers) to appreciate another way of communicating—the French Symbolists' way—a way of communicating that appeals "to the logic of the imagination and not to the logic of reason":

> . . . Knowing of Eliot's admiration for the symbolists I was able to control my frustration: rather than "trying to make logical sense" I allowed the poem's images to bombard me. (That is not to suggest that symbolist poetry "bombards"; that's just the way this poem came to me.) Helen Williams gave me a similar kind of help, in saying that "the poem's tableaux are not self-sufficient, though separately framed." Their relation to each other is emotional.

Although Jan accepts the possibility of "an alternative view of communication," although she knows about Symbolists' appeal to the logic of imagination, although she accepts the possibility that the poem's various tableaux be related emotionally, she doesn't translate this theory into practice. She doesn't, for example, at this point go back to her first reading and re-think in emotional or imaginative terms the relationship between the Antarctic expedition and Christ's journey to Emmaus—the relationship that, because she was unable to solve it logically, got her "stuck."

The negotiation of power is at a standstill. Solidly grounded in her own method of reading, Jan does not allow for the reading method that "The Waste Land" both writes out and is written by to modify it.

Jan's description of her overall response to the poem (until what she reads as the second part of Section V, that is) is also an appropriate description of her act of reading: bombarded by images that don't make logical sense, and by many thwarted expectations that "injure" her ("Much of the poem suggested numbness, perhaps as in the way in which a person's natural protections take over, for instance, to help cope with grief, or as when with terrible injury, the body goes 'into shock,' into a type of numbness"), she finally shakes her defensive numbness off, as she decides to talk about "the other reaction," the one (and she uses a verb that connotes volition) "resorted to when the numbness wears off, and the fear and the loneliness are too much to bear." The rest of the essay is the affirmation of a reading that demands and celebrates solace, comfort, promises of fulfillment and fulfilled promises.

Jan's reading is a "beginning"—a beginning rescued from intransitivity and silence by her attempt to negotiate authority *away* from the text. The fact that her attempt is ultimately flawed—within the course's definition of critical reading—by her rather "blind" preference for a model of reading as straightforward communication, and by her "uncritical," i.e., unexamined, refusal to raise inquisitive questions about the poem's erudition, and about its and her own cultural biases, affirms and confirms the necessity for critical reading/thinking to be critical—i.e., skeptical, inquisitive, reflexive as well as judgmental and evaluative—of itself in the very act of performing the act of criticism.

> The subject of teaching is interminably—a student; the subject
> of teaching is interminably—a learning.
>   Shoshana Felman, "Psychoanalysis and Education:
>   Teaching Terminable and Interminable"

As I bring this essay on students and learning to a *provisional* conclusion, let me reiterate why our students' stories of reading—the difficulties they experience as they try to engage in the critical reading of complex texts— are a subject worthy of theoretical investigation. Insofar as they signal student readers' sensitivity to "difficulties" that even professional critics and expert readers recognize as interpretive cruxes, they bespeak students' potential to be critical readers/thinkers. But insofar as these difficulties turn into entrapments, they bespeak the consequences of an educational system that does not create opportunities for the learner/thinker to reflect on and to act upon the source of entrapment.

For many years, at the end of every term, I would spend time examining my students' papers, scanning them for critical insights that I would read as signs of growth. It was a ritual whose main function was one of self-reassurance. I needed to know (as I still do) that something had happened, something had changed—for the better—so that I could look forward to its happening again. I had constructed a myth that led me to structure little tales of success whose tight narrative form prevented me from seeing a gaping fissure, a meaningful contradiction. If, as I was proclaiming, teaching is a dialectical relationship that engenders learning for the teacher as well as for the learner, I was, at the time, obviously cutting off one pole of that relationship by focusing exclusively on the teacher's teaching: by invalidating the relationship I was denying myself the possibility of learning from my students and of understanding more about the nature of the learning process.

More often than not I would detect signs of learning in "good" students' papers. Much less often would I perceive learning, even only an incipient possibility for learning—for me as well as for the student—in what I read as flawed attempts, or in the language of this essay, "intransitive beginnings." My mythical success was of a dubious type since it often amounted to no more than reproduction of knowledge. It would be fair to say that my pedagogy, what I mistook for pedagogy, was actually didactics: I was teaching techniques, skills, precepts, the end product of a process of learning whose tentative beginnings I had forgotten or chosen to forget. To use Lacan's phrase, I was nurturing my own "passion for ignorance."

This essay records an attempt to enact a different kind of pedagogy: a pedagogy that "reads" students' "passion for ignorance" as a defense against the anxiety of practicing a form of reading that their education and culture has not trained them for, rather than as a form of intellectual deficiency that only somebody else's readings, somebody else's knowledge can "fill"; a pedagogy that seeks ways of transforming that "passion for ignorance" into means of knowing by making it possible for students to learn how to read, as they learn about reading; a pedagogy that, as it claims the necessity for *all* readers, writers, learners to examine and critique their ways of knowing, and their negotiations of authority in the transaction of knowledge, tries not to "forget" the ever lurking possibility of its being or becoming blind to its own "passion for ignorance."

Notes

1. Let me sketch here a distinction to which I will *explicitly* return at the end of this essay—the distinction between *pedagogy* and *didactics*. Because I would like to reclaim pedagogy as a philosophical science, as the theory and practice of knowing that "makes manifest" its own theory and practice by continuously reflecting on and deconstructing it, I will call *didactics* any approach to teaching that shuns the teacher's and the student's critical reflexivity on the act of knowing and promotes the reduction of somebody else's method of knowing into a sequential schematization of that method. Whereas didactics sets up "models" and dictates procedures that will make the approximation of those models possible, pedagogy inquires into the prehistory of those models, and analyzes and assesses their formation. The radically different epistemological assumptions at the basis of didactics and pedagogy determine radically different teacher/learner relationships, classroom activities, projects, and curricula. The conscious or unconscious substitution of didactics for pedagogy may well be one of the reasons for the professional and institutional marginalization of pedagogy.

2. "Introduction to Critical Reading" was designed by Professor Paul Bovè as a course to be offered in the Honors Program at the University of Pittsburgh. Subsequently, Professor Marcia Landy and I adapted it as a multi-section propedeutic course for literature majors. This essay represents my (partial) reading of the course. I assume responsibility for any of the essay's weaknesses. The texts used by the various instructors change from section to section and from year to year. Each section, however, uses three "literary texts" and clusters of "critical readings" of those texts by professional writers. Because there are always going to be particular problems with *any* such selection, the strategy adopted in each section is to make the "problems" a subject of investigation.

3. Because I want to establish from the beginning the complexity of the act of critical reading, on the first day of class, I ask my students to construct in writing their definition of it (I return this brief paper to them at the end of the term, at which time I ask them to assess the adequacy of that definition in terms of their practice in the course). On the second day of class, I distribute a copy of Raymond Williams' entries on "criticism" and "culture" from *Keywords: A Vocabulary of Culture and Society*—a precious book to which I was introduced by Professor Steve Carr—so as to validate and enlarge upon the meanings they attribute to "critical reading." What we discover is that their prevalent reading of "critical" as negatively "evaluative" or "judgmental" ("tearing apart" is their nomenclature) has a "history" since it corresponds to the general sense of "censure" that the word acquired in English, according to Williams, in the last period of the seventeenth century. We also discover that we can trace the history for another of their meanings, i.e., "critical" as "specialized," to a less frequently mentioned definition of the term—that of "critical" as having to do with "culture" (as in a "literary critic's" writings). However, because they tend to think of "specialized"

as natural, spontaneous, genius-like, they have considerable difficulties learning how to understand the connections between a critic's "opinion" and his or her ideology.

4. I am clearly indebted to Said for the idea of "difficulties" as sources of knowledge. However, I use his terms "transitive" and "intransitive" less rigorously than he does. In this essay "transitive" does mean "the first step in the intentional production of meaning" (5). "Intransitive," however, simply means getting and remaining "stuck."

Works Cited

Bartholomae, David. "Wanderings: Misreadings, Miswritings, Misunderstandings." *Only Connect: Uniting Reading and Writing*. Ed. Thomas Newkirk. Portsmouth, NH: Boynton/Cook, 1986. 89–118.

Berthoff, Ann E. " 'Reading the World . . . reading the word': Paulo Freire's Pedagogy of Knowing." *Only Connect: Uniting Reading and Writing*. Ed. Thomas Newkirk. Portsmouth, NH: Boynton/Cook, 1986. 119–30.

———. "I. A. Richards." *Traditions of Inquiry*. Ed. John Brereton. New York: Oxford UP, 1985. 50–80.

Cortazar, Julio. "The Night Face Up." *Blow-up and Other Stories*. Trans. Paul Blackburn. New York: Collier, 1963. 57–66.

Drew, Elizabeth. *Directions in Modern Poetry*. New York: Gordian, 1967. 37–55; 133–47.

Eliot, T. S. *The Waste Land and Other Poems*. New York: Harcourt, 1934. 26–54.

Felman, Shoshana. "Psychoanalysis and Education: Teaching Terminable and Interminable." *The Pedagogical Imperative: Teaching as a Literary Genre*. Ed. Barbara Johnson. *Yale French Studies* 63. New Haven: Yale UP, 1982. 21–44.

Flynn, Elizabeth A. "Gender and Reading." *Gender and Reading: Essays on Readers, Texts, and Contexts*. Ed. Elizabeth A. Flynn and Patrocinio P. Schweickart. Baltimore: The Johns Hopkins UP, 1986. 267–88.

Gadamer, Hans-Georg. *Philosophical Hermeneutics*. Trans. and ed. David E. Linge. Berkeley: U of California P, 1976.

Johnson, Barbara. "Translator's Introduction." Jacques Derrida, *Dissemination*. Chicago: U of Chicago P, 1981.

———. *The Critical Difference: Essays on the Contemporary Rhetoric of Reading*. Lexington: UP of Kentucky, 1983.

Kermode, Frank. *The Genesis of Secrecy*. Cambridge: Harvard UP, 1979.

Leenhardt, Jacques. "Toward a Sociology of Reading." *The Reader in the Text: Essays on Audience and Interpretation*. Princeton: Princeton UP, 1980.

Newkirk, Thomas. "Looking for Trouble: A Way to Unmask Our Readings." *College English* 46 (1984): 756–66.

Pattison, Robert. *On Literacy*. New York: Oxford UP, 1982.

Said, Edward W. *Beginnings: Intention and Method*. Baltimore: The Johns Hopkins UP, 1975.

Salvatori, Mariolina. "Calvino's *If on a Winter's Night a Traveler*: Writer's Authority Reader's Autonomy." *Contemporary Literature* 27 (1986): 182–212.

Williams, Helen. *T. S. Eliot: The Waste Land*. New York: Woodbury, 1968.

Williams, Raymond. *Keywords: A Vocabulary of Culture and Society*. New York: Oxford UP, 1976. 74–82.

Wilkie, Brian and James Hurt, eds. *Literature of the Western World*. 2 vols. New York: Macmillan, 1984. Vol. 2.

8

The Dialogue of Chaos
An Unthinkable Order

HEPHZIBAH ROSKELLY

University of Massachusetts, Boston

In *The Crying of Lot 49*, Oedipa Maas struggles to extract meaning from the frenetic life she lives in California in the Sixties. She is terrified of a complexity that seems without purpose, yet she is paranoid about a purpose that may be malignant as well as inscrutable. One night she is pulled into a hotel ballroom dance. Surrounded by ad executives, deaf mutes, Chinese nationalists, and Harris tweeds, she has a flash of insight that places the dancers' seemingly unconnected movements within a larger pattern:

> Each couple on the floor danced whatever was in the fellow's head; tango, two-step, bossa-nova, slop. But how long, Oedipa thought, could it go on before collisions became a serious hindrance; there would have to be collisions. The only alternative was some unthinkable order of music, many rhythms, all keys at once, a choreography in which each couple meshed easy, predestined.

Oedipa has to accept the chaos around her before she can see pattern; what is more difficult, she has to acknowledge that chaos is an integral part of the pattern, single rhythms part of a comprehensive beat she can't quite hear. Oedipa fearfully probes the relationship between chaos and form, a relationship that is crucial to writing practice, but that has been explored insufficiently by writing theory. Both writing theorists and writ-

96

ing teachers are ambivalent about accepting chaos as a part of the composing process, and even when they do accept it, fail to see it as integral to the pattern of a writer's forming.

Most writing theory describes the connection between chaos and order as linear and chronological, defining chaos as a condition of only early writing life. Chaos is shown to disappear as writers progress to the orderly discourse of final product, as though Oedipa's dancers suddenly abandoned their own steps and began to waltz. Donald Murray, for example, produces a chart in which he diagrams the conflicting forces of chaos and order, as the writer first discovers and collects, and second, clarifies and orders (6–8). Writing finds its own meaning as it negotiates this conflict and moves from the chaotic to the controlled. Linda Flower and John Hayes compare writers to switchboard operators who must learn to juggle competing demands. Writers develop plans to deal with the competing and chaotic constraints of subject, audience, voice and organization as their "best defense against the nature of writing" (40). Peter Elbow's cooking-growing metaphor has become almost a commonplace description of the writing process. Free writing and other open-ended strategies for inventing allow disorientation to "grow" into an "emerging center of gravity" where the writer finds order (12–48).[1]

Although these metaphors for the writing process all explore chaos as an element within it, they encourage composition students and their teachers to believe that the messiness of composing straightens itself out eventually, moving inexorably from the darkness of disorder to the new day of focus, coherence and form. And the inference in this linear conception is clear: the more adept the writer, the more quickly dawn arrives. Consequently, teachers invite writers to grapple with chaos as theory tells us we should, but we insist that writing continually work to shake the chaotic dust from its heels. We tolerate chaos in the writing process with the same sort of irritability that the audience tolerates the clumsy opening act for the featured performer, and our students—good at sensing our moods—learn to tolerate even less patiently than we do.

Giving chaos a place in the writing classroom allows the writer freedom to explore more than one avenue of approach. But a linear, positivistic description of chaos hardening into pattern is simplistic and unrewarding in a classroom that invites critical thinking. Ann Berthoff's work reconstructs both chaos and pattern to make the relationship reflect the writer's constructing, construing mind.

In Berthoff's thinking, chaos represents possibilities for formulation rather than the "blooming, buzzing confusion" of pure sensation; it is therefore generative, rather than entropic in composing.[2] Berthoff clearly

associates chaos with the imaginative construction that derives from ambiguities, "the hinges of thought," in Richards' famous definition. Richards' statement implies a dialectical, paradoxical connection between the
two concepts of chaos and order. A hinge literally determines and orders
movement; thus, for Richards, ambiguity represents a kind of ordering
where thought moves restlessly forward until ambiguity forces thought
onto other paths which both channel and expand it. Berthoff notes the
same "meaningful" tension provoked by the desire to move forward,
sentence after sentence, thought after thought; and the desire to explore
other choices, alternate words, possible responses. Out of this tension
between thought and ambiguity grows lively critical conceptualizing, and
language which illustrates the mind in the process of ordering its own
growth.

To recognize chaos as dialectical and not lower-level thinking requires
redefinition. Chaos is not incoherence, although teachers and students
often apply both words to the same negative concept. Incoherence implies
insufficiency, details without concepts, or generalizations without substance. So defined, incoherence is directly opposed to chaos, which exposes
the relationship of generalization and detail as it promotes tension in the
writing process.[3] Incoherence does not usually result from an overabundant
chaos, but it frequently appears when order is imposed without chaos.
Chaos is tied to Richards' ambiguity—the side streets that arrest, challenge, reorder our one-way writing track. It is then in a dialogue with
"form" or order from the outset, and it remains in the conversation
throughout the writing process.

The dialectic of chaos and form explored by Berthoff exists in the
writer's perception and imagination; the ways in which we perceive and
imagine produce simultaneous impulses to order and to disorder. Susanne
Langer makes the dialogue between the two parts of her definition of the
relational nature of meaning. She first stresses the highly individualized
and chaotic nature of meaning: "We may view a meaning-pattern from
the point of view of any term within it, and our description of the same
pattern will differ accordingly." Yet within the chaos of varying individual
perceptions of meaning, an underlying pattern emerges, a pattern that
results from concepts all perceivers share. Despite the differences in experiences or associations, Langer maintains that we can talk together about
our conceptualizations of ideas or objects because we share the concepts
of those ideas or objects: "That which all adequate conceptions of an object
must have in common is a concept of the object" (68). Langer uses the
mathematician as an example of how perceptions of chaos and order work
together in a conceptual system. The mathematician says, "Let X mean,"

positing an order within the "chaos" of all the possibilities for X. Relationships—meanings—are established with other similar symbols based on the initial meaning the perceiver has assigned. The mathematician might renew the ambiguity by saying, "Now suppose X means," and new relationships to symbols would follow, but a relational order obtains within the system, the same concept "embodied in a multitude of conceptions" (71). For the mathematician, "let" and "suppose" help define the dynamic construct of order and chaos, a Coleridgean unity in multeity. The individual perceiver establishes that construct as she manipulates both unique and shared perceptions.

Those unique and shared perceptions generate the dialogue between chaos and order and are embodied in the language with which we symbolize objects and sensory impressions. In his work on the novel, Mikhail Bakhtin sets the social and psychological terms of the dialectical opposition in language. Because it inhabits a borderline between self and other, language by necessity must appropriate others' contexts as well as the perceiver's own. When some of those other contexts are not easily appropriated, as many will not be, words are "forced to submit to the tension of a difficult and complicated process," one intensely and inherently dialogic (453). Marbled with contexts, nuances and possible answers, the word contains questions and arguments within it, because it has been shaped in interaction with other words. This dialogue keeps language living; "opposing" words interanimate one another. The double-voicedness Bakhtin hears in novelistic discourse is the two voices of "ordered" language (the word produced) and "chaotic" language (the answers, rejections, contexts) in a pattern of discourse that interanimates with other choices, patterns, associations that oppose the order of the discourse. The tension created by the dialogue never resolves itself in order; it depends on irresolution to keep it dynamic. Although Bakhtin finds rhetoric less internally dialogic than novelistic language because rhetoric often defends itself against an outside, hence alien, listener, he notes that in "almost every utterance there exists an intense interaction between one's own and another's word" (353). The double voice, therefore, inheres in all discourse where speakers presume listeners (including speakers themselves), and the interanimation in language depends not on outside hearers, but on the speaker's forming of the discourse "in the atmosphere of the already spoken" (285).

Berthoff's method in *Forming/Thinking/Writing* reflects some of the ideas of both Langer and Bakhtin, and her words interanimate with theirs, to create an approach to the dialectic of chaos and form in the composing process. Langer's contextualized meaning finds expression in Berthoff's desire for organic form in writing: "My guiding philosophical principle is that form-finding and form-creating is a natural activity" (2). Her description of forming, with its accompanying hedging, questioning, responding, paraphrasing, is the compositional translation of Bakhtin's dialogic principle in the novel. "A rhetoric," she says, "should be concerned not just with sorting out topics and places, but with exploring the dialectic of names and purposes, images and concepts, thinking and forming" (6). Berthoff makes the dialogue between form and forming, perception and perceiver into a methodology for the students she writes to and a strategy for her own writing, as she shows how the relationship she establishes between chaos and order works for her.

The most satisfying theorists are often those who are not content to describe operations or behavior but who behave according to their own descriptions, who do as they say. Thus, Kenneth Burke enumerates lots of "not-As" on his way to making a point about consubstantiation. Thus, Peter Elbow revises "aloud" to find his center of gravity as he writes, letting his readers hear the idea bubbling on the page. Berthoff creates a dialogue of pattern and chaos throughout her own prose. Consider this sentence: "Developing a method of composing means explaining explanations, writing about writing, thinking about thinking; sometimes that can make you dizzy" (9). Method as madness. The opposition embodied in the words themselves can make you dizzy. Words and phrases continually turn on one another as Berthoff develops her description of composing, and the turn is not simply a stylistic trick. It is a way of asserting both chaos and pattern, of showing how form and disorder work together as perceptions change and develop. When Berthoff suggests thinking about thinking, a teacher can watch her students' eyes cross, until she helps them apply the idea to their own constructions and reconstructions in writing. Berthoff warns students that "there will be a great deal of repetition," implying that chaos surfaces within the necessarily orderly and linear progression of the text, and (not unintentionally) breaking a sacred composition tenet. "Repetition," she assures, "is, after all, a fundamental aspect of form" (5). But, as she is slyly aware, it is likewise a fundamental strategy for encouraging chaos; repeated statements emerge in varying contexts and create different resonances in readers. Repetition is never precise, anyway, but, as Langer indicates, is always analogue, based on perceptions that are constantly changing. As she characterizes and recapitulates the dialogism in discourse which argues, glosses, and digresses, she follows the characterization in her own composing style, challenging, speculating, reordering, chapter after chapter. And she boldly tells her readers that she's doing it, proving to them that chaos and order work together synergistically as the writer composes.

The dialectic Berthoff achieves between chaos and form in the program she recommends and the one she follows herself may seem deliberately perverse to students unused to believing that chaos should be drawn out, rather than staunched. Her delight in asserting the mutual dependence of ends and means, for example, appears unseemly to students familiar with the Machiavellian epigram that assumes a one-way relationship between the terms. Mutuality negates the logical, chronological continuum that students have been taught to see as a universal truth. It is profoundly chaotic to consider that in writing how you get there depends partly on what happens after you've arrived. If ends and means, parts and wholes, are to become mutually supportive, moreover, the writing has to be kept tentative, and that means that the drive to order must be kept at bay while chaos takes center stage in the dialogue the writer generates.

Like the suggestion to keep writing tentative and mix ends and means, all the methods Berthoff recommends for beginning to form are strategies for hearing the dialogue between chaos and order, and delaying order to make space for chaos. The double entry notebook is the most literal translation of the dialogue because students actually transcribe it, writing on one side of the page and reflecting and commenting on the facing page. Writers become at once agent and agency in a symbolic transaction of thought and hinge, and "purpose"—the writer's *raison d'être*—emerges within the combination of roles. "The continuing audit of meaning"— Berthoff's and Richards' definition of dialectic—produced by these notebooks spills over into all writing, and helps writers respond to an inner dialogue that directs disorderly digression as well as meaningful revision.

Other techniques for concept forming are less obvious as dialogue, but produce the chaos-order dialectic nonetheless. Naming is a strategy for "beginning the chaos" (63). It presents students with a paradox (and a chaos) of their own similar to the paradox of recognizing the symbiosis of ends and means. Students have been taught to believe that naming does not generate chaos, but stems it. The composition teacher announces the essay assignment, a personal narrative. The composition student sighs in relief. "Oh, good. Not a research paper." (Elimination of alternatives, reduction of chaos.) Yet naming insists on symbolizing as well as perceiving; it puts meaning into its relational context. The personal narrative asks students to do internal research, exploring and rejecting possibilities that naming has brought to the surface. Chaos and order have both begun with the forming of concepts. A concept, Berthoff says, using one of her most apt organic metaphors, "is like a hand that gathers. It is also the handful," and naming insists on the recognition of perceiver and thing perceived as inseparable. When writers name, in other words, they don't just begin the chaos; they begin the dialogue between order and chaos, between, as Bakhtin would say, the word and its rejoinder. The paraphrase (recapitulation) and the gloss (commentary) keep the dialogue in motion, as writers generalize and particularize, produce and reflect, at the same time. In paraphrasing and glossing, in all these composing activities, writers must become the perceiver and the thing perceived, the hand and the handful.

Berthoff offers a way to make composition critical forming by helping students jump into chaos rather than fall into it, and employ it rather than fear or deny it. Yet Berthoff herself seems less than happy that the jump is necessary, as she tells students that chaos should not be tolerated for its own sake but "to learn to put up with it while you discover ways of emerging" (65). The mind rebels against chaos, she tells us; it yearns for order. Of course, ordering is a natural activity; the mind fits experience into categories to conceptualize it. And teachers should use that truth, as Berthoff argues, by making their students conscious of what they already do automatically: classify, categorize, find forms within which to express ideas. But if order is "natural" and chaos necessary, it follows that teachers must more consistently acknowledge the hidden truth as well as the more self-evident one. Writers emphasize, omit, stop, and start. They lie, delay, equivocate, deny, and all of these are chaotic impulses, ones that writers fear or despise precisely because they have been taught to see form as the only goal, and chaos as the final defeat.

The natural desire for order creates negative as well as positive behavior in the writing class, as Berthoff acknowledges. Writers form categories and "reach closure" on ideas, but they often close too quickly, refusing to reopen the categories once they have settled them. The compulsion to order keeps writers away from meaningful digression or thoughtful disorderliness. Students and their teachers even impose a kind of pre-order on the writing scene. Think of how quickly the chaos of young women and men walking into the classroom at semester's beginning gives way to the order of students filling in forms, taking notes, getting the first writing assignment. The members of the class categorize form before the first class period ends. Permission has been given to find order and to dispense with chaos as soon as time, or free writing, will allow. Yet chaotic forces within the classroom and within the discourse actually focus writing, determine its shape in product as well as process. As Richards would say, they give hinges to the thought and help writing achieve its own organic form. When writers learn to achieve an awareness of their own composing behavior, they become more critical and creative composers and they learn to see form in a new way, as the dialogue in action, not merely, or even at all, the result of the dialogue. Throughout each phase of the writing process, composing is forming, and forming, the process of thinking about thinking, is at heart more chaotic than orderly.

The importance of chaos to forming indicates that composition teachers must do more than tolerate chaos as a kind of unfortunate buzzing in their students' ears that soon can be stilled with judicious calls to order. Because chaos and order live together in the discourse, both must be explored throughout the writing process to allow the writer the opportunity for true critical thought. Yet most teaching is always an order-affirming, chaos-denying experience for students, with workshop groups on revision containing the implicit imperative to weed out the inappropriate in favor of the meticulously controlled and with free writing inevitably giving way to MAJOR ESSAY #1. We fail to show students that workshops are most exciting and provocative if they become forums for naming and opposing, for addition and quibble, as well as for reconciling. We ignore free writing as end as well as means. I believe that every chaos-generating strategy will fail to make writing more lively, personal, or authoritative, unless all those strategies support a system that acknowledges the intense conversation the writer hears between her order and her chaos. Our students dislike free writing, nutshelling, brainstorming, and other cleverly-named invention techniques if they are made to feel that this discourse is produced only so that it can be skimmed off later. And we often make students feel just this way, as though we say "Get this blithering out of your system, and then you'll be able to write." Students resent the hypocrisy of our insisting they begin with something we later insist will disappear.

Nevertheless, the effort to instill chaos in the classroom is complicated by students' own disposition against it. Students dislike chaos not only because they suspect we don't believe in it. They dislike it because they fear it no less than Oedipa Maas. They are ready to regard the disordered as unpleasant, even painful. Tiana, a student in my upper-level writing theory class, expressed this attitude nicely as she wrote in her journal comparing her own writing process to Nathaniel Hawthorne's: "I don't think Hawthorne's inspiration routine anymore. After reading in the journals, I believe Hawthorne thought a great deal about plot and characters. He wrote in a special place and about mystical overtones to release control of his writing. Everyone who writes goes through the same kind of pain." Tiana sees that composing means manipulating one's context so that the writer invites release, and she designates such release as (paradoxically) hard, painful. Tiana's reflection demonstrates why the composition class needs to make room for chaos, not merely assume it or relegate it to initial writing activities. Chaos does not come naturally in the classroom context, and it is painful to make space for it in an order-dominated pedagogical system, but its dialogic function in composing makes it indispensable for writers. Bakhtin describes the release in the language of the novel that comes through the difficult and complicated process of making word and thought both centrifugal and centripetal, and of balancing the tensions that come from that release. As the imagination names and opposes, it presumes word and response; it creates the context that each inhabits.

We help students negotiate this kind of release of their imaginations by allowing them to participate in their own dialogues of chaos, consciously keeping their ideas tentative and alive. The task of implementing chaos seems particularly difficult in second or advanced level writing classes where students have been rewarded for the orderly discourse they have produced in the past. The sophistication of these students keeps them from wanting to explore beyond the forms that have worked for them. These advanced-level writers were the students, in fact, who forced me to apply Berthoff's generative chaotic dialogue more consistently in my teaching. Recognizing their deep suspicion of unexplored forms, I took the chaos-making strategy of naming literally, and gave advanced composition students the name—a title—for a writing assignment. No discussion of form or content, just title. I was introducing chaos, the dialectical counterpart to the ordered assignment-filling these students were comfortable with. They were disconcerted, obviously afraid of shaking or blurring their categories of response, categories finely tuned and skillfully produced. But during the process of writing and listening to the writing of others, these students learned the freedom that comes from breaking out of pre-fabricated categories; they manipulated the title (which was, I think, "Revision Destroys Invention") to fit subjects and forms that they shaped themselves within the seeming formlessness of a "naked" title.

These advanced writers made me realize that most students are in control, not out of it (freshman writers long for control even more earnestly than these advanced writers); chaos helps them find the release they need to construct and reconstrue their own thinking. If they can oppose as well as order, undefine as well as specify, go on tangents as well as track a point, writers achieve much more than greater control over subject matter.

They begin to learn what Berthoff means by "construct as you construe," by recognizing ambiguity and order in the perspectives they take on. They hear their own voices, find their own authority. Their eyes begin to uncross.

Berthoff once told me of a student who had worked for weeks on a paper about carpentry. He had continued to add details as he had decided first to include an interview and later a survey of tools and uses, fitting all of this into his personal experience as a carpenter's assistant. He had, in other words, generated a lot of chaos, and conferences and workshops showed how engaged he was in the auditing of his own meaning. Late in the semester, he approached Berthoff apologetically, asking for an extension. "I don't have the final paper," he said. "I've got lots and lots of drafts." Berthoff's response surprised and thrilled him. She'd love to have another version because he had captured her interest, but that wasn't the important thing. He had already accomplished his goals for the paper. "You've done it," she said. Berthoff saw that the writer had succeeded when he was critically engaged in making his own meaning, generating chaos and order in a continuing spiral of activity.

Our challenge is to believe in the composing process enough to stop occasionally with the unfinished, the not-smooth, to recognize the effort to embrace chaos rather than suppress it. It is when they stave off the impulse to order that writers find order implicit in the dialogue they make, in the pattern of many combinations, in the rhythm tapped out in the individual dance.

Notes

1. In *Embracing Contraries* (New York: Oxford, 1986), Elbow reconceives his linear cook-and-grow metaphor to include chaos by acknowledging the "hunger" that persists for both coherence and incoherence in the process of conceptualization. He notes that he now views cooking as more than the product of free writing or of simple energy: "I think I've finally figured it out. Cooking is the interaction of contrasting or conflicting material" (40).

2. Both Berthoff and Langer cite William James's phrase in making a similar point about the process of forming, the selectivity and logic which make sense of the bedlam of stimuli comprising our experiences.

3. Lawrence Poston helps make this point in advocating better, more inclusive paradigms for the teaching of English. He argues that we need to negotiate various literacies, that "messiness, unlike fuzziness, offers openings for serious intellectual activity." See "Putting Literacy at the Center," *ADE Bulletin* (Winter, 1986): 13–20.

Works Cited

Bakhtin, Mikhail. *The Dialogic Imagination*. Trans. Caryl Emerson and Michael Holquist. Austin: U of Texas P, 1981.

Berthoff, Ann E. *Forming/Thinking/Writing*. Portsmouth, NH: Boynton/Cook, 1982.

————. *The Making of Meaning*. Portsmouth, NH: Boynton/Cook, 1981.

Elbow, Peter. *Writing With Power*. New York: Oxford UP, 1981.

Flower, Linda and John Hayes. "The Dynamics of Composing." *Cognitive Processes in Writing*. Eds. Lee W. Gregg and Erwin Steinberg. Hillsdale, NJ: Lawrence Erlbaum, 1980. 31–50.

Langer, Susanne. *Philosophy in a New Key*. 3rd ed. Cambridge: Harvard UP, 1963.

Murray, Donald. "Writing as Process: How Writing Finds Its Own Meaning." *Eight Approaches to Teaching Composition*. Ed. Timothy R. Donovan and Ben W. McClelland. Urbana: NCTE, 1980. 3–20.

Pynchon, Thomas. *The Crying of Lot 49*. Philadelphia: Lippincott, 1966.

9

Reading, Writing, and the Dialectic Since Marx

JUDITH GOLEMAN

University of Massachusetts, Boston

However paradoxical it may seem, I venture to suggest that our age threatens one day to appear in the history of human culture as marked by the most dramatic and difficult trial of all, the discovery of and training in the meaning of the "simplest" acts of existence: seeing, listening, speaking, reading. . . . Only since Freud have we begun to suspect what listening, and hence what speaking (and keeping silent), *means*; that this *"meaning"* of speaking and listening reveals beneath the innocence of speech and hearing the culpable depth of a second, *quite different* discourse, the discourse of the unconscious. I dare maintain that only since Marx have we begun to suspect what, in theory at least, *reading* and hence writing *means*.

Louis Althusser, Reading Capital

It is of no little importance to those of us who teach reading and writing that these activities are also concepts, and, as such, have meanings which change. As the privileged status of recent scholarly work which considers reading and writing as interpretive activities would attest, the present "meaning" of reading and writing *has* been changing from that of a simple and linear process to a complex and reflexive act of mind. Seeing ourselves seeing; reading ourselves reading: these are the codifications of the "discovery" of those " 'simplest' acts of existence" to which

Althusser alludes—a discovery of their complexity which for students and teachers alike has certainly constituted a "difficult trial": the trial of learning to think about the sources of our thought conscientiously and problematically, that is to say, dialectically.

It would be a misrepresentation of Althusser, however, to read the passage above only in terms which translate Marx's particular discovery of the dialectic into a call for the cultivation of self-consciousness and a pluralistic perspective among our students. Since Marx, what reading and writing *can* mean is more specific than this. (Marx would say more "concrete.") For what it can mean goes beyond knowing *that* we interpret when we read and write to *how* these interpretations themselves are part of a dialogue in the play of social history whose theater is the world. It is a play, which, for the most part, our students perform in a house darkened and silenced by the bright lights and din of their worldliness. Restoring the dialogue and seeing the play that we are in constitutes a Marxian perspective which, in truth, is not so much a perspective in itself as a means for getting behind our perspectives and analyzing their social and historical functions as knowledge.

Only since Marx, Althusser argues, have we come to suspect that reading and writing—as concepts and as functions—are historically determined and hence, determining constructions of knowledge. They are not natural or timeless acts through which meaning flows, but rather, they are historically contingent acts which compose the meaning we make. As Althusser asserts above, it is only since Marx that we have come to look at these traditionally timeless, neutral, "simple" acts of existence as not timeless but historically contingent, as not neutral but value-laden, as not simple but complex. By turning reading and writing into historical problems themelves, Marx can be said to have discovered a new way of reading and writing which constitutes a new theory of history as well. It is thus to the *reading* of history as discovered by Marx and conceptualized by Althusser that we must turn in order to discover what "in theory at least" reading and writing means since Marx.

Let us begin with what Althusser thinks reading and hence writing does *not* mean since Marx: it does not mean the "immediate reading of essence in existence" on the religious model of Hegel's Absolute Knowledge (*Reading* 9); and it does not mean the abstraction of the essential from the inessential on the empiricist model (37). Because both of these models require that we read knowledge as a real part of a real object, they are, for the purposes of understanding Marx's difference, more alike as idealisms than not (38).

These idealist conceptions of a reality which contains an immediate and discoverable essence—as a nut in a shell or a meaning in a story—imply an epistemology which separates and abstracts a real essence from a real object. Marx's work represents a challenge to these theories of knowledge. In his study of political economy, Marx poses questions that had never been posed before because a theory of knowledge as essence, by its very nature, blocks knowledge from being thought of as a concept, as a *theory*. A belief in knowledge as an essence forecloses an investigation of knowledge as a human production, and it was ultimately Marx's breakthrough to question the historical function of this belief itself. To look at an ahistorical teleology as an historical production constitutes what Althusser has called Marx's "epistemological break" (*For Marx* 33), a break which if we are to understand it, Althusser suggests below, obligates us to reconstruct our own thinking:

> We are thereby obliged to renounce every teleology of reason, and to conceive the historical relation between a result and its condition of existence as a relation of production, and not of expression, and therefore as what, in a phrase that clashes with the classical system of categories and demands the *replacement* of those categories themselves, we can call the *necessity of its contingency*. To grasp this necessity we must grasp the very special and paradoxical logic that leads to this *production*, i.e., the logic of the conditions of the production of knowledges. . . . (*Reading* 45)

Once we have grasped that knowledge itself is a human production, we are forever after on different terrain. Knowledge of an object seen as an act of human production is a type of knowledge that cannot be said to be identical with the object itself. Only by analyzing the specific social and historic logic of the form our knowledge takes—its "contingency"—can we derive insight into the object of knowledge itself. Knowledge then becomes an on-going process of dialectical inference, including inference about our ways of seeing, reading and writing—that is, our ways of forming knowledge. In short, all knowledge, even the knowledge of how we form knowledge, must be understood historically as the particular effects of a social structure.

When we know a structure through essences, we are prevented from asking questions about it which we can ask when we know a structure through our inferred logic of its productions. This explains why Marx wrote of Hegel and the Young Hegelians: "Not only in their answers but in their questions there was a mystification" (40). This also explains why Marx's theories constitute a break from Hegel's dialectic, not a reversal, not a turning of Hegel on his feet again. "A man on his head is the same man when he is finally walking on his feet," Althusser has written, and Marx's interrogation of the terrain itself, the field of the problematic which structures meaning, places him on new terrain and within a different problematic—not on Hegel's terrain or in his shoes (*For Marx* 22).

It is important to pursue the differences between the Hegelian and Marxian dialectic further because the differences have implications for our subject: what reading and writing means since Marx. In *Marxism and Form*, Fredric Jameson takes the position that both the Hegelian and Marxian dialectic are forms of self-consciousness with the Hegelian dialectic raising our awareness of the way thought processes themselves limit thought, and the Marxian dialectic raising our awareness of the political and historical nature of that thought (340). Hegel, Jameson argues, understood the contradiction inherent in the effort to analyze the thought that limits thought while one remains inside those limits. Hegel's "notion of the Absolute Idea, of that 'Sunday of Life' when history stops," Jameson writes, "is clearly the ultimate working out of the contradiction" (364). Marx's rejection of this transcendent place of reflection results in a fully historicized theory of knowing by which to define the problem of history itself dialectically. Jameson writes:

> As soon . . . as one is able to feel one's own thought as a historical action on equal terms with the objects studied, . . . then the Hegelian contradiction is overcome, and one no longer has to posit an end to history in order for historical thought to take place. In the apprehension of all events, mental or otherwise, as profoundly historical and situational in character, Marx's thought represents an advance over that of Hegel, who reserved a single position outside of history for the philosopher of history himself, and was to that extent unable to grasp the notion of being-in-situation in its most paradoxical dimensions. (364–65)

This "being-in-situation" which may appear only to constitute another relativism is, however, no such thing. The Marxian dialectic constitutes neither a numbing skepticism nor a Peircean "contrite fallibilism" (Berthoff *Making* 43). Rather, the Marxian dialectic constitutes a hermeneutic method by which to account historically for the critical limitations of such responses as skepticism and contrition. What, we must ask, are the social and historical conditions which have produced these concepts as solutions and what are the conditions which have produced the forms of the problems which "gave rise to them" as well (Jameson 373)?

By virtue of these questions, then, the Marxian dialectic is not so much a system-in-itself as a response to system, a means by which to analyze the dominant social and historical forces producing structures of meaning. Let us call this hermeneutic method, ideological analysis, where by *ideology* we mean a particular practice, "the practice of representation" (Coward 67). In capitalist society—the object of Marx's study—the practice of representation is dominated by the class which dominates the forces of production and struggles to maintain that position. And so, while ideology, as the practice of representation, may be an organic part of every social structure, it does not function in the same way in every structure. In a structure determined by its contradictory relations of power and privilege, ideology can be "seen" as the representation of these contradictions as normal, as human nature itself.

As the practice of representation and the construction of subjects for those representations, ideology is a material force which naturalizes the unequal relations of production—the on-going, complex, multiply determined interrelations among classes, races, genders, ages, disciplines and more. By virtue of its naturalizing effects, ideology limits individuals to a certain "mental horizon" (Coward 74). The pedagogical function of historical materialism, then, is that it can teach us to "see" ideology in our representations; it can teach us to "read" ideology as a specific organization of reality and therefore to create the possibility of changing that reality. Reading the world ideologically means that we look at the social structure as a structuring; it means that we trace the course from contradictory social relations to their naturalization. This state of contradiction, however, as Althusser has written, is "never simple but specified by the historically concrete forms and circumstances in which it is exercised." In other words, "the apparently simple [Capital-Labor] contradiction is always overdetermined" (*For Marx* 106). Because all contradictions are historically concrete and multiply or overdetermined, ideology cannot exist as a thing-in-itself; rather, it exists only in its own specific effects as the practice of representation. Consequently, ideological analysis is a responsive hermeneutic—even a "negative hermeneutic" by which we can re-construct (or de-construct) the naturalized forms of contradiction where we read them (*Political* 286).

Thus it could be said that a pedagogy of knowing based on the Marxian dialectic makes possible a new way of reading and writing—a way which reads texts closely as part of a social process in contradiction. And here it cannot be said too strongly that the concept of overdetermined contradiction fundamentally differentiates the Marxian hermeneutic from other historical methods of reading and writing where the criterion of truth is coherence. In short, looking for the logic of a text's representations—the relations of the said and the not-said, the seen and the

not-seen, the known and the not-known—in the context of specific overdetermined social contradictions constitutes the Marxian dialectical procedure, a procedure which is wholly different from that procedure which
constructs history on the basis of *"a priori"* or "innate" ideas of coherence
(Collingwood in Berthoff *Reclaiming* 221).

In a decisively Marxian sense, then, all writing thus becomes re-writing
in that it entails re-presenting a cultural artifact's form in terms of the
specific social dialogue it is part of. Seeing the not-seen, hearing the not-
heard, constitutes the Marxian dialectic as an act of dialogical restoration,
one which cannot be accomplished without an understanding of the historical problematic that has structured these visions as non-visions, these
voices as silences. Using the concept of hegemony developed by Antonio
Gramsci to denote the lived experience of cultural contradiction, Jameson
writes: " . . . the stress on the dialogical . . . allows us to reread or rewrite
the hegemonic forms themselves" (*Political* 86). This, then, could be said
to be, if not a stopping point, at least a point of provisional closure for
the student writer engaged by the perpetual motion machine of the Marxian hermeneutic. When a dialogue is restored; when hegemonic relations
are perceived; when a form is understood ideologically as a specific way
of seeing, reading and representing the world—when the student of the
Marxian dialectic has done all this—he or she has entered a new discourse
and can be said to be a participant in "the most dramatic and difficult
trial of all, the discovery of and training in the meaning of the 'simplest'
acts of existence: seeing, listening, speaking, reading . . . " and hence,
writing.

It is, of course, one thing to propose such goals for students of the
historical materialist dialectic and another thing to design a fifteen-week
course which is a means toward those goals. It is one thing to teach that
composing is a dialectical process and another to teach that meaning itself
is dialectical. In her effort to bridge this gap, Ann Berthoff has written
that "writing dialectically encourages as it *requires*, conscientization, the
critical consciousness of oneself as a meaning-maker" ("Reading" 128).
This is certainly true in the sense that writers who are put in a process
wherein they may watch themselves figuring something out are in the
position to watch themselves as figur*ers*, discovering the constitutive power
of their own perspectives, and by extension, the constitutive power of
perspectives beyond their own. In short, the dialectic of composing introduces writers to the historical contingency of meaning, to meaning as
dependent on particular contexts and perspectives. Without a doubt, this
"encourages as it *requires*" new critical consciousness regarding the old

idealism of fixed meaning; that is, of meaning as an essence which resides in its object. Writers who learn through their own composing processes that meaning is situational, which is to say, a matter of specific contexts and perspectives, are writers who are coming into consciousness of history itself, and, indeed, of the complex constitutive relations among history, self, and knowledge.

At this threshold of dialectical self-consciousness, however, where one is both thinking about an object and observing oneself thinking about it, differences emerge in the forms which the self-consciousness may take. These differences broadly distinguish the Hegelian from the Marxian dialectic as Jameson suggests below:

> For Hegel . . . the thinker comes to understand the way in which his own determinate thought processes, and indeed the very forms of the problems from which he set forth, limits the results of his thinking. For the Marxist dialectic, on the other hand, the self-consciousness aimed at is the awareness of the thinker's position in society and in history itself, and of the limits imposed on this awareness by his class position—in short of the ideological and situational nature of all thought and of the initial invention of the problems themselves. (*Marxism* 340)

Let us say then, for the sake of clarity, that dialectical self-consciousness—conscientization—may, but does not have to, stop at the point of Hegelian insight, where the contingency of meaning is discovered. For students brought to this point, tremendous insight may obtain, which over time may lead to questions about the social and historical nature of thought: Why are certain perspectives valued more than others? Or, why are certain contexts more easily imagined than others? Some students, surely, will use the dialectic of composing that they learn in a way which reinvents Marxian historical thinking. It is also possible, in advanced writing classes at least, to teach the Marxian hermeneutic deliberately as an advanced stage of conscientization.

In the conclusion of the first section, I outlined the goals of what we are now calling advanced conscientization. Briefly stated, these goals include: (a) restoring a cultural artifact to the social dialogue it is part of so as to (b) understand the specific hegemonic relations that structure the dialogue, and thereby to enable one to (c) read an artifact's form ideologically as a specific way of representing the world. How can this be done? In her essay on Paulo Freire's pedagogy of knowing, Ann Berthoff suggests a good place to start when she writes that we must teach our students "to look and look again . . . at natural forms and designs, at texts and the topography of their own lives. . . . If we ask our students to name their world and we get digital clocks and designer jeans, that is a place to begin; that is a point of departure for conscientization and dialogic action" ("Reading" 127).

In this section, I'll describe the first two weeks of a course in advanced composition which I have designed in an effort to approach the three goals stated above, a course which began not with clocks or jeans but with the picture of a three-piece suit. The purpose of this two-week project on suits was to introduce the concepts of dialogical thinking, social contradiction and cultural hegemony in an incremental way that would make it possible for the students to see and feel how these concepts complemented and improved their own thinking processes rather than replaced them. For this first stage of the course, there were two texts: Ann Berthoff's essays on the composing process in *The Making of Meaning* and John Berger's critical essays on art and photography in *About Looking*.

I chose a man's suit to begin the course not only because of its obvious semiotic richness, but because of a particular essay in Berger's book, "The Suit and the Photograph." In this essay, Berger restores August Sander's 1914 photograph, "Peasants Going to a Dance," to its social and historical context in such a way as to define the specific hegemonic relations which shape the way the peasants "look" in their suits. What Berger is particularly interested in is the physical contradiction between the peasants' bodies "which are fully at home in effort" and their suits. As a ruling-class costume originating in Europe in the nineteenth century, the suit, Berger argues, was intended "to idealise purely sedentary power" and thus came to look normal on the corpulent bodies of those who administered (34). The fact that peasants and workers adopted these costumes as their own for formal occasions, is, as Berger puts it, an "easily taught example of class hegemony" (35).

As "easily taught" as this example of cultural hegemony may be, I want to emphasize that it constituted the final text of this two-week project; I did not assign it until the students had done so much writing and re-writing about suits that Berger's text could help them to complete analyses *they* had begun, whose gaps could be filled once the concepts of contradiction and hegemony were found. Thus, it was not with a reading of Berger that the students began, but rather, by keeping a dialectical notebook, recording on the right side their thoughts and observations about the picture of a suit and recording their notes about their notes on the left side. In addition, the students were assigned Berthoff's discussion of dialectical notebooks in *The Making of Meaning* (45–46). During class, students read from their notebooks, and on the day the notebooks were due, the students came to class and wrote for thirty-five minutes, setting forth the meaning they had found after four days of being in dialogue with themselves about the suit. At the end of class discussion about what they had written, I handed out the next assignment which included a picture of the same suit, this time, though, with its advertising copy on it. (The students hadn't known the suit came from an advertisement.) The advertising copy included a headline whose pun anticipates Berger's analysis in an interesting way: "To a Continental banker this is a sweatsuit." The assignment asked the students to do two things: (1) to read in Berthoff's "Learning the Uses of Chaos," that "the making of meaning is a dialectical process determined by perspective and context" and (2) to discuss how their perceptions of the suit were affected by the context of the advertisement.

As I learned by reading their papers, this imposed context, coming as it did after four days of writing to imagine their own contexts, caused a dramatic confrontation with the limitations of the advertisement. One student who had written at length about the various ways she had thought about suits—in terms of her love for her father, in terms of funerals and death, in terms of her ambivalent feelings about a man's attractiveness in a suit and in terms of the ways suits, as symbols of male success, exclude women—wrote the following about the suit in the advertisement:

> The banality and self-asserting character of this advertisement threatened to obliterate many of my initial spontaneous responses to the suit, as well as to thwart further thinking processes about it. . . . [The banality] would probably not have been so apparent to me if I'd viewed the ad without having studied the suit first on the blank page. This factor made me aware not only of the significance of context, but also of how dependent advertisements are on the lack of a thinking process. Rather than attempting to stimulate thoughts they seem to appeal to our most passive and unimaginative selves.

In two weeks' time, this student had come to see, through the process of imagining her own contexts and perspectives, that this advertisement itself was only one context for framing a suit's meaning—one context among many that *she* could construct by initiating a dialogue with the object. In her introduction to the same paper, she described what she had learned in this way:

> Before I embarked on this series of suit assignments, I had never given much conscious thought to the concept of the suit. I hadn't spent time

investigating my feelings or associations in relation to suits, what they mean to me, what they mean to other people. . . . One of the most exciting points that became clearly illuminated for me in this process of realizing feelings and associations connected to something as ordinary as the generic suit, is how many thoughts can surface and evolve simply through looking, writing and looking again, then writing some more. I would not have imagined that I could spend two weeks on this process of thinking and writing about something as commonplace and mundane as a man's suit. I became aware that through this method of attention and probing, anything from a candlestick to a lampshade or a flower vase offers this potential for the discovery of all kinds of meanings which seemed not to have existed before, at least consciously.

To be sure, if the project had stopped with these insights, it would have been of considerable value in the way that it shows students how "writing dialectically encourages as it *requires* conscientization." By pursuing a dialogue with an object, this writer and her classmates were in the position to recognize themselves as makers of meaning, finding "all kinds of meanings which seemed not to have existed before." Once again, if the assignment had been limited to these discoveries, it would have been valuable instruction in dialectical awareness. But the project was not limited in this way; it included a more Marxian phase of insight and analysis which the writer above actually mentions in the second sentence where I inserted the ellipsis. The beginning along with the completed second sentence reads as follows:

> Before I embarked on this series of suit assignments . . . I hadn't spent time investigating my feelings or associations in relation to suits, what they mean to me, what they mean to other people, when and how they originated and how and why they're worn.

Once the students read Berger and started re-reading and re-writing their notebook entries in terms of his questions, the whole project advanced dialectically. Berger's interest in such questions as when and how suits originated and how and why they were worn, initiated for the students a new phase of dialogue with their own ideas about suits. In this phase, the students were struggling to make sense of Berger's concepts—a virtually new language—in terms of their own experience and their own language. One student worked through analogy:

> By the time August Sander began his series of photographic "archtypes," the dark suit was a definite part of the peasant/worker life. What Berger is ultimately trying to tell us is that the suit had very

little context in either of their lives. It had become part of their life, he claims, through "class hegemony." The lower classes "came to accept *as their own*, standards of the class that ruled over them—in this case standards of chic and sartorial worthiness." And in doing so "condemned them[selves] within the system of those standards, to being always, and recognisably to the classes above them, second rate, clumsy, uncouth, defensive." In other words, you should stick with the loose, comfortable peasant garb and leave the suits to the sedentary or at least to the wealthy and powerful.

And doesn't this fashion elitism still exist in a far more subtle yet pervasive way? The new '86 fall fashions worn by Harvard and BU students from wealthy backgrounds will be "knocked off," copied by a company in Korea or Hong Kong and put on the shelves next fall at some discount store in a mall and bought by the lower middle class kids going to Framingham State. These kids will in turn be scoffed at by those Harvard kids for wearing cheap imitations of last year's "hot" clothes. Maybe Mao best understood the interaction between fashion and class when he had eight hundred million Chinese wear the exact same uniform.

In this excerpt, the student is concerned with understanding the meaning of hegemony as the lived experience of class contradiction. He looks for a current example of such contradiction in fashion and finds it in the sportswear wars among his peers. Interestingly, he seems drawn to the concepts more than the object of study, suits, and has found his way into his subject by renaming the governing idea for himself as "fashion elitism." What is particularly compelling here is the decisive translation of cultural hegemony into precise terms—"knocked off," "cheap imitations," " 'hot' clothes"—terms which establish the example as both continuous with and different from Berger's. Just as we discussed how the advertisement's play on a suit as a sweatsuit suggests a change over time in the meaning of sedentary power, so too this writer discusses a "subtle" change over time in the meaning of fashion elitism. Reading this fashion elitism in the language through which it is represented, the writer is able to avoid simplistic or deterministic thinking. His depiction retains its historical specificity, and as such its overdetermined quality. By virtue of this overdetermined specificity, the writer has initiated a new dialectic in regard to his key term, "class hegemony": the dialectic of past significance and present meaning (Weimann 9).

In another excerpt, it is possible to see a student rethinking an incident involving jackets after reading Berger. Similar to the preceding writer, she paraphrases the Berger essay first in order to set up her example, which I am including here with only the final sentence of the prior paragraph:

> . . . The suit draws attention to the peasants' position because their bodies make a statement about themselves that they cannot disguise, and because of this, the suit cannot make successfully its statement about privilege and an easy life.
>
> Today suits and jackets are required by some restaurants and clubs as part of the dress code. I think sometimes the men that wear these jackets feel that their clothing makes a statement about themselves. A friend and I were denied admission to one of these clubs because he was not wearing a jacket at the time. We changed our plans and went to a club that didn't require jackets and had a very good time. Weeks later, however, when I mentioned to my friend that I wanted to go shopping for myself, he cautiously remarked that he'd like to go with me. He said he'd been meaning to go shopping for a suit jacket: I couldn't believe that he was still feeling awkward about that night! Obviously, he felt that he did not belong, or was not good enough to be admitted to the club, and that as a result I felt the same way. Somewhat like Berger's peasants, my friend wanted to be a "member of the club," he didn't want to be inferior any more. So even today, in an allegedly classless society, class hegemony still exists.

As this example comes from a personal experience, it is possible to see quite vividly how the writer restores the dialogue to an event about whose meaning it could *also* be said she had been "denied admission." Now, however, rather than not knowing, that is, rather than taking the incident at face value, she re-reads it in terms which examine the said and the not-said dialectically and problematically: "Weeks later . . . when I mentioned to my friend that I wanted to go shopping for myself, he cautiously remarked that he'd like to go with me. . . . I couldn't believe that he was still feeling awkward about that night! Obviously, he felt that . . . he was not good enough to be admitted to that club. . . ."

Interpreting her friend's silences and cautious speech in terms of his feelings of inferiority, the writer is now in a position to avoid the two most obvious responses to this problem, one of which would be to sincerely regret the effects of this particular individual's "inferiority complex," the second of which would be to sincerely regret the unfair ways of the world. Instead, she is able to go beyond a language of individualism and a language of condolence about the way things are because she has begun to learn a language with which she can *analyze* the way things are. And perhaps just as importantly, she has begun to use the language she is learning to imagine—implicitly, at least, in the phrase "allegedly classless society"—an alternative possibility.

If the students in these two excerpts show what it looks like to write their way toward our goals of dialogical restoration and the reading of hegemonic forms themselves, the writer in the following excerpt shows what it looks like to work these dialectical ways of thinking into a more sustained discourse. Dialectical thinking, Jameson has written, involves not only reflection on our thoughts, but also their "fulfillment" (*Marxism* 341) through the discovery that "all events carry their own logic, their own 'interpretations' within themselves" (345). This important point carries us back to Althusser's conviction that to realize Marx's discoveries we must read each particular contradictory result of social life not as the expression of some ultimate truth, but as a necessary and contingent production whose logic is as historically specific as the result itself. When we think dialectically to the point of discovering such contingency, it can feel like whiplash, a sudden reverse motion at which point questions become answers, problems become solutions. In the following excerpt, the writer swings around each paragraph dialectically, in order to explore how the contradictory conditions she examines may "carry their own logic":

> While some aspects of the suit as a fashion and a symbol of formality, authority and success have remained constant since its conception in the late 1800s, other aspects of it have undergone transformations with the development of new values and perspectives, and the shifting of old ones. The nature of class hegemony and people's response to it that Berger illustrates in his essay through the suit, seem to have altered. In the case that Berger presents, peasants blindly accepted standards set by the ruling class. Consequently, peasants looked clumsy and ill-proportioned in the suits developed by the ruling class. . . . Conversely, the ruling class "gentlemen" were physically flattered by the fit of this costume which they developed. Peasants were generally speaking much more fit and better proportioned than the ruling class because of their physical lifestyle. Because of this, it seems they *should* have looked better in whatever they wore. This physicality, however, was not what the suit was designed for. Yet as Berger and the photograph portray, the peasants and country men did not *feel* clumsy wearing their suits but wore them with pride and felt well-dressed in them. This fact

seemed to be caused by the unquestioning acceptance of ruling class standards and a lack of awareness that what was good for the ruling class was not necessarily suitable for them.

Today, a fashion of the suit has developed which has many characteristics in common with the way peasants wore their suits. The peasants however did not choose this particular formless fashion to be "hip" or stylish. This ill-fitted oversized look of suits which I am referring to *is* very specifically and consciously chosen by people, i.e., young people, of today. This anomaly could be indicative either of a decrease in the class hegemony Berger refers to, or simply of an altered response to it. While the "ruling class" no longer sets the trends in fashion and no longer is blindly accepted as the ultimate authority of standards in general, the element of rebellion to their standards as exemplified in this purposely contradictory suit style may in fact illustrate the enduring presence of class hegemony. . . .

In each paragraph, the writer finds the logic of a contradiction in terms of hegemonic relations. In each paragraph, she swings herself around so as to see a conflict as a relationship, a problem as a solution within historically specific limits. Reading the effects of history in social relations, she is reading dialectically. Like the other students, she eschews the common-sense response for one which reads for the origins and functions of such contradictory relations: "This anomaly could be indicative either of a decrease in the class hegemony Berger refers to, or simply of an altered response to it." This sentence, we should remember, was written two weeks into the semester by a writer who begins and ends her essay by expressing wonder not only at the breadth of her own thinking but at the recognition that she could write still more:

> As I conclude this essay, I realize how much more could be written in relation to the suit in terms of how and why it is worn, what peoples' various responses to the suit are and why people respond to suits in the way they do . . . how people feel when they wear suits and why they feel the way they do in them and much much more.

It is perhaps one of the most interesting contradictions of all that explanations of the Marxian dialectic can be crabbed and excruciatingly abstract while practicing the Marxian dialectic can be an experience of suspenseful unraveling and prolific writing—as it was for this student. We can explain the contradiction this way: the Marxian hermeneutic is, as Jameson has written, "dialectically linked to untruth, to that mystification of which it is the determinate negation . . ." (*Marxism* 372). This mystification includes the full spectrum of our philosophies and episte-mologies and thus, to theorize the Marxian dialectic requires that we look historically at the complex network of our own abstractions while at the same time explaining why we should. Writing students, however, are not put in a position to theorize the Marxian dialectic; they are put in a position to use it and thus to let it explain itself.

Students given the means to use the Marxian dialectic are given the means to re-read and to re-write the world historically. Through the dialectic, they are given the means, as Marx wrote, for "rising from the abstract to the concrete" (*Political* 98). This desire for rising to the concrete was not only Marx's; it is our students' desire too. And while I have tried here to describe my experience of "rising from the abstract to the concrete" with my students, it is perhaps best left to Tolstoy, a teacher of the "historical imagination" reclaimed by Ann Berthoff, who most eloquently observed a long-standing contradiction between the desires of teachers and students which we should certainly want to understand the logic of:

> . . . to the teacher the simplest and most general appears as the easiest, whereas for a pupil only the complex and living appears easy. (*Making* 146)

Works Cited

Althusser, Louis. *For Marx*. Trans. Ben Brewster. Great Britain: Verso, 1979.

Althusser, Louis, and Étienne Balibar. *Reading Capital*. Trans. Ben Brewster. Great Britain: Verso, 1979.

Bakhtin, M. M. *The Dialogic Imagination*. Trans. Caryl Emerson and Michael Holquist. Austin: U of Texas P, 1981.

Berger, John. *About Looking*. New York: Pantheon, 1980.

Berthoff, Ann E. *The Making of Meaning*. Portsmouth, NH: Boynton/Cook, 1981.

―――. *Reclaiming the Imagination*. Portsmouth, NH: Boynton/Cook, 1984.

―――. " 'Reading the world . . . reading the word': Paulo Freire's Pedagogy of Knowing." *Only Connect: Uniting Reading and Writing*. Ed. Thomas Newkirk. Portsmouth, NH. Boynton/Cook, 1986.

Coward, Rosalind and John Ellis. *Language and Materialism*. Boston: Routledge, 1977.

Jameson, Fredric. *Marxism and Form*. Princeton: Princeton UP, 1974.

―――. *The Political Unconscious*. New York: Cornell UP, 1981.

Marx, Karl. *The German Ideology*. Ed. C. J. Arthur. New York: International Publishers, 1978.

Weimann, Robert. *Structure and Society in Literary History*. Charlottesville: UP of Virginia, 1976.

III

Weekend: The QC Center
for Writers at Caumsett

We wake in the mansion
restored destroyed mansion.
It sees the joke of us in its age of gold.
Ghosts nudge each other & hint they're as
indestructible as their drains of real
lead shipped from a real castle
here to the long island,
to its north shore, east of lost Gatsby
by two buoys (by night a 10-second
red & a 3-second turquoise;
2 black nuns, bobbing, by day).

Practicing poets need: each other,
and a way to empty time.
As if I had time I stroll down the lawn.
Close up, it's weeds: mustard, dandelion, lots
of mowed briar. I cross a meadow
past a fellow poet bent to his book.
His laugh at catching a poem goes unexplained.
It pleases the houseghosts' benevolence.

Dressed in her smallness as a body of freshness
Poet A says, "I saw the sun rise today & it jumped,
it looked as if it jumped up." Her poems now
though deep in the urban century
can have sun jump from their beaches.
Above a bay the wind gives tongue to,
Shakespeare & Wordsworth swoop to listen as

Poet B comes to the edge of a daffodil galaxy.
Her son, Ben, shows them starry in his face.
His friend John is littler,
his face still closer
to the poignant & temporal blossoming.
He touches one. It nods. He nods.
The Sweet Williams are nodding.
She watches & keeps & speaks to
boys & the many of daffodils.
Such abundance, like her own abundance,
nods & gives liberty, herself responsible.

Ghosts of the thing-minded sigh wishing
they'd spent their time like her, wisely.

Yet their elegance minds us.
I lunch in their gameroom.
It reflects waters where catboats skim yachtless
behind heads of poets crowned
by the beams of spirits envious enough
of the work we do to allow us ketchup on
our choice of hand-held sandwiches
& recourse to coffee all afternoon.

o jazz generation
you're coming back
as ancestors, mamas & papas
rich in spooked conscience;
welcome; it's twilight;
all wander, ethereal; your roof overshadows
your mansion, many & occupied;
the osprey have nested close by & mated
this time successfully maybe;
poems, pocketed, electric, crackle
no louder than your whispering money;
& each of our houses has its own power house
housing a generator; each has, under ground,
its own house reservoir, glimmering.

MARIE PONSOT

10

Metaphor and the Order of Things

PAUL KAMEEN

University of Pittsburgh

Discussions of metaphor—there are not many of them—often strike us as superficial. Not until we ourselves have made the attempt to get further do we begin to realize that the investigation of metaphor is curiously like the investigation of any of the primary data of consciousness: it cannot be pursued very far without our being led to the borderline of sanity. . . . The earth trembles and yawns beneath the explorer's feet.

John Middleton Murry, "Metaphor"

I have glanced for a moment at these deep waters into which a serious study of metaphor may plunge us, because possibly fear of them may be one cause why the study has so often not been enterprising and why Rhetoric traditionally has limited its inquiry to relatively superficial problems.

I. A. Richards, *Philosophy of Rhetoric*

It is not so much the apocalyptic flash of these passages—the trembling earth, the deep waters, the plunging and pursuing—that attracts our attention these days. We have, after all, what with the latest critical sophistications, become connoisseurs of catastrophe. No, it is more the earnest, almost paranoiac, urgency, and the genuine uncertainty with which the risks of the enterprise in question are being measured. What

stakes could be so high, what losses so threatening, to inspire such fear
and trembling? Especially in discussions of metaphor, which hadn't,
among rhetoricians and literary critics at least, amounted to much of a
walk on the wild side for a very long time, maybe even since Socrates
put a lid on things by deciding to kick the poets out of his Republic. I
will be coming around to this issue of the stakes, the potential losses, as
the essay goes on; but I want to begin with the problem of superficiality,
which from both of these writers' points of view has afflicted prior investigations into the subject, and which both of them seem hopeful of rising
above.

Unfortunately, it is not all that simple. In Murry's case, for example,
it is not merely, given his critical system, some "gap" in a "text" that
threatens him as a "reader"; it is the earth itself, about to open up and
swallow him wholly. One can understand, and even forgive, his failure
of courage when, in the face of such a fate he beats a hasty and complete
retreat from the heady prospect he had momentarily assumed, choosing
instead to search over steadier and more familiar ground for what he calls
a "middle way." His discussion of metaphor is thereby doomed to the
same superficiality he admonishes in his predecessors. Richards is more
explicit about what looms in the watery depths he stops for a moment
to fathom. He is willing to entertain the possibility that not only might
"the mind and all its doings" be "fictions," but likewise for "matter and
all its adventures" (91). These are extraordinary claims for Richards to
be thinking about making in 1936, guaranteed, it would seem, to get
his discussion of metaphor off the dime of superficiality. As the essay
proceeds, however, Richards takes a step back here, a stroke back there,
until, by the end, his is more a brisk dip in the shallows than a plunge
into deep waters. But he does at least, unlike Murry, get the discussion
off the ground.

No matter, though, the degree to which, by our standards, Richards
and Murry fall captive to the very vice they bridle against, the question
remains: Just what about prior (and perhaps subsequent) discussions of
metaphor has been so "superficial"? This essay is no place for a point-by-
point survey of all of those discussions, but a map of their general structure
is not that difficult to sketch. For there are two primary categories into
which most traditional approaches to metaphor fall. The first defines
metaphor as an act of renaming one thing in terms of another; it is therefore
a sort of conveyance for transferring meaning from a familiar place—the
"thing" to which it properly belongs—to a strange place—something,
almost anything, else. The second defines metaphor as a agency for re-

constituting one thing in terms of another; it is therefore a medium for synthesizing new meanings from old materials.

Our most commonplace ways of thinking about metaphor fall, of course, into the first category, and they are largely derivative from 18th- and 19th-century rhetorics, which are themselves little more than repetitive appendices to Aristotle, in this case to his definition of metaphor as "the transfer of a word belonging to something else" (*Poetics* 39). In Aristotle's system the context within which metaphor takes on its identity then is a mimetic theory of language. "For words," he says, "represent [imitate] things" (*Rhetoric* 184); and "one word may come closer than another to the thing described, may be more like it, and being more akin to it, may set it more distinctly before our eyes" (*Rhetoric* 184, 189). Though the qualifier "may" seems to leave in doubt the degree to which a word can actually and always maintain a one-to-one correspondence with its proper "thing," the mimetic theory certainly presumes, as the ground for discourse, such a primary and univocal linkage, and, further, that the world of "things," of non-words, exists prior to, independent of and uncontaminated by the linguistic instruments we deploy to mimic it. Metaphor is, in the context of such a system, necessarily an impertinence, a purposeful mis-naming of the thing, the effect of which is to add an air of dignity (*Poetics* 41–42) or a dash of novelty (*Rhetoric* 186) to the otherwise competent but drab canvas of literal discourse.

For Aristotle, metaphor is in fact merely a subset of "lexis"—diction or style—the final step in the production of discourse, the means by which meanings are made to "appear" in actual language. Its proper function has then, by fiat, been radically circumscribed: to redeem the diction arising from "authorative" words—normal, referential language—from "abjectness," i.e., to make "idiomatic" discourse less boring (*Poetics* 41– 42). As long as the potentially subversive power of metaphor—its capacity to estrange the word from its proper thing—is held so strictly in check (in this case by making it the last rather than the first thing one does with language) there is not much of a problem. Any discussions, of course, on the subject are likely to be pretty formulaic, pretty brief, pretty superficial, as in fact they were, at least among rhetoricians, for a couple of thousand years after Aristotle.

In our own century, Max Black has labeled the structure (impertinence for the purpose of ornamentation) as the "substitution view" of metaphor, according to which "the focus of a metaphor, the word or expression having a distinctly metaphorical use within a literal frame, is used to communicate a meaning that might have been expressed literally" (32).

This view, as Black points out, assumed enough authority to serve as the prototype not only for almost every definition of metaphor in our rhetoric textbooks, but also even as the framework for the only definition of metaphor provided in the *OED*: "The figure of speech in which a name or descriptive term is transferred to some object different from, but analogous to, that to which it is properly applicable." Here we have in capsule form all of the essential elements of the substitution view of metaphor: the notion of a meaning being "transferred" from its customary place to a new and strange place, of objects as discrete and "different from" one another, a spatial isolation that can be transfigured by the artifice of analogy, and finally of "names and descriptive terms" as "properly applicable" in one place by some unspecified but clearly metaphysical necessity—and presumably improperly applicable, impertinent, elsewhere. Thus metaphor remains, as it was for Aristotle, a small sub-set of language, the study of which is confined to the linguistic analysis of the odd disjunction between the literal and semantic aspects of such expressions. In Wayne Booth's terms, metaphor remains a "deliberate rhetorical deviation" from "normal discourse," a kind of verbal aberration that packs its meanings elsewhere than on the surface and doubly mediates between what is said and what is meant (52).

The extent to which this view has informed and constrained the way we talk about metaphor is suggested when even Owen Barfield, whose conception of metaphor is generally quite rich, can lapse into the habit of claiming that metaphor involves "saying one thing in terms of another" (111). Even Max Black, who criticizes this sort of semantic polarization, advances only slightly beyond it in his own "interaction view" of metaphor, which simply enlivens the interplay between the two planes of the metaphor by complicating the processes by which the subsidiary and primary "foci" interact in their contextual "frames" to produce a semantic overflow. Such bi-focal conceptions of the functional structure of metaphor do, of course, provide it with some potential as an epistemological agent. When what is meant is compelled to lurk in the shade of what is said, the very act of comprehension must require a "way of knowing" first of all that what is said is not what is meant, and second of all for construing what is meant despite the fact that it is not what is said. In effect, "reading" a metaphor involves recognizing and approving of the "creativity" of such an intentional mistake. Discussions of how and why such interpretive activity should take place can range from the very simple— along the information-processing model, for example—to the very complicated—along the lines of literary criticism, for example. But they are unlikely to rise ever, as long as this structure remains intact, above the charge of superficiality that Richards and Murry so astutely accuse them of.

The principal alternative to this view of metaphor has arisen more recently, in a variety of guises, two of which are of specific interest to me here: the proto-new-critical definition proposed by Richards himself and the phenomenological definition offered by Paul Ricoeur. What these two systems, so obviously different as they might otherwise be, share in common is the assertion that metaphor, as Richards would have it, is not merely "a grace or ornament or *added* power of language, but rather its constitutive form" (90). His first gesture in fulfilling this promise is to redefine metaphor as a mental rather than a lexical or linguistic function:

> The traditional theory noticed only a few of the modes of metaphor; and it limited its application of the term *metaphor* to a few of them only. And thereby it made metaphor seem to be a verbal matter, a shifting and displacement of words, whereas fundamentally it is a borrowing between and intercourse of *thoughts*, a transaction between contexts. *Thought* is metaphoric, and proceeds by comparison, and the metaphors of language derive therefrom. (94)

This does functionally transform metaphor from the stage hand of invention—moving words from here to there to enhance an effect—into, at least, the leading actor, giving voice to what meanings we can make. As to the making of those meanings, though, that capacity appears to reside elsewhere, in "thought" for example, which seems here, as elsewhere in Richards, much as he keeps trying to avoid it, to pre-figure the language, figurative or otherwise, with which it is ultimately represented.

In the same vein, Richards argues that "a word is normally a substitute for (or means) not one discrete past impression, but a combination of general aspects." Thus, "in the simplest formulations, when we use a metaphor we have two thoughts of different things active together and supported by a single word, or phrase, whose meaning is a resultant of their interaction" (93). Once again it is metaphor that is the product of, not the maker of, the "interaction" of these "two thoughts of different things." And we now have an added layer of not-language in the equation: those "things" which there are "thoughts of" resulting, by their interaction, in a "meaning."

The problems continue to mount in Richards' effort to distinguish between the "two ideas that any metaphor, at its simplest, gives us" (96). He calls these the "tenor and the vehicle," a tandem that does in fact allow him to do considerably more with his analysis of the potential range of metaphor than his predecessors (100, 118). But still there intrudes this problematic dissociation of the linguistic aspect of metaphor—the figure itself—from that to which it refers, or perhaps more appropriately defers: "The tenor," for example, becomes "the underlying idea or principal subject which the vehicle or figure means" (97). Where before it was the thoughts of things which the whole of a metaphor enacted, it is now the "idea" or "subject" which intervenes, under the mask of the tenor, between the figure and its ultimate meaning. It would seem that what is gradually being recuperated is a stable, non-verbal realm to which language refers, i.e., the concept of representation, and, with it, the bifurcation of language itself into two modes: the literal, which keeps close ties to this extrinsic reality, and the figurative, which doesn't.

Richards presumes just such a bifurcation when he argues:

> Whether, therefore, a word is being used literally or metaphorically is not always, or indeed as a rule, an easy matter to settle. We may provisionally settle it by deciding whether, in a given instance, the word gives us two ideas or one. . . . If we cannot distinguish tenor from vehicle then we may provisionally take the word to be literal; if we can distinguish at least two co-operating uses, then we have metaphor. (119)

Richards goes on to suggest that "by this test, of course, most sentences in free or fluid discourse turn out to be metaphoric. Literal language is rare outside the central parts of the sciences" (120). This does, obviously, attribute to metaphor a great deal more frequency and authority than does the "substitution view." On the other hand, we're still left with an irreducible core of literal language, belonging primarily to the sciences, which, small as it might be, remains the ground against which metaphoric language establishes, as figure, its identity. The nemesis that Richards seemed ready to face down when he imagined the intrinsic fictionality of what we call "mind" and "matter," gradually re-emerges over the course of these two lectures to take most of it back.

Richards makes a genuine effort at the close of his argument to reverse this trend of capitulation. "Words," he asserts, "are not a medium in which to copy life. Their true work is to restore life itself to order" (134). Once again, Richards tries to deny that language is primarily mimetic in its functions, that metaphor, consequently, is not solely ornamental. But what interests me most here is the reference to "order," a recurrent motif in this final lecture.

In Richards' system, it seems, psychological order, social order, political order, all reflect, he proposes, their microcosmic double in linguistic order:

Thus in happy living the same patterns are exemplified and the same risks of error are avoided as in tactful and discerning reading. The general form of the interpretative process is the same, with a small-scale instance—the right understanding of a figure of speech—or with a large-scale instance—the conduct of a friendship. (136)

One must need, of course, a system of privilege within which such loaded terms as "error" and "right" can take on any particular meaning. And it looks like it falls to Rhetoric to provide that system:

It seems modest and reasonable to . . . hope that a patient persistence with the problems of Rhetoric may, while exposing the causes and modes of the misinterpretation of words, also throw light upon and suggest a remedial discipline for deeper and more grievous disorders; that, as the small and local errors in our everyday misunderstandings with language are models in miniature of the greater errors which disturb the development of our personalities, their study may also show us more about how these large scale disasters may be avoided. (136–37)

The dissimulations and complications characteristic of metaphor are a big problem as long as "misinterpretation of words" pre-figures "grievous disorders," as long as "local errors" pre-figure "large scale disasters." Only the proper "remedial discipline" can hold such threats in abeyance, and metaphor, in Richards' system, seems to be held in check by its subordination to something, on the one hand, that is language but not-metaphor—literal discourse—and to something, on the other hand, that is metaphoric but is not-language—"thinking." To abandon such a base, such a ground, is to risk the very order Richards is interested, finally, in preserving here. That is what is at stake for Richards, as it was for Aristotle and most of the rhetoricians that came between. In that light, Murry may not be overstating things to suggest that even "sanity" is jeopardized whenever one is trying to draw the borders around metaphor—at least as long as one's concept of sanity presumes an extant reality that supersedes and outlasts the ephemera of language, figurative or otherwise. To allow metaphor to overrun its bounds is to threaten, then, the orderliness of discourse, which is, ultimately, to threaten the orderliness of the mind, of society. One can see why Richards, no matter his courage, must resist his most extreme temptation: to define both mind and matter as fictions, originating rather than culminating in language.

Forty years later Paul Ricoeur seeks to pick up this conversation where, in his view, Richards left it off:

My thesis is that it is not only for theories which deny metaphors any informative value and any truth claim that images and feelings have a *constitutive* function. I want instead to show that the kind of theory of metaphor initiated by I. A. Richards in *Philosophy of Rhetoric* . . . cannot achieve its own goal without including imagining and feeling, that is, without assigning a *semantic* function to what seems to be mere *psychological* features and without, therefore, concerning itself with some accompanying factors extrinsic to the informative kernel of metaphor. (141–42)

Ricoeur's ambition is to assess "the semantic role of imagination and eventually feeling" in the "work of resemblance" (143), to locate the "constitutive function" of metaphor in a context different from, and presumably more powerful than, the one Richards chooses. But it seems hardly likely, even at this early moment in his essay, that Ricoeur can achieve the "goal" that Richards falls short of. For despite the obvious differences in their philosophical agendas—Richards is heir to the Anglo-American pragmatists and semiologists, Ricoeur to the European phenomenologists and existentialists—we can begin to see already a structural resemblance in their epistemic systems. Whereas for Richards it is (usually) "thinking," for Ricoeur it is (usually) "feeling" that prefigures and supercedes the production of metaphoric discourse. For both then it is in factors "extrinsic," rather than intrinsic, to language that meaning-making originates.

Ricoeur does, though, make some headway against one of the long-standing inhibitions to the investigation of metaphor: the stigma of impertinence:

> . . . it seems to me that we are still only halfway to a full understanding of the semantic innovation which characterizes metaphorical phrases or sentences if we underline only the aspect of deviance in metaphor. . . . The decisive feature is the semantic innovation, thanks to which a new pertinence, a new congruence, is established in such a way that the utterance "makes sense" as a whole. . . . In other words, metaphorical meaning does not merely consist of a semantic clash but of the *new* predicative meaning which emerges from the collapse of the literal meaning, that is, from the collapse of the meaning which obtains if we rely only on the common or usual lexical values of our words. (144)

This is not much different from what Richards seems to want to argue on behalf of the originary power of metaphor, though Ricoeur's mode of discourse allows him to get it out more slickly. But still, at the center of things, is this hobgoblin of the "literal," which seems in this case, as it was for Richards, the unchallenged base against which metaphor must run counter to generate its "new pertinence." Conflicts between the literal and the metaphoric erupt in fact throughout the essay, with the former retaining consistently its hierarchical priority in relation to the latter, a structure that is established in Ricoeur's opening paragraph, where he defines the concept of "semantic theory," so crucial to his argument, as "an inquiry into the capacity of metaphor to provide untranslatable information and, accordingly, into metaphor's claim to yield some true insight about reality" (141). As long as metaphor's highest ambition is to earn the right to be "about reality," as long as it has to argue on behalf of its claim to "yield some true insight," as long, that is, as it takes on its identity by contrast with the more reputable and prudent modes of literal discourse, it may achieve the status of "pertinence" that Ricoeur countenances for it, but it will never, any more than it did for Aristotle, escape the stigma of "deviance," "acceptable" or otherwise.

Ricoeur goes on to do a lot of complicated things with "proportionalities" and "ratios," which are in fact somewhat more sophisticated versions of the traditional bi-focal systems for describing the operations of metaphor. And his notions of the "split reference" and "*epoché*" likewise allow him to do and claim certain things that elude his predecessors, including Richards. But in the final analysis Ricoeur's treatment is afflicted by the same strictures that have dogged discussions of metaphor from the start: Metaphor remains a subset of lexis, aberrant in its essential structural relationship with "normal" discourse, requiring, therefore, a complicated set of strategies both for its invention and its interpretation.

Like Richards, Ricoeur flirts with a concept of "fiction" as the locus for his ultimate argument on behalf of the originary powers of metaphor:

> It is to . . . the image as fiction that is attached the power of symbolic systems to "remake" reality. . . . But this productive and projective function of fiction can only be acknowledged if one sharply distinguishes it from the reproductive role of the so-called mental image which merely provides us with a re-presentation of things already perceived. *Fiction* addresses itself to deeply rooted potentialities of reality to the extent that they are absent from the actualities with which we deal in everyday life under the mode of empirical control and manipulation. (152–53)

We have here another re-enactment of the scene in which figurative language has always found itself: bragging about its superiority to the language of "everyday life" while at the same time boxing itself into a position from which it must plead feverishly for some concessions to its claims to be "about" the same "reality" it is feigning contempt for. This structure is reinforced when Ricoeur turns to the concept of poetry, the epitome, it seems, for him, of figurative/fictional discourse. As he explains:

> poetic language is no less *about* reality than any other use of language but refers to it by means of a complex strategy which implies, as an essential component, a suspension and seemingly an abolition of the ordinary reference attached to descriptive language. (151)

We have here the customary plea to admit poetry into the realm of discourse that is "about reality," followed by the equally familiar excuse that it only seems not to belong there because it is more "complex" in its strategies, must accomplish its goals by means of "suspension" and "abolition," which are not, it seems to me, much different from the sorts of things—like subterfuge and dissimulation—that poetry is often faulted rather than applauded for. The inevitable consequence of such a stance is to define "poetry" (and in Ricoeur's system both "fiction" and "metaphor") in terms of and by contrast with some other primary mode of discourse, one that deploys language descriptively or referentially and which is therefore more obviously and legitimately "about reality." The only role that metaphor can play in such a context is deviant and, finally, ornamental, which is where this all started in the first place. No wonder then that while discussions of metaphor have gotten more and more specialized, more and more complicated, denser and less accessible, they have remained equally "superficial."

Ricoeur's reasons for ending up in such a defensive posture are, I think, not unlike Richards': There is an "order" at stake, one he is committed to and would prefer not to put at risk. While for Richards—as one would expect given the impetus of his leading concept, thinking—it is the mental health, the sanity, if you will, of both the individual and of society that is at stake; for Ricoeur it is the emotional health of both the individual and of culture.

> To *feel*, in an emotional sense of the word, is to make *ours* what has been put at a distance by thought in its objectifying phase.
> . . . Feeling is not contrary to thought. It is thought made ours. This felt participation is a part of its complete meaning as poem. (154)

It seems to be via this notion of meaning-as-poem that the potentially destructive possibilities of *epoché* are overcome, that unity is restored, that our feelings are " 'attuned to' aspects of reality which cannot be expressed in terms of the objects referred to in ordinary language" (156). Thus, it is by a kind of transcendence that emotional order is restored, that cultural order is maintained. The very elitism of poetry that Ricoeur could be said at the outset to be trying to overcome has now, at the close here, been reinstated, crucial to the "order" he hopes to preserve.

We see a clue to the primary threat to that order in his earlier discussion of the concept of *epoché*:

> Imagination *is epoché*. As Sartre emphasized, to imagine is to address oneself to what is not. More radically, to imagine is to make oneself absent to the whole of things. Yet I do not want to elaborate further on this thesis of the negativity proper to the image. (152)

The demon of "negativity," of "absence," then is something Ricoeur hopes to elude, or at least elide, if only by refusing to talk about it. This concept, which deconstructionist systems have seized upon to overcome many of the inhibitions that seem here to silence Ricoeur, may in fact be his own "borderline of sanity," the line he'd just as soon not have to cross. For to do so would be to violate the traditional hierarchical relationship between poetic and representational discourses, a structure that is even more endemic to Ricoeur's argument than it was to Richards'. And it would probably mean admitting that there is no clear line that can be drawn between what is metaphor and what is not in any mode of discourse. To preserve the order of his system against the ambitions of absence, Ricoeur must ask awkward questions and generate convoluted answers in explaining how and why metaphor works. And that has been, it seems to me, the unfortunate fate of all our efforts at non-superficial discussions of metaphor.

But why not simply invert that hierarchy and install figurative discourse as the ground against which referential modes of discourse, and the "literal" "reality" they have, historically, engendered, figure problematically. This is, in one sense, what Richards was tempted toward by his vision of ubiquitous fiction; and it might be what Ricoeur senses in Sartrean negativity. But the cost, the penalty, for such gestures is just too steep for them: "reality," "thinking," "feeling," even "things," all become products of, rather than antecedents for, figurative discourse, for, i.e., all discourse. Language then, like Middleton Murry's explorer, has no longer any solid ground to stand on, no "sanity" to measure its madnesses against. Deconstructionist systems have, of course, already taken us this far, and further. But what even they can't seem to shake are the strains of elitism that seem always to show all over our definitions of "poetry," "literature," "fictions." Simply to make *all* texts potentially literary, to make the process of "reading" "texts" universally complicated, to institutionalize the role of "teacher" or "critic" or, most generally, "expert" in all interpretive transactions, is not really much of an answer. But how to do the opposite is surely, at this stage of our longstanding cultural conversation about the proper role and status of figurative discourse, not an easy matter to imagine. I am thinking now, for example, about a conversation that begins by presuming the "everydayness" of fiction, the unproblematic givenness of "metaphor," the simplicity and straightforwardness of "poetry," that treats in fact literature not as a problem for subtle analysis and critical circumspection, but as what we as humans most naturally make and do. I am thinking about a conversation in which we might be saying how odd and tremendously exciting it is that we have, as a civilization, invented, almost perfected, an array of linguistic instruments and discourses, from "everyday" idioms to sophisticated scientific jargons and methods, to domesticate the various "realities" we have found it necessary and useful to constitute. I am thinking about a conversation in which we would have none of the dense and long-winded "defenses" of poetry we have become accustomed to, the ones that elevate the status of poetry to the realm of exotic, precious uselessness; a conversation that would more likely involve explanations and defenses of the "literal," the univocal, the referential; I am thinking about a conversation that would not acknowledge the customary distinction between rhetoric and poetics, the bifurcation of "composition" and "literature," to say nothing of "creative" writing, that would not isolate writing from reading, that would not even have us in charge of the "reading" of our "culture," responsible for the cultivation of reading.

There seems to me no better place, no more appropriate occasion, to imagine this new discussion, this escape from the superficial, than a celebration of the contributions made already on its behalf by Ann Berthoff.

Works Cited

Aristotle. *Poetics*. Ed. Kenneth A. Telford. South Bend: Gateway, 1961.

———. *The Rhetoric of Aristotle*. Ed. Lane Cooper. Englewood Cliffs: Prentice-Hall, 1932.

Barfield, Owen. "Poetic Fiction and Legal Fiction." *Essays Presented to Charles Wilson*. Oxford: Oxford UP, 1947.

Black, Max. *Models and Metaphors: Studies in Language and Philosophy*. Ithaca: Cornell UP, 1962.

Booth, Wayne C. "Metaphor as Rhetoric: The Problem of Evaluation." *On Metaphor*. Ed. Sheldon Sacks. Chicago: U of Chicago P, 1978. 47–70.

Murry, John Middleton. "Metaphor." *John Clare and Other Studies*. 1927. Reprinted in *Essays on Metaphor*. Ed. Warren Shibles. Whitewater, WI: The Language Press, 1972.

Richards, I. A. *The Philosophy of Rhetoric*. London: Oxford UP, 1936.

Ricoeur, Paul. "The Metaphorical Process as Cognition, Imagination, and Feeling." *On Metaphor*. Ed. Sheldon Sacks. Chicago: U of Chicago P, 1978. 141–57.

11

The Discovery of Meaning
Emerging Evaluative Structure in a Student Narrative

ELEANOR KUTZ

University of Massachusetts, Boston

In composition courses, narrative has traditionally been approached first as form, as one of the rhetorical modes, rather than as a process by which people come to understand and reflect on themselves and their world. Yet the very act of narration, of selecting from the flux of experience, and re-presenting that experience in narrative form, is, like any other act of composing, "a process of discovery and interpretation, of naming and stating, of seeing relationships and naming meanings" (Berthoff 20). This paper will focus on the relationship between that process of interpretation and the emergence of structure in narrative, on "forming" as a process which emerges in relation to the discovery of meaning.

If we follow the first of Ann Berthoff's maxims, "Begin with where they [our students] are . . . as language animals, endowed with the form-finding and form-creating powers of mind and language" (9), then we will begin with narrative, for as E. L. Doctorow tells us: "Narrative is the art closest to the ordinary daily operation of the human mind. . . . Everyone all the time is in the act of composition, our experience is an ongoing narrative within each of us" (22). Embedded in these narratives is a meaning or multiple meanings—narrative is not without meaning. "No human, under normal conditions, fails to make sense when narrativizing his or her experience" (Gee 11). Rather, Hayden White

suggests, "the absence of narrative capacity or a refusal of narrative indicates an absence or refusal of meaning itself" (2).

All students can "tell a story," and these stories, selected from personal
experience, are about something which is inherently meaningful. Some
clues as to that inherent meaning are usually present in the telling, whether
they represent a constructed understanding (even if unexpressed) of a
significant event or a puzzled restatement of something felt to be significant but not yet understood. I assume, then, that students have narrative
competence, that their narratives have embedded meanings, and that as
these meanings emerge, so will appropriate forms. I will refer to such
patterns, emerging as part of a process of interpretation and evaluation
of experience, as an "evaluative structure."

Because narrative is so fundamental to our processing of human
experience, to our ways of reflecting on and making meaning from
that experience, there is, in the most inchoate student narrative, the beginning of meaning as structure. First of all, the meaning lies in the events
chosen for retelling, not in what lies outside of the story. In deciding
where to begin and end, the teller has already begun to link meaning and
structure, to say that the meaning which he wants to communicate or
discover lies in these events as opposed to those which came before
or after (though such meaning may be shared, even among widely scattered events). Similarly, through the selection of details from within
the event has come some movement toward matching events and meanings, details and significance—even though student narratives often
include details which more accomplished tellers might take to be insignificant.

William Labov, in "The Transformation of Experience in Narrative
Syntax," examines narratives of personal experience told by black, urban
adolescents. He finds a common structural pattern to these narratives,
with fully formed versions containing an abstract, orientation, complicating action, evaluation, resolution, and coda. (Other researchers have
found this pattern applicable to narratives produced by narrators from
quite different backgrounds. See, for example, Gee, Heath, Michaels,
Scollon & Scollon, Tannen.) While I draw on these terms in my analysis
of student narratives, the aspect of structure which I wish to focus on
here is the evaluation. Labov defines the evaluation as "the means used
by the narrator to indicate the point of the narrative, its *raison d'être*: why
the story is told and what the narrator was getting at" (366). In other
words, the evaluation offers an indication of the meaning of the story to
the narrator at the time of this telling. Labov finds that although evaluation

is often lacking in narratives of vicarious experience (recounts of TV stories given in response to an interviewer's question), it is strongly present in self-generated narratives.

Labov points out that, unlike the other units of narrative structure, evaluation can appear anywhere, scattered throughout the narrative and embedded in its syntax. Some of the evaluation will be external, as the narrator stops the narrative and tells what the point is, from the perspective of the present. (Labov sees this method as common to middle class narrators; Scollon and Scollon link it to the larger patterns of western "essayist literacy." Certainly in our expository writing classrooms we try to draw out explicit statements of meaning.) Often the evaluation is partly embedded in the narrative, presented as occurring to the narrator at the moment of the action or as a statement addressed to someone else or made by someone else at that time. Or it may be further embedded in actions of the participants or fully embedded within narrative syntax.

Basic narrative syntax consists most often of subject, verb, (indirect object), object sentences with verbs in the past tense (or the narrative/historical present). Other syntactic elements are likely to be evaluative, to point toward meaning. As Labov explains, "Since syntactic complexity is relatively rare in narrative, it must have a marked effect when it does occur" (378). He describes in detail the syntactic devices which he finds to represent such fully embedded evaluation, but for my present purpose I will make only a general distinction among external, partially embedded and fully embedded evaluation. My concern is to show that as the meaning of the narrative becomes clearer to the narrator with successive versions, the evaluative portions of the narrative become more clearly ordered and sharply defined (though not necessarily fully explicit), and that they come to provide the structure for the central portion of the narrative—a meaning-based, evaluative structure.

Here I will examine two versions of a student narrative, one produced in class on the first day, in response to an assignment to "tell of an event that happened in your family—a family story," the second a later version of this story produced at mid-term for a formal class collection. In between, students used their own narratives, in oral as well as written versions, as data for a series of investigations into the nature of language. The sequence of activities was designed, in part, as an outgrowth of a project I had been collaborating on with Shirley Brice Heath, in which students undertook ethnographic and other studies of language. I was not directly "teaching" narrative form as rhetorical mode, nor did students receive explicit instructions for revising their narratives, though they produced several different versions over a period of six weeks.

My purpose here was to allow students to draw, from the study of their own uses of language, some general conclusions about rhetorical principles and constraints. In comparing their own different tellings of a story, students began to see and formalize, for example, what they already knew "intuitively" about uses of language in relation to audience and purpose. They discovered that, through subtle variations, the same story can express multiple meanings as they gathered several versions of an often-told story from other family members. And, by reading examples of family stories from a folklorist's collection while collecting their own, they began to develop a sense of genre.

For freshman writers the discovery of meaning is often limited by their rush to premature closure. We must get students to allow the many possible meanings and many possible ways of showing those meanings in a piece of writing to percolate for a while, to let shapes and forms emerge along with meaning, to discover that "meanings change as we think about them; statements and events, significances and interpretations can mean different things to different people at different times" and that "the making of meaning is a dialectical process determined by perspective and context" (Berthoff 71). Working with these texts as data allowed the narratives to stay open; each version provided more material for analysis, and no version had to be definitive. At the same time the identification of differences between most oral and written narratives, for example, fostered a growing awareness of formal concerns. Yet because this attention to form was not focused directly on revising the narrative, any changes in form would grow out of the "cooking" that was going on, out of the unidentifiable ways in which meaning emerges and can be represented in a structure.

Aqeelah's first and last written versions of her "family story" illustrate a developing writer's alterations in evaluative structure. Her story tells of the time that she and her mother accompanied her father, who was taking flying lessons, on a solo flight. The first version begins with an orientation which places the characters in the setting of the event. "We moved back to the West Indies two years ago and a few months ago my Dad decided that he wanted to start taking flying lessons." Movement in time and place are both important, and the chronological structure demands that her family's return home included, even though it occurred well before, the central event of her story. It is followed by background explanation to the lessons themselves, why the father needed a pilot's

license and the fact that this required his making a trip from Antigua to
St. Maarten. The opening paragraph ends: "My mother and I decide to
accompany him."

Following this orientation, narrative clauses, often in the narrative
present, recount the main events:

> We start out early one Sunday morning. . . . We leave Bird Interna-
> tional Airport for St. Vincent. . . . The flight to St. Vincent went
> smoothly. . . . the trouble started after leaving the St. Vincent airport.
>
> My dad notices this great big cloud. . . . He decides to sidesweep
> the cloud by going around to the left of it. . . . He sidesweeps this
> cloud and we notice that we seem to be going on forever. . . . We find
> out that the identification code that the tower gave us was the wrong
> one. . . . We spend a few minutes circling an island that no one could
> identify. . . . We finally get a new code. . . . My Dad then hooks into
> this frequency. . . . We're in St. Maarten.

The narrative, as presented here, contains some embedded evaluation
of the events. There is trouble, they seem to be going on forever, they
have been given the wrong identification code. Interspersed with these
narrative clauses are further evaluative statements, some from the present
("I often say that if I had prayed that morning then none of this would
have happened." "Now, from the ground clouds look small and fluffy, but
up in the air they can be gigantic"); and some from the time of the events
("So needless to say [the cloud] looked rather threatening"). Connectors
such as "anyway" and "needless to say" return the focus to the central
narrative after such interjections. The narrative concludes with one sentence which ends the event but which implicitly evaluates the whole: "I
hate to embarrass my dad like this but, accidents do happen and when
we landed, the first stop we made was for a new pair of pants for him."

The evaluative statements which are embedded or interspersed in the
narrative show that there was trouble and that the narrator was concerned
about this at the time ("the cloud looked rather threatening") as well as
later ("I often say"), but there has been no preparation for the evidence
of the father's concern which appears at the end. While the surprise ending
is potentially effective, it is tacked on to the narrative: there has been
some general thematic preparation for it in this account of trouble, but
nothing in the structure of this narrative, which moves from a paragraph
of orientation to a paragraph on the first (uneventful) portion of the flight
to a third and final paragraph on the trouble and return, leads the reader
to see it as other than a straightforward story of complication and resolution. And the final evaluation, because not anticipated structurally,

remains only surprising, rather than combining that sense of discovery with the sense that you almost knew it all along, a combination which a more effectively structured narrative might evoke.

I asked a separate series of questions about these initial narratives, not as instructions for revision but as part of our collection of data on why people—i.e., our class members and their families—tell stories: "Why do you think you chose that particular story? Does it have a special meaning for you or your family? Does it show something that is typical of your family or a family member? Is it told often? Under any particular circumstances? What do you think the point of the story was?" In responding, Aqeelah focused on the demands of the audience: "It was simply a humorous incident that was worth telling to other persons." While she saw the incident as "typical of my family's ability to control emotions at times that other persons would consider stressful," she twice insisted that "the story has no particular meaning," that "I don't believe that there is any particular point to the story."

Nevertheless, in the next versions of Aqeelah's story, changes appear which indicate that one meaning which this story has for her is in fact her family's ability to control emotions. What emerges in these succeeding versions is a tension between that ability and the clear indication that her father was not wholly successful in exerting that control. This tension emerges as the meaning of the story, and as it emerges it is built into the evaluative structuring of the narrative. In fact, two effective tensions emerge: the first between troubling events and being in control; the second between seeming to be in control but really not being. As the "being in control" is explicitly worked through the events, as part of the first tension, it prepares the reader simultaneously for the surprise ending—the second meaning.

In her final version Aqeelah has reduced the orientation to one sentence: "My Dad had to fly to St. Maarten in order to add flight hours towards receiving his pilot's license." She has reduced the amount of explanation and has added narrative clauses to provide a more detailed account of the events themselves. But the most significant changes occur within the evaluative structure of the story. Where in her first version Aqeelah had included several statements evaluating different aspects of these events, insofar as such evaluation was from anyone's perspective it was from her own, and these evaluative statements shifted back and forth between a present and external perspective ("I often say") to a past and embedded one ("The trouble began"). The intrusiveness of the external evaluation was demonstrated by the forcible return to the narrative ("Anyway"). Here, in contrast, the evaluative statements focus on the whole family's responses, and those responses are effectively situated within the narrative (in Labov's terms, partially embedded or embedded). The narrator no longer steps outside of the events ("I often say") but remains within them ("Despite this news we all remained calm"). Now there is no need to pull the reader abruptly back to an interrupted story.

But even more significant is that these partially embedded statements of evaluation emerge as a structural principle within the narrative and are repeated and varied at key junctures. Now the narrative has four distinct movements. It recounts the events up to the first sign of trouble—the incorrect pass code—and follows this with the evaluative statement: "Despite this news we all remained calm." It moves through a second cycle of seeming control into a problem with an echo of the earlier evaluation: "We were now officially lost. Yet still we remained calm." And through a third, ending with "They had no sight of us on their scanner. Still no one panicked." And a fourth, which moves to a resolution of the real-life problem—"The tower gave us new coordinates and we were on our way to St. Maarten"—and of the explicit level of tension and meaning, ending with the resolution of the hidden tension and statement of hidden meaning:

> The first place we went after leaving the plane was to a gift store in the airport in order to buy a pair of shorts for my father. It seems that for some strange reason, the pants he had on during flight had developed an odd stain right in its seat. But, no one panicked.

Thus Aqeelah has effectively built both meaning and form by using evaluation as a structural element in the narrative. She had discovered simultaneously both her meaning and a form which supports it, and as a result she has told a story whose meaning is clearly but organically expressed without the sort of external statement of "the moral of the story is" which I used to receive in response to my attempts to instruct students about how to write an effective narrative.

Later units of this course moved to other discoveries and constructions of meaning, in projects which focused on other uses of language (e.g., studies of greetings). But the principle remained: a form would emerge as meaning began to emerge. This integrated discovery of meaning and form—of evaluative structure—in narrative can provide a model for the emergence of form in any act of knowing or interpreting or understanding.

Works Cited

Berthoff, Ann E. *The Making of Meaning*. Portsmouth, NH: Boynton/Cook, 1981.

Doctorow, E. L. "The Passion of Our Calling." *The New York Times Book Review*, August 25, 1985.

Gee, James. "The Narrativization of Experience in the Oral Style." *Journal of Education* 167 (1985): 9–35.

Heath, Shirley Brice. *Ways With Words: Language, Life and Work in Communities and Classrooms*. Cambridge: Cambridge UP, 1983.

Labov, William. "The Transformation of Experience in Narrative Syntax." *Language in the Inner City*. Philadelphia: U of Pennsylvania P, 1972. 354–96.

Michaels, Sarah. "Narrative Presentations: an oral preparation for literacy with first graders." *The Social Construction of Literacy*. Ed. Jenny Cook-Gumperz. Cambridge: Cambridge UP, 1986. 94–116.

Scollon, R., and S. B. K. Scollon. *Narrative, Literacy and Face in Interethnic Communication*. Norwood, NJ: Ablex, 1982.

Tannen, Deborah. "Oral and Literate Strategies in Spoken and Written Narratives." *Language* 58 (1982): 1–21.

White, Hayden. "The Value of Narrativity in the Representation of Reality." *On Narrative*. Ed. W. J. T. Mitchell. Chicago: U of Chicago P, 1981. 1–24.

12

Reaching for Understanding

A "Capacity-Based" Approach to Learning

PAT D'ARCY

Wiltshire County Council, U.K.

For the last decade at least, I have consciously been trying to find some way of interpreting learning that is helpful for me as a learner, for students in their classrooms and for the teachers of those students with whom I now work. In the sixties my perceptions were already shifting as an educator, from being a good teacher to becoming a better facilitator of students' learning. In that endeavour and since, I think I have slowly become more aware of the varied and often complex processes that "reaching for understanding" involves.

At school and at university, I was content, indeed happy as I look back, to be a receiver—not entirely a passive recipient—as I always questioned, challenged, bucked the system, receiving such remarks on my school report as, "Pat should remember when she asks questions that she is not the only member of the class." Nevertheless I accepted until well into my twenties a "transmission" approach to learning: experts passed on what they knew and I absorbed as much of that knowledge as I could. When I first became a teacher I simply switched and did it the other way round; I expected my pupils to sit still and listen as they absorbed the benefits of the knowledge that I had in this way dutifully acquired.

It was not by any means a duff system; my teachers passed on a great deal and I absorbed and responded to that knowledge as best I could, sufficiently so to leave college with a first class honours degree and teaching distinctions in both "the theory and practice of education," even though I knew very little about education at the time. So why did I not continue to be a "successful" teacher in the same mould that had led me to be a "successful" student? I think it's an important question to which the rest of this short essay will seek to respond.

Looking back, I changed first of all because in my fifth year of teaching I had the good fortune to meet two university tutors at the London Institute of Education who related and responded to practicing teachers like myself, as equals—equal in the sense that we had experiences to share with each other that could be, indeed were, mutually enlightening and beneficial. Those two tutors, James Britton and Nancy Martin, changed my life—certainly my life as a practicing school-teacher but because such changes are fundamental, my life as a human being as well. What I learned from sharing my work in schools with Jimmy and Nancy, and from sharing also their work with student graduates and other practicing teachers, was an openness to learning, an acknowledgment (intensely stimulating) that *no one* had all the answers, let alone the right ones. Also that sharing whatever insights we were all struggling for helped everyone: the children in our classrooms, those of us who were looking for ways of educating more effectively, the postgraduate students and yes, also those at the top—the university tutors. Jimmy and Nancy rarely if ever lectured; they *shared* and asked questions instead of always giving answers. They were the academics who first shifted my perceptions of learning from being told to finding out.

Subsequently, after three years working with them on the *Writing across the Curriculum Project*, I moved back into a school as a head of English and then into my present job as an English Advisor. By that stage I had a very different view of what education was all about than I had first envisaged when I took on the role of teacher. That doesn't mean to say that everything was plain sailing. Neither is it now, after eight years as English Advisor for the Wiltshire Education Department. But the shift I was encouraged to make from a preoccupation with teaching to a fascination with how any of us make sense has rooted itself deeply. I did not succumb in the sixties to the woolly-minded liberalism that is said so often (and often so falsely) to typify progressive educators: "Let it all hang out." If sheep provide the image of a student flock, perhaps the slogan should have been, "Let it all hang on: we're not going to fleece you of your confidence as learners any more."

Shifting from teacher to learner did not reduce the necessity for a theory of what I was about. On the contrary, it increased it, and it's the theory to do with learning about learning that has grown for me through my work with primary and secondary teachers, in their classrooms, at Summer Institutes and at workshops outside school hours, that I want to share. I hope that it makes sense in terms of classroom practice in contrast to some of the other theories about learning that currently confront us on both sides of the Atlantic. It stems from the years through which the *Learning about Learning Project* has developed in Wiltshire and Somerset. The idea for the LAL Project came from my links with the Bay Area Writing Project and the respect with which BAWP treated classroom teachers. I am deeply grateful for all these contacts with teachers in the United States and nearer home, who have made the sharing of ideas both possible and productive.

What I want to offer is a "capacity based" approach to learning which is still evolving. I make no apology for that as I now believe that learning is an organic process. It stops only when we stop. I would rue the day when those of us who actually *work* in the field of education conclude that we've finally worked it all out—in spite of present pressures from government to petrify and compress learning into rigid sets of objectives and checklists. This is how it goes: (I wish I had appropriate music—not so much Wagner as improvised jazz with Frank Smith on the trumpet!)

The New Rs—Not the Traditional 3 but the Brainpower 5

- The brain's capacity to RETAIN all sensory experiences—taste, touch, smell, sights and sounds—especially the last two as the brain develops its ability to sequence both, in images and words. Our capacities to think in pictures and in language, transposing one form of thought readily into the other, make us very audio-visual creatures.
- The brain's capacity to RE-COLLECT. Each of us can "program" our brain with conscious messages to trawl for selections or networks drawn from that hugely rich sea of retained experience.
- The brain's capacity to RE-CREATE, to take recollected memories and to change them into a different kind of experience. (Why would we weave extended anecdotes around our most traumatic experiences if each time the recollection caused pain?) The act of re-creation can transmute and transform.
- The brain's capacity to RE-CONSTRUCT, to take the jigsaw pieces of new information that come to us piecemeal and to build them, gradually, into a coherent picture that "makes sense."
- The brain's capacity to RE-PRESENT, to take what has been recollected,

recreated or reconstructed and to give it a new shape in one form or another, verbal or non-verbal, and to make the past present again.

How the New Five Rs Operate

As well as possessing these innate capacities for meaning making, the brain's multiple helix of mental processes can utilize the five Rs potentially from birth and in practice within days or months of being born. The mental processes which coil and spiral around the axis of meaning, continually and inextricably inter-relating are: THINKING, VERBALIZING, VISUALIZING, FEELING, and DOING or ENACTING. I choose the helix metaphor because it has a dynamic quality. In their handbook for teachers (K–13) James Moffett and Betty J. Wagner observe that "Biology is the most appropriate field from which to draw a model of education because mental growth parallels the growth of the total organism in which it occurs." Their model is the human embryo which "grows from a single cell to an extraordinarily intricate organism"; mine is the helix which has, physically speaking, magnetic as well as genetic connotations.

Through our continual deployment of all these processes we are able to retain, recollect, recreate, reconstruct, and re-present the world to ourselves and ourselves to the world. All children, whatever their age, country, or culture, can think in words and pictures and are active talkers and doers whose every word and action is coloured by their feelings. For this reason, in our schools in Wiltshire we are encouraging teachers to develop "learning policies" (both for their own classroom programs and wherever possible for their schools), which take the whole helix into account rather than pulling out separate strands such as "language" for special attention, in what we believe to be mistaken isolation.

Modes of Expression

Thirdly, as well as the R capacities and the helix of processes, there is the wonderfully wide range of media from which we can choose to give a shape to our meanings, as we seek to bring the *what* and the *how* together. We can use spoken or written words, film, photography, drawing, painting, modelling, math symbols, dance . . . all modes of *expression* rather than the compartmentalized content boxes that secondary institutions have turned them into.

When I visit some of our most exciting primary schools (including some two-class village schools still in the same buildings the children's great-grandparents attended), I can look around and see signs of active learning everywhere. Some children may be writing, others busy with brushes or cardboard and glue; there will certainly be all kinds of conversations taking place, around the tables, in the Wendy House, with the teacher, other children, the pet hamster. The classroom will truly be a hive of activity. Sometimes I silently compare it in my mind with visual recollections of the many secondary rooms that I still know where the desks are in rows, students face the teacher but look at the backs of each other's heads all day, and the only talking comes from the front or subversive muttering in corners.

To be fair, many secondary teachers are changing, and as they change so do their rooms and the students who inhabit them. I would like to think that if more of us adopted a capacity-based approach to learning, based on a firm belief in the innate powers that *all* humans possess, immeasurable, unchecklistable, but *meaningful*, then such changes might come about with a greater sense of certainty and optimism. Teachers are great anguishers, and certainly we all have plenty of cause for hand-wringing. But we also need to celebrate what is positive about education— including the wonderful educability of the human brain.

13

Auditing the Meaning of the MOVE Report

SUSAN WELLS

Temple University

The mind in action selects and orders, matches and balances, sorting and generating as it shapes meanings and controls their inter-dependencies.

Ann E. Berthoff,
"I. A. Richards and the Audit of Meaning"

This essay responds to two moments in Ann Berthoff's work. The first, represented in my epigraph, is her insistence on the relation between the formative powers of language and the possibilities of knowledge, a relation which she mediates through a formidable, complex, and quite contro-versial notion of the mind. The second moment is the discussion in *Forming/Thinking/Writing* of the logic and structure of lists. To propose so marginal a form as the object of study and the subject of a pedagogy widens our discipline, opening to rhetorical reflection a range of previously invisible inscription practices, from the coded vials of the biologists' "DNA library" to those lists of "bests and worsts" and "ins and outs" that fill the Sunday papers with scripts for social dramas of membership and exclusion.

The writers of the report of the Philadelphia Special Investigations Commission, the MOVE Commission, were faced with problems in con-necting events and organizing evidence. This essay will use those questions of arrangement and style to consider how the report organizes our understanding of events, how it performs its own audit of the meaning of the MOVE catastrophe. And, since even though the MOVE report is full of selections and orderings, matchings and balancings, sortings and generatings, this group-written document cannot be seen as the production of a "mind in action"; this essay also engages the continuing debate on Berthoff's use of that concept.

Let me begin by providing some background. On May 13, 1985, the Philadelphia police surrounded a row house at 6221 Osage Avenue which was occupied by members of MOVE, a radical sect headed by John Africa. When the occupants of the house failed to surrender, a bomb was dropped on its roof from a police helicopter, igniting a cache of gasoline. The resulting fire killed all eleven occupants of the house, including six children, and destroyed much of the densely populated city block on which it stood. After the MOVE catastrophe, Philadelphia Mayor Wilson Goode appointed a city commission to investigate the event. They issued a short report on March 6, 1986, which was read as a condemnation of the mayor, other city officials, and the police. The report reversed a popular understanding of the MOVE catastrophe as a tragic series of miscalculations and provoked the resignations of the Police Commissioner and the Managing Director of the city.

Such a successful document repays study. Like Berthoff's list, it arranges materials according to a principle of selection: the report is a series of "findings" that narrate the story of May 13 as thirty-one independent items. The report shapes meanings by controlling the relations among these findings, establishing patterns through selection and ordering. This essay will examine one segment of the MOVE report, the findings numbered three to six, which describe the events leading up to the planning for May 13. These findings are appended to my essay in the form in which they were originally published.

Although the MOVE report is organized chronologically, it borrows the format of the administrative report, with its conventions of segmentation, numbering, and graphic emphasis. In fact, the commissioners had in mind a specific format (personal interview, Graham Macdonald, June 1986), the "pyramidal report" devised by Barbara Minto (Minto 1982); that format suggested, especially, the hierarchical arrangement of each finding, with a central idea supported by more specific "dot points," some of which are in turn supported by "check points." The arrangement of these somewhat static forms, however, and the power of their situational referent (Berthoff 58), prompts the reader to compose the report as a narrative, a compelling and tragic story that leads inexorably to a violent close.

This narrative is both interrupted and enabled by the pyramidal format of each finding, which organizes the document thematically, rather than presenting events in temporal order. Instead of following a normal sequence (Mayor Goode met with the neighbors, who went to the press), we read in the report general summaries followed by their expansions. Thus, findings 4, 5, and 6 expand a statement in finding 3: there, the city's policy is described as "appeasement, non-confrontation, and avoidance." These terms initially read as synonyms: all three denote inactivity. But each term is also subject to independent expansion, to development on lower levels of the hierarchy of supporting points, or in subsequent findings. When those expansions are arranged as a series, they take on narrative force. Each term refers to a separate line of action, understood from a distinct point of view: *appeasement* refers to the Osage neighbors; *nonconfrontation*, to MOVE, and *avoidance*, to the city's self-understanding.

Appeasement collocates with other terms we can find in the report, such as "mollify," "superficial," "frustration," "diffuse" (for *defuse*), and "benign avoidance." It presents the neighbors as minor characters in these events: the neighborhood will be warned off in finding 4, emerge as unauthorized mediators in finding 5, and hold angry meetings with the mayor in finding 6. *Appeasement* is a process which is, by definition, both extended and unsuccessful. And so it is not surprising that, in finding 9, the neighborhood forces the mayor to "abandon his policy of nonconfrontation and avoidance." This assignment of agency to the neighborhood will be crucial in the characterization of Goode; as we will see, it will preserve the report's economy of initiatives at a difficult moment. The segmentation of the report transfers initiative through a round of locations: the mayor's *appeasement* is developed as a series of actions negated and avoided, actions which prompt the neighborhood's anger in finding 6. This anger reverts upon the mayor, forcing an end to the policy of *appeasement*, which is tacitly dropped from the description of Goode's policy in finding 9.

The other two substantives, *nonconfrontation* and *avoidance*, are each also developed separately. *Nonconfrontation* relates to the city's treatment of MOVE: MOVE is expected to "weary of unanswered challenges"; during talks with MOVE, the Mayor would "listen, but not act." The negated term here, *confrontation*, is a technical term in MOVE's political vocabulary. Associated with John Africa in finding 1, *confrontation* is a combat that reveals the truth about both parties, an exchange of hostilities in which each party faces possibilities of gain and loss. *Confrontation* is a kind of violence which is also discourse. By pursuing a policy of *nonconfrontation*, Goode abstains from any exchange with MOVE, refuses to risk power, hides the true nature of the city's authority, and encourages the recklessness of MOVE. Goode has become the narrative locus for a disruption of the economy of discourse. He is the figure that, listening but not acting, enforces a rule of silence, substituting a sterile receptivity for the civic exchange of talk. Choosing *nonconfrontation* to describe the mayor's policy, rather than denotationally equivalent terms like *abstention* or *restraint*, the commissioners adopt for the moment the vocabulary of MOVE; they also set in motion a series of actions that can have only one outcome. A policy of *nonconfrontation* resolves in *confrontation*.

Avoidance, the final substantive describing the city's policy, operates reflexively, to describe the administration's relation to itself. The city administration restricted itself from engagement with MOVE and tried to contain the problem. This policy of *avoidance* is described by expanding the term: we learn first that city officials did not discuss MOVE, even among themselves. Then, different branches of city government are shown handing the problem off: the Mayor delegates the Managing Director to be his "eyes," the Managing Director declares MOVE to be a "police matter," and the city commissioners adopt a "hands off" attitude. The report has created a body politic, and that body is paralyzed. Finally, a "rule of silence" emerges: city officials will not speak about MOVE. The disruption of discourse associated with Goode is generalized into a civic disorder. In summarizing these episodes under the topic *avoidance*, the report uses a term from a register different from the political one which supplied the words *appeasement* and *inactivity*. *Avoidance* is a therapeutic term rather than a political one. On this level of the narrative, the silent body of the city is constituted as a neurotic subject, divided against itself, prey to uncontrolled behavior, the sources of its pain inscribed upon it as symptoms. The commissioners have become therapists of that subject, diagnosing the illness and sagely pointing out its source in a forgotten trauma.

That trauma is an injury associated with Mayor Goode, the focus of these early findings. All the characters in the report—MOVE, the neighbors, the city administrators—met with Goode, and their meetings accelerated in tempo and urgency. Just as the mayor abstained from any exchange with MOVE, in all these meetings he remained the passive receiver of messages, the enforcer of a rule of silence. But in the domain of the investigative commission, the transmission of discourse virtually defines character, since it is by discourse that the commission lives and dies. Goode's silence establishes his complicity in the discursive crisis that it both narrates and rectifies.

The action of that narrative, in findings 3–6, is a repeated circuit of initiative, which begins with MOVE, travels to the mayor, is delegated to his agents, and then returns to the mayor through the neighbors' intervention. This circulation of initiative through the closed universe of the report secures its cohesion quite simply, by making sure that one thing leads to another. Such elementary narrative connection is consistent with administrative reason. But it also invokes a scheme for a more overarching narrative coherence, a structure of meaning formed by neither contingency nor contiguity. Such a structure would satisfy a more global desire for understanding, for a meaning that would withstand an audit. If we find in the MOVE report a story that hangs together, we are also prompted to look there for a story that makes sense. That search is prompted by our desire for intelligibility, for readerly coherence, a desire that administrative reason can only satisfy formally. The MOVE report arrives at the scene of this desire after the fact; the commissioners encounter a wreckage of language, property, and lives that does not promise any tragic redemption, any translation into significant action. Sorting through this wreckage, the MOVE commissioners faced a problem. They had to construct a narrative that could transcend both the instrumental limits of administrative prudence and the ideological paralysis that divorces our understanding of these events from politics. Such a document would fulfill the traditional cultural tasks of narrative history; it would also collapse the satisfaction of narrative completion with that of intelligible explanation. But although the Commission produced a document that seems to accomplish just such a fusion, transforming extremely unpromising materials into a highly articulated narrative structure, it created that structure only by shifting initiative and reasonability among agents, and by refashioning the events that it reports. It would take an especially painstaking use of Berthoff's master question, "How does who do what and why?" (/1) to trace out all of these shifts. In the case of the findings we have been examining, the work of refashioning and reorganizing was undertaken quite consciously. Commission staff member Emerson Moran, who was responsible for drafting many of the findings, described the three terms, *appeasement, nonconfrontation*, and *avoidance*, as a "trinity": each of them could be expanded and supported, and the series of expansions would also suggest a narrative. The relations among events, then, would be clear, even though the segmented pyramidal form did not favor normal adverbial connections. As Moran put it, "If the order is there and the connections are there, you don't have to spell it out" (personal interview, May 1986). And another MOVE staff member, Graham Macdonald, spoke of the "drumbeat of narrative" that the writers of the report sought to achieve in its opening section (personal interview, June 1986).

It is with finding 6, however, that the persuasive force of the trinity emerges. There, we are told that the Mayor was presented with evidence that his policy was "doomed to fail." This finding presents itself as patent truth. A policy of *appeasement* is already a policy that will fail; a policy of *nonconfrontation* can only lead to *confrontation*, and a policy of *avoidance* establishes its agent as an object of therapy. The narrative staging of these three elements as separate stages in an unfolding disaster, rather than as three inflections of the same policy, makes the mayor's persistence in that policy seem not only wrongheaded, but virtually demonic. Even though he could have known that his policy was (triply) a failure, the Mayor (triply) persisted in it. The narrative has been reinflected: it is translated into a problem, a problem whose inadequate solution has been explicated, a problem for which there must in principle be an adequate solution. Paradoxically, at the moment that the commissioners invoke the language of tragedy (*compelling, doomed, intransigent, desperation*), they also mobilize the customary forms of administrative discourse, forms for which there are no tragedies, but only mistakes (*briefed thoroughly, response was inadequate*).

My analysis suggests that the report's audit of meaning was blocked or circumvented, that a series of forms which was invented to organize evidence and to provoke reflection functioned instead to derail reflection as each form cancelled the other. But this critical analysis is, of course, also an act of auditing. It might therefore be well to remember the etymology of *audit*, which invokes the hearing of testimony and the solemn examination of witnesses. *Audit*, then, is an apt analytic term for a report that is based on testimony that fixed the attention of a city for weeks. But is *audit* also the proper term for the work of a rhetorician analyzing this document? Who, after all, is the speaker of this document? Whose voice is being heard? It was written by two staff members, debated by a large and active committee, reviewed by other staff members—all of whom, to this day, are compelled by that work, all of whom feel the most intense identification with the words they produced. To hear the voices of those writers, voices that disagree and continue their polemics, is to call into question the unitary "mind" that orders and selects by itself, to suggest that a more plural notion of the writer and the scene of writing might do more justice to the difficulty and the work of writing as it appears in this text.

Appendix

1. BY THE EARLY 1980s MOVE HAD EVOLVED INTO AN AUTHORITARIAN, VIOLENCE-THREATENING CULT.

- John Africa and his followers in the 1980s came to reject and to place themselves above the laws, customs and social contracts of society. They threatened violence to anyone who would attempt to enforce normal societal rules. They believed that only the laws of John Africa need be obeyed.
- The members of MOVE saw themselves as the targets of persistent harassment by regulatory agencies, unjust treatment by the courts, and periodic violent attempts to be suppressed by the police.
- John Africa and his followers believed that a catastrophic confrontation with "the system" was necessary, if not inevitable, because of the campaign by "the system" to force MOVE to conform to society's rules.
- MOVE's last campaign for confrontation began in the fall of 1983, and was predicated on (1) the unconditional demand that all imprisoned MOVE members be released; and (2) that harassment of MOVE by city officials cease. The stridency and extremism of individual MOVE members escalated during the first years of the Goode Administration.

2. THE RESIDENTS OF 6221 OSAGE AVE. WERE ARMED AND DANGEROUS, AND USED THREATS, ABUSE AND INTIMIDATION TO TERRIFY THEIR NEIGHBORS AND TO BRING ABOUT CONFRONTATION WITH CITY GOVERNMENT.

- The death of Officer Ramp and the wounding of many police and firefighters in the 1978 clash confirmed that MOVE members would use deadly force when confronted.
- On Osage Avenue, the occupants of 6221 Osage Ave. committed violent acts against their own neighbors and threatened violence against public officials and private citizens in a manner which was intended to shock and intimidate both the general population and the city's officials.
- MOVE's deliberate use of terror included the intentional violation of the basic rights of those living in the Osage Avenue neighborhood. This was achieved by:
  - √ Both verbal and physical assaults upon targeted individuals living in the neighborhood.
  - √ The periodic broadcast over outdoor loudspeakers of profane harangues against the government and threats of violence against public officials.
  - √ The public acclaiming by MOVE of the 1978 death of Officer Ramp, and the repeated threat that, if the police come to 6221 Osage Ave., "we'll put a bullet in your motherfucking heads."
  - √ The prominent fortification of an ordinary row house.
  - √ The aggressive display of a weapon by a hooded man at mid-day in a normally peaceful neighborhood.

√ The compelling domination of the neighborhood by MOVE's rooftop bunker, which, by itself, became a commanding public notice of imminent confrontation.

• Through this use of terror, MOVE, in some respects, held Osage Avenue "hostage" for nearly two years. During that period, the city's leadership chose not to secure the neighborhood's release, and, instead, drifted toward the confrontation that MOVE had declared was preordained.

3. MAYOR GOODE'S POLICY TOWARD MOVE WAS ONE OF APPEASEMENT, NONCONFRONTATION AND AVOIDANCE.

• The Goode Administration assumed that any attempt to enforce the law would end in violence. MOVE-related issues thus became "too hot to handle," and the Administration pursued a do-nothing and say-nothing policy. Avoidance of the problem was so pervasive that city officials did not even discuss the issue among themselves.

• The Mayor attempted to mollify neighbors with claims that a proper legal basis for action was being sought, and with superficial actions that were designed to diffuse neighborhood frustrations without addressing the crux of the problem.

• With this policy of benign avoidance, the Mayor hoped that the problem might dissipate on its own, particularly, that MOVE would weary of unanswered challenges, modulate their confrontational behavior and/or relocate. To a great extent, then, MOVE effectively paralyzed the normal functioning of city government, as it applied to MOVE and to the Osage neighborhood.

4. THE MANAGING DIRECTOR AND THE CITY'S DEPARTMENT HEADS FAILED TO TAKE ANY EFFECTIVE ACTION ON THEIR OWN AND, IN FACT, ORDERED THEIR SUBORDINATES TO REFRAIN FROM TAKING ACTION TO DEAL MEANINGFULLY WITH THE PROBLEM ON OSAGE AVENUE.

• As early as March, 1984, the Mayor treated the problem on Osage Avenue as a "police matter."

• The Mayor assigned the responsibility of monitoring the problem to the Managing Director who was to be his "eyes on things out there through the police department."

• In May of 1984, Managing Director Brooks instructed his task force (established to coordinate and focus the city's programs related to neighborhood problems) that "MOVE is not an issue for this group, it is a police matter."

• The Osage Avenue situation was never raised prior to May 13th in any of the weekly commissioner meetings during the Goode Administration. The Commissioners of Licenses and Inspections, Human Services, Water and Health each adopted, without question, this "hands off" attitude. Not a single city commissioner ever questioned the Mayor or the Managing Director about the rationale for this policy.

5. THE CITY ADMINISTRATION DISCOUNTED NEGOTIATION AS A METHOD OF RESOLVING THE PROBLEM. ANY ATTEMPTED NEGOTIATIONS WERE HAPHAZARD AND UNCOORDINATED.

- The city's experience with MOVE in 1978, and MOVE's insistence on making release of its members from jail the sole basis for negotiation in 1985, promoted a view that rational discussion and compromise were impossible. Because the situation was believed to be inherently volatile, with no hope of acceptable compromise, it was thought that active negotiation would accelerate rather than postpone an ultimate confrontation.
- All occasions on which the Mayor met with MOVE were instigated by MOVE members or sympathizers and were held for the sole purpose of airing MOVE's grievances. The Mayor's posture was to listen, but not act.
- Formal and informal city groups chartered to deal with these kinds of problems were rebuffed and discouraged by the Administration from mediating or otherwise offering their services.
- Into this vacuum stepped a number of community mediators with no active mandate from the city administration.

6. IN THE FIRST SEVERAL MONTHS OF HIS ADMINISTRATION, THE MAYOR WAS PRESENTED WITH COMPELLING EVIDENCE THAT HIS POLICY OF APPEASEMENT, NONCONFRONTATION AND AVOIDANCE WAS DOOMED TO FAIL.

- In March of 1984, the Mayor and the Managing Director were briefed thoroughly by the Police Commissioner and told the following:
  - √ That, since late summer, 1983, the alley behind the MOVE house was blocked by fencing.
  - √ That MOVE was barricading its house, including putting slats on all the windows.
  - √ That a bullhorn had been affixed to the front of the home and was being used to harangue and threaten the neighbors.
  - √ That construction material was visible on the roof.
  - √ That, since Christmas, 1983, MOVE had been in a self-proclaimed confrontation with the city.
- In May, 1984, a hooded MOVE member appeared on the roof of 6221 Osage Ave. brandishing a shotgun.
- On Memorial Day and the Fourth of July, 1984, the Mayor met with Osage neighbors who gave him a detailed and emotional report of the difficulties of living on Osage Avenue and told him the city's response was inadequate.
- In the summer of 1984, the Mayor met with Louise James and learned that John Africa and Frank James had become increasingly violent and intransigent. She told the Mayor that the failures of MOVE to obtain the release from prison of its members had provoked a sense of desperation in the MOVE leadership.

Works Cited

Berthoff, Ann E. *Forming/Thinking/Writing*. Portsmouth, NH: Boynton/Cook, 1982.

———. "I. A. Richards and the Audit of Meaning." *New Literary History* 14 (1982–83): 63–79.

Minto, Barbara. *The Pyramid Principle: Logic in Writing and Thinking*. 1978. 3rd ed. London: Minto, 1981.

Philadelphia Special Investigation Commission. *Report*. Philadelphia, March 6, 1986.

IV

Hangzhou, Lake of the Poets

Morning

Reading the bones, wetting a fingertip
to trace archaic characters, I feel
a breeze of silence flow up past my wrist,
icy. Can I speak here? The bones say I must.
As the first light strikes across the lake, magpies
scream, & the cast bones say the work must come true,
it's been true all along, we are what we do
out on our digs. Dictor, inlooker, all eyes,
with spade and a jeweler's loupe I sift mud & dust
for bone, for shellcast. Spy, archeologist
of freshness, I expect sight-made-sound to reveal
fear cold at the throat of change, & loosen its grip.
Mind rides the stream of language. Mind wells up
into the stream that bears it and is telling.

Evening

Magpies scream. Though the tongues of birds
say Now and warn forward, free of a live past,
we seek back and forth for change, the ghostly sparkling
of our watertable under everywhere.
If I don't speak to tap & ease it out,
I go dry & dumb & will die wicked.
On the lake of the poets a stone lamp flickers.
It casts eight moons dancing, casting doubt
on the moon that rides above the winter air.
Ice thaws in a poet's throat; the springing

161

truth is fresh. It wakes taste. If the taste lasts
it presents the present in a cast of words
& focuses the human face whose discourse
speaks with the tidal power of its source.

MARIE PONSOT

14

Interpretation
in a Place Between

ANGELA G. DORENKAMP
Assumption College

In *The Cheese and the Worms*,[1] Italian historian Carlo Ginzburg describes the trials of Domenico Scandella, also known as Menocchio, a sixteenth-century miller from northern Italy who lived in relative obscurity until he was accused of heresy. Interrogated by the Holy Office of the Inquisition in trials held fifteen years apart (1584 and 1599), Menocchio was advised to say as little as possible, but he ignored such counsel; instead, he shared his somewhat bizarre ideas freely and with enthusiasm. Because of his generosity and because of the full records kept by the Inquisition,[2] Ginzburg has been able to reconstruct the miller's interpretation of the world, an interpretation which is especially interesting because Menocchio was literate. A little more than a hundred years after the invention of printing,[3] an Italian miller had learned to read and write, representing for Ginzburg the conjunction of oral and literate cultures. During his trials, the miller frequently referred to the books he had read, sometimes blaming them for his curious ideas (35, 37, 42). From such comments, we can draw some inferences about the relationships among reading, writing, and thinking within the peasant culture of sixteenth-century Italy as well as raise some questions about these connections in our own time.

Menocchio's beliefs were not only heretical; in some respects, they were beyond heresy. He did not, for instance, believe in divine creation, but in a process closer to that of spontaneous generation: in the beginning, all was chaos, and from the chaos a mass formed, out of which came the angels and God, like worms out of putrefying cheese. He did not believe in original sin, in the divinity of Christ, or in the Real Presence. Under questioning, he said that his parish priest had told him that the host was the body of Christ, but he believed it was the Holy Spirit "because I believe the Holy Spirit is greater than Christ, who was a man, whereas the Holy Spirit came from the hand of God" (11). He preached a kind of pantheism and a tolerance for all religious beliefs.

Ginzburg makes it clear that Menocchio's ideas cannot be traced to Anabaptism, Lutheranism, or any other Reformation religious movement, although he does cite parallels to the miller's vision of creation (56–58). From the beginning of the first trial and even under torture, however, Menocchio had insisted that no one else was responsible for his ideas: "Sir, I have never met anyone who holds these opinions; my opinions came out of my own head" (21). And he is quite clear about his motives, too: "My mind was lofty and wished for a new world and way of life, because the Church did not act properly, and because there should not be so much pomp" (13). Menocchio wanted to change things, and he knew that literacy was a key to power. He assailed the courts, for instance, which, by using Latin, betrayed the poor. A villager quoted him as saying, some years after the first trial, "Can't you understand, the inquisitors don't want us to know what they know!" (59).[4] Menocchio knew that printing had made knowledge a commodity which could be purchased on the open market and that with such access, it might be possible to build "a new world," a utopia.

The world that Menocchio himself built owed something to his reading of books, most of which had religious themes and had been directed toward popular audiences, works such as *Rosario della gloriosa Vergine Maria*, *Legendario delle vite de tutti li santi*, *Fioretto della Bibbia*, *Historia del Giudicio*, and the *Travels* of Sir John Mandeville.[5] These texts seem uninteresting to us now, but they were vital sources of images and ideas to Menocchio. As a reader, however, Menocchio did more than "write the text," as many modern theorists describe the act of interpretation. "Any attempt to consider these books as 'sources' in the mechanical sense of the term," says Ginzburg, "collapses before the aggressive originality of Menocchio's reading" (33). The historian theorizes that the miller unconsciously placed an interpretive screen between himself and the text, filtering out certain words and concepts, altering or modifying meanings. He concludes that it is the explosive "encounter" between the oral and print cultures, rather than the texts themselves, which enabled Menocchio to formulate his ideas. But it is perhaps helpful to note that in addition to filling in the blanks in the printed work, the miller as reader used the text to fill in the blanks in his mind, in his construing of reality.

Menocchio, for example, said he didn't believe in the Virgin Birth because "many men have been born into the world, but none of a virgin woman" (36). Mary was called a virgin, Menocchio explained to his questioners, because she had been kept in a temple of virgins who, when they grew up, were married. In the *Rosario della gloriosa Vergine Maria*, which Menocchio referred to several times, there is an account of Mary's parents, St. Joachim and St. Anne, leaving her in the temple with other virgins. Although the account also says that she was visited by angels there and treated as a queen, Menocchio focuses on Mary's inclusion with the "other virgins," who eventually married, and not on her special treatment.

It was Menocchio's own knowledge—"many men have been born into the world, but none of a virgin woman"—which guided his selectivity in interpreting the printed text. In another instance, Menocchio says he doesn't believe in the divinity of Christ because he read in *Fioretto della Bibbia* that "St. Joseph called our Lord Jesus Christ his son." Ginzburg points out that in the chapter immediately preceding the one Menocchio refers to, Mary is asked if Jesus is her son, and she replies: "Yes, he is my son, his father is the one God" (36). Menocchio selects those details which accord with his own images of daily life—putrefying cheese and worms—and with knowledge gleaned orally from preceding generations and from his contemporaries—women who give birth are not virgins, men who call boys "sons" are their fathers. He also filters out whatever does not accord with his political ideals and receives whatever his vision of the world can accommodate. Because he believed that printing had made accessible to the peasants knowledge which those in power had previously kept for themselves, he adjusted his filter, designed to respond to such attitudes, to reveal hitherto "unrevealed" truths.

In a sense, Menocchio lived in a place between, between oral and print cultures, unable to identify fully with either one, he partook of both. Undoubtedly, perceptions and ideas retained from the oral context in which he lived reinforced certain concepts which he found in his reading. On the other hand, his reading may have given him access to much of the "tacit" knowledge gleaned from an oral culture by providing the language which enabled him to articulate his world. Walter J. Ong says that "Interpreting a text means inserting it somehow into the ongoing conversations you live with. No matter how difficult of access the meaning or meanings in a text from an unfamiliar milieu may be, no matter how bizarre, the text has to be related in some way to what the reader knows of actuality, if only by contrast, or it cannot be understood at all" ("Reading" 175). Menocchio, for instance, knew that virgins did not give birth. If Mary's "virginity" could be explained away, then Joseph would be Christ's biological father, which would make Christ human rather than divine. Menocchio's rejection of the divinity of Christ, then, depended in some measure on his interpretation of the temple of virgins. He brought to his text what Robert Crossman's dairyman brought to his interpretation of Ezra Pound's "In a Station at the Metro": his life's experience as context for the poem (153–54). And just as that context altered the poem's "meaning," so did Menocchio's experience alter the meaning of the printed texts he read. The contexts of orality, in other words, overrode those of literacy.

Although Menocchio "wrote" a text, it is a self-generated text of the mind, supplemented by the printed text but not proceeding from it. In some sense, the process is reversed, and it is the printed text which "fills in the blanks" of the mental one. The miller's vision provides the framework; his reading is the "filler." And although the text may have triggered his idiosyncratic interpretations, the interpretations themselves often have connections with pre-existing images. Since the reader can't learn from a text how accurate or inaccurate his interpretation of it is, Menocchio, who lived in a very small community of readers, could remain confident of his interpretation.

Although his writing does not attain the same level of confidence, it reveals the influence which the printed page has had on him. The appearance of a letter Menocchio wrote to his judges, with "the letters set side by side, almost without ligatures (as is usually done by 'ultramontanes, women, and the aged' according to a contemporary writing manual), clearly demonstrates that their writer didn't have great familiarity with the pen" (89). Ginzburg says that the manuscript bespeaks the enormous effort which the physical act of writing must have required of the miller. But the style and structure of its argument differ markedly from those which characterize his recorded testimony.

The letter begins with a statement emphasizing his commitment to Christianity; acknowledges the "false spirit" which led him into error; re-tells the story of Joseph as an analogy for his own situation (like Joseph, Menocchio was "sold" by his brothers, but he sees this as the will of God and forgives them so that God will forgive him); gives four reasons for his imprisonment; cites Christ's mercy as the standard for judges; pleads for forgiveness; and notes six causes of his errors. The ordered arrangement is reinforced by rhetorical devices such as alliteration and repetition, and the letter is free from the everyday metaphors which characterize Menocchio's speech as it is recorded in the trial record. It is obvious that the letter was, as Ginzburg says, "conceived as written words" (90). In his testimony, Menocchio had revealed his confusion concerning the concepts of soul and spirit. Sometimes he said that spirit and soul were the same; at other times, he said the soul dies with the body but the spirit remains. In light of the careful arrangement and connection of his ideas in this letter, one wonders whether or not Menocchio would have resolved such contradictions if he had been able to write his theology.

In our post-Gutenberg age, the image and orality have become powerful again. The writing of personal letters and keeping of diaries or journals have been replaced by the telephone or by messages taped on cassettes. Executives "dictate" letters, memos, and reports, and computer software which provides business letters for every occasion is readily available. Young people read less and less, watch TV, VCRs, and MTV more and more. Walter Ong says that the "electronic transformation of verbal expression has both deepened the commitment of the word to space initiated by writing and intensified by print and has brought consciousness to a new age of secondary orality" (*Orality* 135). But if this secondary orality is shaping our students' interpretation of the world, then perhaps some of them are closer to Menocchio than they are to us. Most of the time, we presume our students can read, though we might complain that they read passively, merely tracing the graphic symbols on the page rather than engaging the text. But perhaps some of the difficulties of interpretation spring not from passivity, but from too much activity: some students may actively use the text, as Menocchio did, to fill in the interstices of their preconceived visual and aural constructions. Are we sometimes puzzled by the "aggressive originality" of their reading? Do some of them override textual constraints so that communication between text and reader is not successfully accomplished?

Obviously, most of us would answer those questions in the affirmative. Recently, a teacher cited as a failure an assignment which asked students who had just finished reading and discussing *Jane Eyre* to re-tell the story from the point of view of Bertha Mason Rochester. The assignment failed because most of the students *invented* a story and a Bertha Mason, neither of which "fit" the Brontë story. The students, in other words, were not constrained by the text; they used what they wanted and ignored what did not accord with their visions. In some sense, these students are Menocchio's heirs, expressing their own ideas outside the limits imposed by print.

What can the story of this Italian miller teach us about reading, about construing, about interpretation? It can tell us that our students may also stand in a place between, between print culture and the technological future. Partaking fully in neither, but engaging in a dialectic with both, they put on earphones, turn on the television set, and read. It is impossible to pull them away from sound and image, even if we wanted to do so. Rather, we need to help our students find a method which will enable them to distinguish between misinterpretations and variant interpretations even as they hover between print and the newer technologies.

Notes

1. Trans. John and Anne Tedeschi. Harmondsworth: Penguin Books, 1982. Originally published in Italy under the title *Il formaggio e i vermi: il cosmo di un mugnaio del '500*, Giulio Einaudi Editore, 1976. The English translation first published in the U.S. by The Johns Hopkins University Press, 1980. References will be to the Penguin edition. I am indebted to my colleague in history, John McClymer, for calling my attention to Ginzburg's work.

2. According to Ginzburg, a notary was a required member of each inquisitorial court. He was responsible for transcribing "in writing as the legal manuals required 'not only all the defendant's responses and any statements he might make, but also what he might utter during the torture, even his sighs, his cries, his laments and tears' (E. Masini, *Sacro Arsenale* [Genoa, 1621]: 123). The notary's charge was to transcrebe everything that transpired verbatim. On occasion, however, . . . both questions and answers were reported in the third person" (ix).

3. Printing was invented in 1465 in Germany, but by 1470 Italian printers were already producing their own texts. By the turn of the century, there were 150 presses in Venice. S. H. Steinberg, *Five Hundred Years of Printing*. 3rd ed. 1955. Harmondsworth: Penguin, 1974. 65.

4. Menocchio's ideas about power and literacy are reminiscent of those of Paulo Freire. See *Pedagogy of the Oppressed*. New York: Seabury, 1970.

5. During his trials, Menocchio mentioned eleven books. We know that he bought at least one of them—the *Fioretto della Bibbia*—and that several were loans or gifts (Ginzburg 29–31).

Works Cited

Crosman, Robert. "Do Readers Make Meaning?" *The Reader in the Text*. Ed. Susan R. Suleiman and Inge Crosman. Princeton: Princeton UP, 1980. 149–64.

Ginzburg, Carlo. *The Cheese and the Worms*. Trans. John and Anne Tedeschi. Harmondsworth: Penguin, 1982.

Ong, Walter J. "Reading, Technology, and Human Consciousness." *The Yearbook of English Studies* 10 (1980): 132–49. Reprinted in *Literacy As a Human Problem*. Ed. James C. Raymond. University, AL: U Alabama P, 1982. 170–99.

———. *Orality and Literacy: The Technologizing of the Word*. New York: Methuen, 1982.

15

On Filters,
Hinges,
and Windows

ANN RAIMES

Hunter College, CUNY

Mina Shaughnessy wrote eloquently in the late 1970s of how teachers in open admissions freshman composition classrooms were "stunned" by the problems in the essays their students wrote. These students were "strangers in academia, unacquainted with the rules and rituals of college life, unprepared for the sorts of tasks their teachers were about to assign them" (3). Since that time, we've been able to come to grips with the problems these students posed. We've examined what they write and how they write, we've devised special programs, we've written textbooks and trained teachers, and we've invented teaching strategies and reported on them at length in our journals.

Now in the eighties, another group stuns us. College writing programs find growing numbers of non-native speakers of English in their courses and debate ensues about how these English-as-a-second-language (ESL) students should be treated administratively and pedagogically. First-language (L1) and second-language (L2) students share the problem that they have to become familiar with the demands of written communication, as opposed to the oral skills that they have acquired. In addition, though, L2 students have what Paul Ammon calls "double trouble" (83): they are still language learners while they struggle with the rigors of composition.

Researchers have been examining what it means to compose in a second language. They have found that, like native speakers, L2 writers explore and discover ideas through writing just as native speakers do (Zamel, Raimes). Their planning skills are similar to those of L1 writers, and, indeed, planning skills in L1 transfer to L2, helping the process of writing and not inhibiting it (Jones and Tetroe). In fact, the difficulties of ESL writers appear to stem less from the contrasts between L1 and L2 than from the constraints of the act of composing itself.

Few researchers have yet explored in depth what the significant differences between the two groups of students might be; to date, they have observed that unskilled ESL student writers are not necessarily preoccupied with error and with editing (Raimes) and that they negotiate between L1 and L2, sometimes using their knowledge of L1 writing to help them form hypotheses in L2 (Lay). Meanwhile, practical concerns overtake theoretical ones. Since there are more than 300,000 foreign students enrolled in American colleges,[1] as well as many thousands of immigrants and refugees, teachers are frequently faced with L2 students in their composition courses and have to devise teaching strategies.

A dilemma has arisen for composition teachers: how can they address the constraints of composing, how can they help their students "learn the uses of chaos," and "find the forms of thought by means of language," as Ann Berthoff says (39, 69) when ESL students have so much else—so many errors!—to contend with. As one despairing teacher put it: "How can we do process and do grammar?"

Of course, that's not really a very helpful question, but it illustrates the dilemma teachers face with L2 students. A better question would be this: "What do we need to know about L2 students' composing?" I see three key areas here. First, we need to know how students learn—or don't learn—a new language. Second, we need to know how cultural and rhetorical knowledge contributes to what and how our students write. Finally, we need to know how our students' errors reveal their strategies for language learning and for composing. These three areas provide the title and the framework for this essay.

Filters

The filter is that part of the internal processing system that subconsciously screens incoming language based on what psychologists call "affect": the learner's motives, needs, attitudes, and emotional states.

Heidi Dulay, Marina Burt and Stephen Krashen,
Language Two

We'll begin with that "internal processing system" that determines second language learning or acquisition. The distinction is crucial in current theories. According to those who have presented the dominant and pedagogically influential hypotheses most comprehensively (namely Krashen; Dulay, Burt and Krashen[2]), language acquisition arises from "meaningful interaction in the target language" (Krashen 1) or from picking up knowledge through real communication, and is distinct from conscious language learning. The latter, achieved through rules and explicit error correction (that is, through traditional language classroom practices), is only a minor part of language acquisition, operating for the learner in the form of a "monitor" that can alter the production of the acquired system but not generate it. For acquisition, "comprehensible input is the crucial and necessary ingredient" (Krashen 9). Such input consists of language that focuses on communicating meaning, on getting a message across; it is language at a level that is comprehensible linguistically and culturally to the learner. But even when the input is comprehensible and plentiful, obstacles might occur to hinder acquisition. The learner's emotions, anxiety, motivation, and attitude to the new culture and the new language can set up a subconscious "filter," which serves to block out acquisition.

For acquisition to occur, that "filter" must be as inactive as possible. Even those who do not accept the acquisition/learning distinction will agree that attitude and motivation play a large part in language learning. An L2 learner who seems to be having trouble in a composition class could be a student for whom more visits to a tutoring center and more grammar drill would be counterproductive. Teachers at Hunter College have observed that among the ESL students in the basic writing courses, those who repeat courses over and over again do so not so much because of a clearly identifiable writing problem, such as difficulties providing evidence or specific details, but because they never appear to be actively engaged with writing. They seem to see it simply as a tiresome academic requirement, the imposition of a dominant culture. Immigrant minority group students often feel alienated from the new language and see themselves as hovering between two ethnic groups for a variety of reasons, such as lack of identification with the social group of the target language, in this case with English-speaking college students and professors. They can even view a competent second-language speaker as a kind of "ethnic traitor" (Loveday 77). In addition, they tend to "fossilize" at defined points in their interlanguage—the linguistic system learners adopt as an intermediate system between the native and target languages, one which they gradually refine to approach the target language (Selinker). This fossilization occurs particularly when learners are confronted by new language situations; sometimes they will stop acquiring the target language as soon as they can function well enough in it for their perceived daily needs. They acknowledge no motivation to improve their writing ability either for a utilitarian purpose, such as getting a job, or for the purpose of becoming a member of the L2 language community. Yet such "instrumental" or "integrative" motivation (Gardner and Lambert) is seen as crucial for successful second-language acquisition.

Alienation can also be caused by instructional method and past experience. One of my students, who wrote, "I can say that my English learning is built on the punishment basis . . . " and explained how she had to recite her English lessons to her father every night and was scolded or beaten if she made any mistakes, could hardly be expected to have a positive attitude to grappling with "making meaning" in English. In fact, this student admitted to having restricted her own possibilities for language acquisition: "Gradually I seldom talk to others. Always I try to learn English from reading newspapers, novels and magazines. Mostly I find difficulties to understand. However, I still keep trying this way because I believe that it is the ideal way which I suppose to learn better English."

Obviously, L2 acquisition is a complex business. There is no one formula, no nice neat description of "the" ESL student. When we have ESL students in our composition classes, we need first to ensure that we provide an acquisition-rich environment, one in which there is a great deal of reading and discussion, and where the language the students produce is interpreted as their expression of meaning, not just as linguistic data. A classroom in which an incident could occur like the one told by Doug Brown is not an acquisition-rich classroom:

> Asked to write something down, a student comments, "I ain't got no pencil." The teacher immediately responds: "I don't have a pencil, you don't have a pencil, we don't have any pencils . . . " and so on. The student's response is a bewildered, "Ain't *nobody* got no pencils?" (35)

Here the learner's motives and needs were being ignored. How many such incidents would it take for the student to put a block on language production, a block on risk-taking, a block on the communication of anything meaningful?

It is not enough, though, to provide an acquisition-rich environment. We need to ensure that students do indeed acquire the language. We need to devise a curriculum that establishes clear short-term goals, ones that the students agree on and share. Often, even if L2 students reject the idea of "integrative" motivation (they have no desire at all to become part of the target language society), they do perceive that career interests will be served by learning how to write in English. We also need to find out as much as we can about our students' experiences with learning English and with writing. I use questionnaires and interviews as a basis for discussion and writing about prior education and experience with writing. I ask students to recall when and under what circumstances they last learned something new about English. I ask them to read an article about motivation and attitude in language acquisition. Then students write to describe their own attitude and motivation and to assess the effects on their language learning. All of this guides students towards "executive procedures for planning and reprocessing text" (Ammon 80). And frequent and meaningful engagement with English in discussion, reading, and writing is not only acquisition-rich; the activities are also "instructionally rich," a feature Ammon observes to be the basis for explaining the "superior writing gains" he observed in two out of thirteen third-grade ESL classrooms (82–83).

In asking students to use their new language to observe their attitude to language and to explain it to others, we provide them with the chance to use their new language as a heuristic. What Ann Berthoff says about "assisted invitations" to writing applies to L2 learners, too: as students perceive, they form concepts. Thus in observing their own language use, they can learn about language acquisition and what inhibits it.

Hinges

Words and ambiguities are "the very hinges of all thought."
                    I. A. Richards, *How to Read a Page*

A frequent and false assumption made about second language acquisition is that the first language is a villain—the source of "interference" and thus the major cause of ESL students' problems with the new language. However, studies show that only about 20 percent of the grammatical mistakes adults make can be traced to L1 features (Dulay, Burt and Krashen 102). And even then, it is not so much that the native language interferes with and impedes second language production; rather, L2 writers rely on what they know from their L1 only when they have not yet acquired competence in the second language (Krashen 7). Thus L2 writers produce text mostly by means of their acquired competence in L2; when that is lacking, they turn to their L1 competence. Both routes can be assisted by what has been consciously learned about L2, usually in the form of

Producing L2 Writing

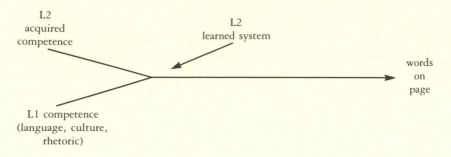

the "monitor" that applies learned rules to the editing of written text (see figure above, "Producing L2 Writing").

The words we see on the page, then, emerge from a kind of hinge point between what learners have acquired about L2 and, failing that, what they know about L1. Moreover, that point of putting L2 words down on the page is the point of commitment to a system not only linguistically different but also culturally and rhetorically different from L1.

Those cultural and rhetorical influences on L2 writers are important for teachers and students to consider. For instance, when bilingual Japanese women married to Americans were asked to complete sentences, first in Japanese and then in English, they gave markedly different responses. One woman's responses in the two languages are reported as follows (Ervin-Tripp 203–4):

1. When my wishes conflict with my family . . .
   (Japanese) it is a time of great unhappiness.
   (English) I do what I want.
2. I will probably become . . .
   (Japanese) a housewife.
   (English) a teacher.
3. Real friends should . . .
   (Japanese) help each other.
   (English) be very frank.

Writing, then, may be a way of "making meaning" as Ann Berthoff reminds us, but we have to remember that L2 students might have more than one meaning in their heads. This ability to form concepts in two languages, this hinge point between two sets of cultural expectations, is, however, a very real strength that can be turned to advantage in a writing class. An interesting experiment with a class of L1 and L2 students is to have everyone in the class respond to a topic in two different languages, or if the native speakers cannot do that (quite likely, given the current state of foreign language instruction) from two different viewpoints. The resulting texts can then be used for comparison and analysis.

A sense of rhetorical appropriateness can also affect L2 writers' production of language. Kate Parry tells of a Nigerian student whose English skills were advanced but who wrote a letter in English that was extremely difficult to comprehend, with sentences like: "Am with much greatful to issued this few lines of words to you and to know the agent of my mine." She attributes the cause to the fact that the writer was expressing profound respect—"far deeper than any native English speaker is likely to feel in a personal relationship." To convey that respect, he used formal vocabulary and complicated syntax, the meaning becoming less important than the formula. What an opportunity we would lose in the classroom if we did not ask the student to explore the differences in the ways of expressing respect to help him understand the influences on his own language production.

A growing body of literature exists on the rhetorical systems of different languages and cultures, known as "contrastive rhetoric" (see Kaplan, and Connor and Kaplan). We know that differing rhetorical patterns occur in different languages. Arabic uses coordination more than subordination, and paragraphs are developed with parallel constructions (see Ostler for examples). Chinese writers, with their emphasis on paragraphs containing a turning point or change, "dislike structure that is too direct" (Tsao 111). In Japanese, it is regarded as the reader's responsibility to create connections and to see the relationship between the parts and the whole (Hinds 146); would-be writers are advised by the novelist Junichiro Tanizaki not to be too clear but to "scorn the bald fact" and to "keep a thin sheet of paper between the fact or the object and the words that give expression to it" (10).

However, what we don't know is how much of a system of L1 rhetorical conventions our students have actually acquired—we seldom investigate how much they have read and written in their native language. Nor do we know how much such knowledge, if held, might transfer into the production of L2 text. If learners use more of their acquired or learned knowledge of L2 grammar when they speak, then the same might be true for the production of rhetorical strategies in written discourse.

At any rate, it is useful for teachers to remember that ESL students

will bring to the classroom not just grammar problems but, more posi-
tively, native knowledge of L1, some acquisition of L2, and their knowledge of L1 culture and rhetoric, all of which can affect how they write
and what they write in L2. So while Japanese students might need explicit
instruction in using coherence markers and transitions, they might also
need to be made aware that "the writing process in English involves a
different set of assumptions from the ones they are accustomed to working
with" especially since Japanese writers frequently write only one draft
(Hinds 152). In class discussions of rhetorical form, the ESL students'
knowledge of alternate systems is of interest to other students and can
become the basis for pointing out to L1 students that with forms of
organization, style and argumentation they are dealing with academic
convention rather than any inherent superiority of one convention over
another (Purves 50).

One of the best ways I have found to direct students' attention to
these interesting dimensions of their writing is to ask them to use
the double-entry notebook recommended by Ann Berthoff (45). With
this, ESL students can write on one page in L2 and use the facing
page for an L1 or L2 paraphrase or comment to try to explain any
points of difficulty or to note where conflicts arise between the two
language systems.

Windows

> Errors in the speech and writing of foreign students are "windows into
> the mind."
>
> > Barry Kroll and John C. Schafer,
> > "Error Analysis and the Teaching of Composition"

One misconception that we have discussed about acquiring a second
language is that L1 is the source of interference. Another is that ESL
students, even more so than L1 freshman writers, are obsessed with errors.
In my own study of unskilled ESL writers I found far less obsession with
application of the grammatical system than Perl found with native speakers. When we consider errors, though, what is important to note is that
L2 writers, even when engaged in an early draft, have an acute awareness
of audience. For if they were truly writing for the purpose of making
sense of the world and gaining access to their own ideas, they would
surely choose to do that in L1, not L2. The language of intimacy, of
writing for oneself, is L1. When students write in L2, they use their
public voice. Consequently, ESL students rarely see it as stigmatizing

when teachers point out errors. In their grappling with learning a new language, they understand that words are only labels. They are not tied to what Dell Hymes calls the monolingual's "naive acceptance of fixed habits of speech as guides to an objective understanding of the nature of an experience" (74). They can thus be encouraged to use their double-entry notebook while composing to engage in dialogue about linguistic options and difficulties. They can practice seeing their own errors as windows into their minds, into their language learning and composing processes.

To encourage this dialogue about language use, I do not save comments on errors for the final draft, contrary to current recommendations about focusing only on meaning at the beginning. However, I do try to separate comments on content from language comments by using those adhesive editorial tags—"Post-It Notes"—to ask questions and make comments about errors. Students address these in their notebooks and keep a running dialogue about their own use of language. Once they have done that, they remove the tag and the text is still untouched by red pen, still theirs to revise as they see fit.

One of my ESL students wrote these entries in his double-entry notebook in response to one of my comments on a draft:

> My teacher asked me to look again at this sentence that I wrote last time: "Are those assumptions can be generalized?" and to look at it with the following sentence: "Can we really learn about people's personality without considering what may or may not have affected their past?" I see here that I wrote two questions, and both contain *can* but *can* is in first place in only one. Why are these different?

And on the facing left-hand page:

> The first sentence is wrong. It should be "Can those assumptions be generalized?" I think I wrote it this way because I began to say something else, like "Are those assumptions possible?" but I didn't know the word that related to *generalize* so did it this way.

The opportunity for dialogue about alternatives is important. When L2 students compose, they need to be able to move beyond their first thoughts. In my study of composing aloud I found that a frequent cause of errors was that students began writing (not just rehearsing) before they knew how to express their propositional content in L2. Often they had to change direction to accommodate their ideas to the language at their disposal. They backed into a sentence and then were imprisoned in it. One of the students in my study wrote this sentence: "When I came to the U.S. I didn't feel the welcome of the American people." I could imagine that some teachers might suggest a change here to "American people didn't make me feel welcome." But the protocol reveals that the latter part of the student's sentence was a device to deal with a difficulty:

> I didn't feel that the Americans were like my . . . like Peruvians always welcome the tourists when someone goes to Peru, usually they have good times. When I came to the United States, I didn't feel that Americans were . . . how can I? I don't know how to say when a person doesn't welcome another. Someone goes to my house, I welcome him. But if I go to his house, and he doesn't welcome me . . . is there a word that I can use to say that? Ah: "the welcome of the American people."

The student had wanted to write "I didn't feel that Americans were hospitable" but got sidetracked because the term was not available to her in L2.

Here the double-entry notebook used during the writing of the draft would make it possible for the student to write in L1 or L2 on the left-hand page as a way of preserving a record of the concept the writer had in mind. ESL writers often feel that as they write they are locked in by their limited knowledge of the language and thus forced into syntactic derailments. A regular use of interpretive paraphrase, or what Berthoff calls responding to the question, "How does it change your meaning if you put it this way?" (81) helps students unlock the seemingly intractable L2. At the problem points in the writing, students use the opposite page to try to say it another way. When they are at the same time urged not to back into their sentences but to paraphrase with a clear subject/agent and verb/action, they find ways of sorting out the structure of their derailed sentences. Since subjects and agents coincide in most languages, L2 writers have few problems learning how to do this type of paraphrase. They obviously don't write every sentence in that way in their final draft, but once they have expressed each proposition as a kernel, they then have a basis for examining other ways to express that kernel to fit a variety of sociocultural contexts.

The double-entry notebook and interpretive paraphrase also help L2 writers deal with the problem of avoiding error. If the prose of ESL students sometimes appears simplistic, it could be that the writer is playing it safe and avoiding using any structures that are problematic. This makes sense, perhaps, in an essay exam, but in a classroom that offers guidance and feedback, opportunities to develop syntactic and grammatical knowledge are lost if students continue to avoid problem areas. In Japanese and Chinese, for instance, a relative clause is pre-nominal and left-branching while in English it is post-nominal and right-branching. So when a researcher found that Persian and Arabic speakers produced far more relative clauses in their compositions than Japanese and Chinese students, she concluded that "the students may have had so much trouble with these constructions that they refused to produce them" (Schachter 210). The double-entry notebook would allow students to use the left-hand page for notes in L1 and to explore alternative ways of expressing the meaning that is clear to the writer in L1. So L1 can illuminate L2, with the double entries throwing light on errors.

The hardware of "filters, hinges, and windows" has served to build a scaffold for discussing what we need to know about L2 students in composition classrooms. We need to know first how they acquire a new language—and how an attitudinal filter might block acquisition. We need to know, too, how culture and rhetoric might also influence writers, so much so that conflicts and ambiguities appear at the hinge of L1 and L2. And we also need to know that ESL students' errors are not just a "language problem" but indicators of process and progress, in fact, "windows into the mind" of the writers who are engaged in mastering new linguistic, cultural, and rhetorical conventions. To explore all this, the double-entry notebook is recommended; it provides the opportunity for dialogue and for constant L1/L2 interaction. L2 students are then made directly aware that "there is no study which is not a language study." For them, and for their teachers, thinking becomes forming becomes writing.

Notes

1. This figure is quoted in *Open Doors 1985–86: Report on International Educational Exchange* (New York: Institute of International Education, 1986), 5.

2. Their hypotheses, while dominant in theoretical literature and in pedagogical practice, are far from being accepted as *the* theory or even *a* theory of how a second language is learned (or acquired). Many dissenting voices are heard. Some argue that learning precedes and causes acquisition (McLaughlin) or they question the distinction made between acquisition and learning (Omaggio). Kevin Gregg questions whether Krashen's five hypotheses (the Acquisition/Learning Hypothesis, the Monitor Hypothesis, the Natural Order of Acquisition Hypothesis, the Input Hypothesis, and the Affective Filter Hypothesis) together make up a coherent linguistic theory (95), but he acknowledges that the hypotheses are "probably the most ambitious

and most influential attempt in recent years to construct an overall theory of second language acquisition" (79) and concedes that Krashen "is often right on the important questions" (94).

Works Cited

Ammon, Paul. "Helping Children Learn to Write in English as a Second Language: Some Observations and Hypotheses." *The Acquisition of Written Language.* Ed. Sarah Warshauer Freedman. Norwood, NJ: Ablex, 1985. 65–84.

Berthoff, Ann E. *The Making of Meaning.* Portsmouth, NH: Boynton/Cook, 1981.

Brown, H. Douglas. *Principles of Language Learning and Teaching.* Englewood Cliffs, NJ: Prentice-Hall, 1980.

Connor, Ulla, and Robert B. Kaplan. *Writing Across Languages: Analysis of L2 Text.* Reading, MA: Addison-Wesley, 1987.

Dulay, Heidi, Marina Burt, and Stephen Krashen. *Language Two.* New York: Oxford UP, 1982.

Ervin-Tripp, Susan M. "An Analysis of the Interaction of Language, Topic and Listener." *Readings in the Sociology of Language.* Ed. J. A. Fishman. The Hague: Mouton, 1968. 192–211.

Gardner, Robert C., and Wallace E. Lambert. *Attitudes and Motivation in Second-Language Learning.* Rowley, MA: Newbury House, 1972.

Gregg, Kevin R. "Krashen's Monitor and Occam's Razor." *Applied Linguistics* 5 (1984): 79–100.

Hinds, John. "Reader versus Writer Responsibility: A New Typology." *Writing Across Languages: Analysis of L2 Text.* Eds. Ulla Connor and Robert B. Kaplan. Reading, MA: Addison-Wesley, 1987. 141–52.

Hymes, Dell. "Speech and Language: On the Origins and Foundations of Inequality Among Speakers." *Daedalus* 102 (1973): 59–85.

Jones, C. Stanley, and Jacqueline Tetroe. "Composing in a Second Language." *Writing in Real Time: Modelling Production Processes.* Ed. Ann Matsuhashi. Norwood, NJ: Ablex, 1987. 34–57.

Kaplan, Robert B., ed. *Annual Review of Applied Linguistics 1982.* Rowley, MA: Newbury House, 1983.

Krashen, Stephen D. *Second Language Acquisition and Second Language Learning.* Oxford: Pergamon Press, 1981.

Kroll, Barry M., and John C. Schafer. "Error Analysis and the Teaching of Composition." *College Composition and Communication* 29 (1978): 242–48.

Lay, Nancy Duke S. "Composing Processes of Adult ESL Learners: A Case Study." *TESOL Quarterly* 16 (1982): 406.

Loveday, Leo. *The Sociolinguistics of Learning and Using a Non-Native Language.* Oxford: Pergamon Press, 1982.

McLaughlin, Barry. "The Monitor Model: Some Methodological Considerations." *Language Learning* 28 (1978): 309–32.

Omaggio, A. "The Proficiency-Oriented Classroom." *Teaching for Proficiency, the Organizing Principle.* Ed. T. V. Higgs. Lincolnwood, IL: National Textbook Co., 1984. 43–84.

Ostler, Shirley E. "English in Parallels: A Comparison of English and Arabic Prose." *Writing Across Languages: Analysis of L2 Text.* Eds. Ulla Connor and Robert B. Kaplan. Reading, MA: Addison-Wesley, 1987. 169–84.

Parry, Kate J. "Letter from Mohammed: An Example of Interlanguage." Paper presented at the New York State TESOL 7th Annual Applied Linguistics Winter Conference, New York City, January 1985.

Perl, Sondra. "The Composing Processes of Unskilled College Writers." *Research in the Teaching of English* 13 (1979): 317–36.

Purves, Alan C. "Rhetorical Communities, the International Student, and Basic Writing." *Journal of Basic Writing* 5 (1986): 38–51.

Raimes, Ann. "What Unskilled ESL Students Do as They Write: A Classroom Study of Composing." *TESOL Quarterly* 19 (1985): 229–58.

Richards, I. A. *How to Read a Page.* 1942. Boston: Beacon Press, 1959.

Schachter, Jacquelyn. "An Error in Error Analysis." *Language Learning* 24 (1974): 205–14.

Selinker, Larry. "Interlanguage." *New Frontiers in Second Language Learning.* Eds. John H. Schumann and Nancy Stenson. Rowley, MA: Newbury House, 1974. 114–36.

Shaughnessy, Mina P. *Errors and Expectations.* New York: Oxford UP, 1977.

Tanizaki, Jun'ichiro. Trans. Edward G. Seidensticker. *Some Prefer Nettles.* New York: Berkeley Medallion Books, 1960.

Tsao, Fen-Fu. "Linguistics and Written Discourse in English and Mandarin." *Annual Review of Applied Linguistics 1982.* Ed. Robert B. Kaplan. Rowley, MA: Newbury House, 1983. 99–117.

Zamel, Vivian. "The Composing Processes of Advanced ESL Students: Six Case Studies." *TESOL Quarterly* 17 (1983): 165–87.

16

Thinking Beyond Imagination

Participating in the Process of Knowing

VIVIAN ZAMEL

University of Massachusetts, Boston

Life as a whole is too complicated to teach to children. The minute it is cut up they can understand it, but you are liable to kill it in cutting it up.

C. E. Beeby

A tree is composed of a stem, branches and leaves. A paper, just like a tree, is also composed of a stem, branches and leaves. If we have too many limitations, the paper is just like a tree without leaves, a naked tree—unlived. If more serious limitations, it is like a tree with all branches cut, only a stem left, a totally dead tree.

Peter Chew

Both quotations, the first from Sylvia Ashton-Warner's *Teacher* (51), the second from a paper written by a student writer whose native language is not English, appear in my reading journal. It serves as my dialectical notebook, a place where I can record passages from my reading, react to them, and, in the process, discover why I recorded them in the first place. It is not by coincidence that these passages and others like them appear throughout my journal. They are often juxtaposed to other pieces about mechanistic models of teaching, in particular, the teaching of writing, and serve to explain how and why these approaches can undermine and "kill" the process of learning (to write).

To get some sense of the impact that reductionist and lock-step pedagogies, what Ann Berthoff calls a "pedagogy of exhortation" (743), have on students, I often ask ESL students to consider their writing experiences, the kinds of problems they have encountered, their attitudes toward writing and their feelings about themselves as writers. The following was written by a student who was having considerable difficulty in the composition class he was taking at the time:

> Thinking about my writing problems is like a devastating experience, and writing about it, knowing fully well that someone is going to read it, seems to me a great confession. If thinking about these problems and making these confessions will free me from this writing hardship, I will not hesitate to make them.
>
> I thought I was a good writer, but circumstances have kept on disproving me, and there is no confidence that I know of now. Apart from the writing exercise in this class, which took me nearly half the time allowed, to think about what to write, how to get started, who my audience was, and how to present a well-organized idea in a logical sequence, I've had at least two papers which I wrote in my other courses that caused me lots of embarrassment and disgrace.
>
> Generally, I don't feel bad nor enjoy writing, but I wish I know how to write, then all my beautiful ideas which will die when I am gone will be left behind.
>
> However, I don't feel I have enough confidence in myself about writing and this generates all my fears to the extent that I even doubt the few writing rules I've acquired.
>
> Writing takes me hours and sometimes days to produce something I consider meaningful to pass on to people to read. It has now become a habit to write and rewrite on any particular topic, even in an exam where the time allowed is so minimal. In most cases, I've ended up doing nothing.
>
> My most critical point in writing is getting started. Then I've to think of a suitable introductory sentence. This first sentence becomes a hard nut to crack because I feel I think beyond imagination. For instance, what are the best structure to use in order to capture the attention of any audience immediately, how to structure the paragraphs so that the points in each link neatly with the preceding and the succeeding paragraphs? Under this situation, sitting down to write seems an unsurmountable obstacle, especially if procrastination cuts in.
>
> I believe I've good ideas, but how can I prove that unless I can express them in a communicable manner. These fantastic ideas bump

each other in my mind each time, increasing my heartbeat, while I struggle with organizing and outlining my points on paper. Most of the time the outlines are scarcely followed because even when I sit down to write, ideas still doesn't stop coming. For this reason, I shy away from making outlines for my work.

I have never failed to consider my audience in my writing. However, the more important or highly I hold them, the more agonizing my writing becomes and I have always ended not pleasing them.

Obviously this student experiences a tremendous amount of anxiety when he attempts to compose, and this anxiety has undermined his confidence and convinced him that he cannot write, this despite his acknowledgment of the "beautiful ideas" that he wants to leave behind when he is gone. He remarks that he once thought he was a good writer, but that "circumstances" have proven him wrong. These circumstances, I discovered during an interview with him, refer to his experiences with school-based writing instruction, instruction that expected him to attend to predetermined sets of conditions and concerns while attempting to write. He explicitly mentions these: presenting a well-organized idea in a logical sequence, writing a suitable introductory sentence, capturing the attention of an audience immediately, linking paragraphs neatly with one another, and outlining his thoughts before writing.

Despite the fact that this student is still acquiring English, the kinds of problems and difficulties he has identified are similar to the blocks to writing experienced by other writers. Rose ("Rigid") and Bloom, for example, have revealed what happens to these writers when they operate by strategies and rigid assumptions that restrict and virtually paralyze their attempts to write. The research on composing processes likewise demonstrates that less skilled writers apply ineffective behaviors and strategies that "truncate" the flow of discourse (Perl 22). These writers, concerned with teacher-generated rules, seem to view composing as mechanical and formulaic, and hence to revise in the most limited way. Even studies of ESL students suggest that it is not primarily language but composing constraints that impede their development as writers (Jacobs; Jones and Tetroe; Zamel "Composing Processes"). These studies reveal what happens to students who have acquired debilitating notions about writing. And they raise serious questions about classroom practices that continue to promulgate principles, guidelines and rules which seem to be counterproductive to the development of these students as writers, and about prescriptive approaches that view writing as the static transcription of pieces of text, as a means for displaying and re-presenting language and form, as a subset of skills taught *seriatim*. For example, composition textbooks, which at least suggest how writing is taught, subvert the highly fluid and context-oriented process of composing by presenting students with formulaic, arbitrary statements, artificial rhetorical modes, and discrete, underconceptualized tasks (Rose "Sophisticated"; Stewart; Weaver).

In the case of ESL textbooks, this lock-step model of teaching is aggravated by additional concerns with language acquisition, and language itself is treated in the same rigid ways that writing is. Specific forms and techniques become obligatory, objectives are stated as performance competencies, the mastery of the various components of writing is monitored and controlled, and revising becomes confused with proofreading for error. Very often the main purpose for composing is to practice and reinforce grammar and vocabulary. Readings, too, are used for test-like purposes; rather than developing in students the notion that reading is a creative, reconstructive and individualized practice, whereby meaning is derived from interaction with the texts, they give students vocabulary and word form practice, cloze exercises, and comprehension questions that either test their recall of unimportant details or their ability to identify structural features.

Surveys of writing instruction (Burhans), too, reveal the persistence of product-oriented concepts, methods and goals. Studies of teachers' responses to student writing (Sommers) indicate that students' texts are perceived as fixed and final products and are evaluated according to predetermined and often unarticulated assumptions about good writing. In the case of ESL teachers' responses (Zamel "Responding"), the focus on language concerns or on other local features of texts distracts teachers from reading students' texts as whole pieces of discourse and perpetuates the notion that good writing is correct writing. Finally, studies of classroom teaching (Applebee) demonstrate that traditional models still predominate, that writing is occasioned by drills, exercises and low-level writing tasks, and that school curricula continue to be marked by a mechanistic view of education. While there are some classrooms in which meaningful writing is promoted within an encouraging and non-threatening environment (Perl and Wilson), these are isolated rather than representative cases. It is in fact *because* they are so markedly different from the classrooms observed by Applebee that they are being studied by writing researchers working to demonstrate that alternatives to the teacher-dominated paradigm are possible.

Given what we have discovered about the actual behaviors and strategies of writers, it is no longer appropriate to subscribe to a pedagogy that sets up inflexible standards and performance objectives and that uses sequential and systematic means for achieving these goals. Writing instruction must take into account the purpose, function and communicative effectiveness of a written text, the relationship among the writer, the text and the audience, and how and why that text took the form that it did. It is only by beginning with what individual writers do in the context of particular writing acts that we can give them some understanding of the fluid, changeable and exploratory nature of writing. Prescription, literally meaning that which is written before, and as applied to the teaching of writing, that which we provide our students even before we have seen their writing, is therefore not only inappropriate but may preclude genuine writing development.

A useful and instructive analogy here is the behavioristic model that still underlies much language instruction. Such a model reduces language to a system divisible into its constituent parts, which then form the basis of curricula: students are exposed to the various components of the system, beginning with the simplest forms and progressing to more complex ones; through rote memorization and drill, it is believed, these structures are internalized. In the same way that language structures are hierarchically presented, language use is separated into four discrete skill areas (listening, speaking, reading, and writing), and writing and reading are basically treated as the orthographic transcription and decoding of language already practiced. Meaning, purpose, function, and context of language use are largely ignored; individual, motivational and sociolinguistic factors are left unaddressed; and errors become the "quirks" in the system that need to be eradicated. Such a pedagogical stance, not surprisingly, affects teacher and student roles: the teacher becomes the authority, determining and controlling instruction; students are expected passively to feed back the material presented. This model fails to take into account the conditions, constraints and strategies that affect language acquisition.

Obvious parallels can be drawn between this behavioristic language teaching and writing instruction (Bartholomae "The Study"; Raimes; Krashen). Given that writing instructors are now being asked to view the teaching of writing as the teaching of language, the lessons we are now learning from recent work in second language acquisition take on particular relevance, particularly that language is acquired in the process of *meaningful* attempts to communicate. Analyses of first and second language acquisition emphasize learners' active roles in this process; it is these *learners'* needs, not those of the teacher or curriculum, that determine actual acquisition. Furthermore, these studies demonstrate that error is both inevitable and essential, that each learner's "interlanguage" is valid in its own right. To focus on empty form and to ignore how and why we acquire language in the first place is futile.

By failing to take into account the implications of research and emerging theory in writing and language acquisition, we perpetuate a building-blocks model of teaching that limits learning to and defines progress by the correct and systematic application of procedures and forms. Teachers become authorities by virtue of their knowing these procedures and forms, and, as a result, they are the sole determiners of whether these have been applied correctly or not. Such a pedagogy represents what Freire calls a "banking model of education," whereby the focus is on the transmission and retrieval of information, and students are the recipients of what their teachers have determined they need to learn. Our surveys of writing instruction and writing achievement in our schools indicate this system has gone bankrupt. Instead of predetermining *what* needs to be taught, as in rule-based and product-oriented instruction, therefore, we need to predetermine the conditions and opportunities for acquiring and developing writing.

Students need to come to understand that all writers experience the process of discovering ideas both before and after they begin to search for them, that it is the writing itself that leads to this discovery and that generates these ideas. A preliminary draft or free-writing can help students explore their topics and can serve at the same time to model the open-ended nature of writing. Student-teacher working journals help reduce students' writing anxiety, and, because they require teachers to write, make teachers participants in the writing process and collaborators in the making of meaning. Furthermore, these dialogue journals give teachers insight into individual students and their unique strengths, which might otherwise not be revealed. Dialectical or double-entry notebooks provide students a method for considering, weighing, and interpreting their reading and give rise to reactions that they may not have been aware of. They allow for dialogues with a text so that students come to discover that the meaning of texts is not fixed "out there" but is made while readers react to them. This gives them insight into how all texts, including their own, are understood on the basis of individual readers' interpretations. These types of reading/writing experiences encourage students to take risks, explore or experiment (which are prerequisites for language acquisition), since these first attempts will not be judged as finished products.

Students further need to be provided time and opportunity in order to work with their tentative ideas. By doing a number of drafts, they are able to move closer to approximating what they realize they want to say. (This process is like language acquisition itself, which requires time and opportunities that foster hypothesis testing and the formulation of approximations of the target language.) And our responses to these drafts need to reveal to the writer our attempts to make meaning of his or her text, the confusion that we may have experienced, and the means by which these problems can be dealt with. By genuinely enabling students to go beyond their first attempts, we give credibility to the claim that texts do not exist in the writer's head, but evolve or unfold in the process of construction. By providing assistance before an essay is considered finished, we are facilitating more writing and reinforcing the idea that continual clarification and exploration may be necessary before one's meaning becomes articulated.

If we try to convince students that they are writing in order to develop into more autonomous, proficient and confident writers, writers who will be able to demonstrate their competence and confidence in other writing contexts, their attempts should be shared with other student writers in collaborative activities. In this way teachers come to be viewed not as the sole authority, with what seems to be specialized and inaccessible knowledge about writing, but as one representative of a varied audience.

Beginning writers of course need some guidance as to how they should respond to their peers' writing. In my own composition class, I duplicate student papers and role-play my own responses in front of the class. The students pay attention to my responses and determine those features of writing that I have addressed. In one way, I am modeling for them a method of reading and responding to papers, making them aware of the issues that are important, helping them understand the kinds of responses that can be used as a basis for revision, demonstrating, as I share with them what I took away from (and gave back to) the text, how readers interact with texts. But again I am not predetermining *what* they should say to each other, but suggesting *how* they should do so. The *what* arises from the particulars of the written texts themselves. This is as it should be if papers are approached as real texts rather than the "Ur" texts that product-based teaching encourages.

Just as students share their writing with each other, they can be writing about and discussing their actual experiences. This inquiry into their behaviors as writers thus becomes a course topic radically different from textbooks' abstract exegeses about writing. They share the strategies underlying and perhaps inhibiting their own performance as writers, and teachers thus gain critical information about the ways in which these strategies affect this performance. Students also learn about strategies that prove to be effective. They begin to realize that their frustrations and concerns are not unique and find out how others deal with the anxiety or blocks that so often accompany writing. It is comforting to discover that other writers—including the teachers—get stuck or have trouble getting started, just as it is helpful to hear about ways others have found of getting past such blocks.

Experiences of this sort give students to understand that one does not need to attend to surface-level concerns until the writing is ready to be proofread, edited and then evaluated. Attention can thus be devoted to the representation and articulation of meaning without the premature obsession (characteristic of beginning writing) with mechanics, grammar and usage which leads to serious writer's block. This attention to meaning is particularly crucial in the ESL writing classroom, where students and their teachers may be convinced that accuracy and correctness are of primary importance, and where, because of their concern with language and their inexperience with writing, students may be trying to attend to all of the various demands of composing simultaneously. We therefore need to help them realize that what is true for language acquisition also applies to learning to write: that monitoring output while it is developing may not only be unproductive, but may also inhibit further development. Furthermore, by focusing on the making of meaning, we are likely to be more effective teachers of language, for students are engaged by their writing and genuinely committed to creating reading for others. I have often heard teachers complain that their students seem unable to transfer to their writing the skill and accuracy with which they complete grammatical exercises and quizzes, and of course this inability is partially the result of the numerous demands that composing makes on the writer. However, in the case of my own composition students, I have found that the opposite may be just as true: students do not perform very well on written drills and exercises but are quite capable of demonstrating good grammatical control as they work toward their final drafts. (An ESL tutor recently reported the same phenomenon: she observed that students who had performed poorly on an exam testing their mastery of the passive voice had used the passive voice remarkably well in their narratives about the histories of their countries.) As student writers become more absorbed and involved with meaning, the various concerns of writing, even the surface-level features, are taken more seriously.

I propose a writing course based on the premise that behavioristic non-contextualized, prescriptive rules and directives are ineffective, that a curriculum dividing writing into its constituent skills and defining these in terms of sequences (first words, then sentences, then paragraphs, then essays, then the research paper) fails to take into account how writing (all language) is acquired. Instead we must take into consideration the stu-

dent's own built-in syllabus and his or her own attempts at creating and
negotiating meaning, which is exactly what language acquisition theorists
consider essential for effective language teaching and learning (Corder;
Brumfit). As Bartholomae argues, such a pedagogy "begins by making
the soundest possible speculation" about the individual learner "rather
than imposing upon [the] learner a sequence serving the convenience of
teachers or administrators" ("Teaching" 89). This is the way Peter Chew,
the ESL student whom I quoted at the outset, argues for a pedagogy that
values individuals' attempts to use language meaningfully:

> I can never forget that last semester. I could write freely. Under the
> instructor's guidance of creative writing and her encourage, I really
> tried to write as much as I could, hoping that I could expand my
> writing skill in order to express my unbounded thought. Though my
> English was poor and my writing skill was weak, I did not care how
> many mistakes I made. I just wanted to write more. Because I dared
> to write, gradually writing became easier to me.
>
> In order to obtain a better writing skill, according to my experience,
> creativity is much more important than the rules and format. How can
> a student who is troubled by such rules and format write a good paper?
> Rules and limitation easily give "self-defeating thinking" to students.
> Self-defeating thinking affects students' creative thinking and writing
> skill. They may give up almost as soon as they start, "Am I doing all
> right?", "It is too hard for me to write.", "I am foolish because I can't
> follow the rules.", "I don't dare to write. . . . " In order to encourage
> students (especially ESL students) to write, a teacher should not em-
> phasize the rules and format and other limitations, but try to understand
> students' mistakes and help them to be creative. Actually, students are
> able to improve their creativity by stopping self-defeating thought and
> replacing them with self-encouraging ones. A creative person is less
> concerned with what other people think. He does not care what anyone
> else thinks, he just wants to come up his own idea. A teacher should
> encourage students not to be scared to make mistakes in writing.
> Nonsense thought or crazy ideas may hold the key to creativity.

If only the student whose "confession" appears at the beginning of this
paper, who "feel[s] that [he] think[s] beyond imagination," were given
to understand that this was not cause for despair, that "nonsense thought
or crazy ideas may hold the key to creativity."

Unlike a "banking model of education," an approach that recognizes
the learner's potential for autonomous thoughts and action is representative
of what Freire has called a "pedagogy of knowing" (Berthoff 744), whereby

teaching and learning begin with the forming of a thematic universe based on students' needs, problems and perceptions. This, of course, is only possible when writing is viewed as a mode of inquiry and learning, and when students are recognized as participants in the process of knowledge-making. It is this perspective that has turned writing theorists' attention toward an examination of "discourse communities," and the ways in which students, particularly basic and beginning writers, can be introduced to and collaborate in the specialized discourse of the university, for it is this very discourse from which these inexperienced writers have been excluded (Rose, "The Language"; Bizzel). But this does not mean exposing students (as banking models would have us do) to so-called models of expository prose or assigning them "academic" writing tasks about alien and alienating topics. Instead, students become engaged in writing (and reading and speaking, of course) that helps them make connections between what they already know and what they have yet to explore.

This engagement can be achieved through sequences of writing that build on or extend previous writing, thus legitimizing the texts students produce as points of reference in their exploration. For example (and this is only an example, for what students are involved in needs to be informed by who these students are), we can have students produce their own narrative accounts of their work experiences, but this represents the beginning of their inquiry. They read Studs Terkel's *Working*, develop their own questionnaires, conduct surveys, and then, exploring the relationship between work and satisfaction, produce essays that raise questions about their own or popularly-held assumptions about work. Or, they may begin by considering an important instance of learning in their lives, but again this is only a beginning. They go on to read Holt and other educational philosophers, observe and analyze the discourse of their classrooms, and attempt to explain the extent to which this discourse allows for involvement and real learning. For students who come from cultures with very different norms and expectations about educational processes, such a project may reveal why they are experiencing difficulties. Last year several teachers at UMass/Boston had their beginning and ESL writers observe and explore language itself. A rich body of data was produced which students analyzed in reports that revealed how much they had learned about language use. They were able to differentiate the kinds of constraints brought to bear on different types of discourse and drew articulate and astute conclusions about the importance of these distinctions. They *discovered* language rules, forms and processes, and as a result of studying about language, they become better language users.

Providing students the opportunity to collect data, to become ethnographers, to become researchers and explore issues together, as members of the same discourse community (in the same way that sociologists, anthropologists and linguists engage in inquiry), is an extremely powerful approach. What we are helping our students do is experience the process of not only creating a text but creating knowledge, for it is the very process of inquiry that creates knowledge. It is by beginning with a particular topic, question or problem, by allowing students to reconsider these reflections from a broader intellectual perspective and then to recast these reflections as part of a developing store of knowledge, that these students are empowered both as writers and knowers.

A pedagogy of knowing promotes the development of "literate-ness" rather than the mastery of isolated literacy skills. This is a critical distinction, especially because so much instruction, particularly for students whose previous schooling and/or home experiences put them at academic risk, is still based on the limited understanding that literacy has to do with mastering the surface and technical features of reading and writing (and language). Such a view of literacy fails to take into account what students bring with them to the schooling experience and the extent to which the problems they experience have less to do with their "deficiencies" than they have to do with the conflict between their expectations and assumptions and those of their teachers (Heath). Such a view perpetuates a deficit model of education whereby teachers possess "privileged knowledge" (Hartwell) which confers on these teachers their traditional authoritarian role. But literacy, in its much fuller sense, has to do with the "human capacity to make meaning" (Robinson 485). It has to do with a rich, deep and complex engagement with language (and reading and writing) within a community of other learners (Bruffee; Reither). It has to do with the critical ability not only to "read (and write) the word" (texts), but to read the word in relation to the students' own world (Freire and Macedo), since meaning resides not in the text but in the interaction between text and reader/writer. A pedagogy of knowing, since it acknowledges and values students and the worlds they represent, since it encourages an examination of how these worlds connect with the new worlds they are entering, since it involves students in collaborative experiences through which meaning is generated, promotes this more profound version (the deep structure) of literacy. And in the process, because teachers no longer own and control the "answers," because they are freed from the constraints of passing on a predetermined package of information, they become learners participating in their students' analyses, observations and investigations. They learn about what their students already know so that instruction can address and build on this knowledge. (I keep a list entitled "illuminations," which records my students' logically derived but erroneous hypotheses about language use, because it informs my pedagogy.) Finally, they learn about their own practice, examining students' work in relation to their own, raising question about their attempts to take into account students' strategies, behaviors and intentions. Although they have given up one kind of control, their questioning stance has empowered them, just as it has empowered their students, as researchers and theory-builders in their own right, continually retesting and reevaluating their efforts to help students create/re-create texts that confirm the act of writing/reading as an act of knowing.

Works Cited

Applebee, Arthur N. *Contexts for Learning to Write*. Norwood, NJ: Ablex, 1984.

Bartholomae, David. "Teaching Basic Writing: An Alternative to Basic Skills." *Journal of Basic Writing* 2 (1979): 85–109.

———. "The Study of Error." *College Composition and Communication* 31 (1980): 253–69.

Berthoff, Ann E. "Is Teaching Still Possible?" *College English* 46 (1984): 743–55.

Bizzell, Patricia. "College Composition: Initiation into the Academic Discourse Community." *Curriculum Inquiry* 12 (1982): 191–207.

Bloom, Lynn Z. "Anxious Writers in Context: Graduate School and Beyond." *When A Writer Can't Write*. Ed. Mike Rose. New York: Guilford Press, 1985. 119–33.

Bruffee, Kenneth A. "Collaborative Learning and 'The Conversation of Mankind.'" *College English* 46 (1984): 635–52.

Brumfit, Christopher. "'Communicative' Language Teaching: An Educational Perspective." *The Communicative Approach to Language Teaching*. Eds. Christopher J. Brumfit and Keith Johnson. London: Oxford UP, 1979. 183–91.

Burhans, Clinton S. "The Teaching of Writing and the Knowledge Gap." *College English* 45 (1983): 639–56.

Corder, S. Pit. "The Significance of Learners' Errors." *International Review of Applied Linguistics* 5 (1967): 161–70.

Freire, Paulo, and Donaldo Macedo. *Literacy: Reading the Word, and the World*. South Hadley: Bergin and Garvey, 1987.

Hartwell, Patrick. "Creating a Literate Environment in Freshman English." Unpublished paper delivered at the Conference on College Composition and Communication, New Orleans, March 1986.

Heath, Shirley Brice. *Ways With Words*. London: Cambridge UP, 1983.

Jacobs, Suzanne E. *Composing and Coherence. Linguistics and Literacy Series 3*. Washington, D.C.: Center for Applied Linguistics, 1982.

Jones, Stan, and Jacqueline Tetroe. "Composing in a Second Language." *Writing in Real Time*. Ed. Ann Matsuhashi. Norwood, NJ: Ablex, 1987. 34–57.

Krashen, Stephen D. *Writing: Research, Theory and Applications*. Oxford: Pergamon, 1984.

Perl, Sondra. "A Look at Basic Writers in the Process of Composing." *Basic Writing*. Eds. Lawrence N. Kasden and Daniel R. Hoeber. Urbana: NCTE, 1980. 13–32.

Perl, Sondra, and Nancy Wilson. *Through Teachers' Eyes*. Portsmouth, NH: Heinemann, 1986.

Raimes, Ann. "Tradition and Revolution." *TESOL Quarterly* 17 (1983): 535–52.

Reither, James A. "Writing and Knowing: Toward Redefining the Writing Process." *College English* 47 (1985): 620–28.

Robinson, Jay L. "Literacy in the Department of English." *College English* 47 (1985): 482–98.

Rose, Mike. "Rigid Rules, Inflexible Plans, and the Stifling of Language: A Cognitivist Analysis of Writer's Block." *College Composition and Communication* 31 (1980): 389–401.

————. "Sophisticated, Ineffective Books—The Dismantling of Process in Composition Texts." *College Composition and Communication* 32 (1981): 65–74.

————. "The Language of Exclusion: Writing Instruction at the University." *College English* 47 (1985): 341–59.

Sommers, Nancy. "Responding to Student Writing." *College Composition and Communication* 33 (1982): 148–56.

Stewart, Donald. "Composition Textbooks and The Assault on Tradition." *College Composition and Communication* 29 (1978): 171–76.

Weaver, Barbara T. "Bibliography of Writing Textbooks." *Writing Program Administration* 6 (1982): 25–38.

Zamel, Vivian. "Responding to Student Writing." *TESOL Quarterly* 19 (1985): 79–101.

————. "The Composing Processes of Advanced ESL Students: Six Case Studies." *TESOL Quarterly* 17 (1983): 165–87.

17

Structuralism, Mediation in Psychoanalysis, and the Student "Who Just Can't Write"

NEAL BRUSS

University of Massachusetts, Boston

"Linguistics ha[s] nothing to teach us about the composing *process*," Ann Berthoff has warned composition researchers attracted to structuralism's power in analyzing composition *products* (*Forming* iii; my italics). Berthoff's warning, I would argue, is valid because structuralism's scientific base lacks a provision for mediation, for the individual's adaptation of resources furnished by the pre-existing language to the making of meaning in actual settings (Berthoff, *Reclaiming* 167–87). The defining activity of linguistics is writing grammars. A provision for mediation would undermine grammar writing if it meant that each use of a language had to be seen as diverging from all others. Better to disregard uniqueness and concentrate on similarity. But structuralism has long held that every language use *is* unique, and has studied the uniqueness in individual style-shifting, dialect difference, and historic change. It has found the variation in these areas limited and orderly. However, without a provision for mediation, structuralism cannot give this orderliness a satisfying explanation.

Berthoff's emphasis on mediation, then, may have a good deal to teach linguistics about itself. But her emphasis on the composing *process* rather than on the structure of language *products* has not inclined her writings to furnish linguistics with a provision for mediation. Such a provision, I believe, can be found in psychoanalysis, which studies texts such as dreams, neurotic symptoms, slips of the tongue, covert messages in literature, rituals and ordinary discourse. These data of psychoanalysis are not the ordinary uses of language which linguistics studies, but they are communicative products nonetheless.

Mediation is so important to psychoanalysts that they provide for it in their "basic assumption" and carry it forward as a major construct: the ego. I believe that because of this centrality of mediation, psychoanalysis can help us understand why structural linguistics cannot explain variability data such as the style-shifting of the "Oscar Brothers"; why "linguistics has nothing to teach us about the composing process"; and how to deepen our understanding of mediation in even the most difficult challenges of the composing process, that of the student who "just can't write."

I

In the late 1960s, William Labov's sociolinguistics (*Language* and *Sociolinguistic*) emerged as a rival to Chomsky's approach to language. In studies that delicately analyzed large quantities of actual speech (rather than dismissing it in the Chomskyan mode as "performance error" [*Aspects* 4]), Labov demonstrated that the dialects and historical stages of English were continuous, and that every person style-shifted among several dialects, in relation not only to phonological and syntactic features of utterances already well understood by structuralism but also in relation to speakers' social identities and the social levels of their contexts of speaking. Labov's explanatory construct, the "variable rule," encompassed speaker identity (an amalgam of age, socioeconomic class, gender, ethnicity and race), context of speaking, and linguistic environment as predictors of whether speakers would use particular linguistic forms. As illuminating as Labov's work was for understanding dialect and language history, it was equally suggestive as an approach to individual style—whether the individual was Shakespeare or the freshman composition student. Style-shifting was the theory's point of access for an application to idiolect.

Labov analyzed style-shifting data from two opposed types of speech, informal group conversation and more formal one-on-one conversation. He studied speech from black males of three different ages: pre-adolescent boys who organized themselves in clubs such as "the Thunderbirds," a less organized late adolescent group called "the Oscar Brothers" (named for basketball great Oscar Robertson), and some adult men. Labov found that speakers of all three ages varied their speech in relation to the style—formal or informal—in which they spoke (*Language* 65–129). They varied between standard forms and those of vernacular or so-called nonstandard English, features like double negation, "r"-less pronunciation, loss of final "-ed," and "be"-deletion, the occasional non-pronunciation of inflections of the verb "be" that were already subject to contraction (particularly present tense "'re" "'s"; the nasal "'m" resists deletion). Labov argued against the assumption that for a speaker to delete "be" or use other vernacular forms implied that he suffered a cognitive deficit. Labov provided evidence of the linguistic and logical richness of the vernacular culture. He explained nonstandard variants as semantic equivalents of standard English forms, or products of sound changes moving through the English-speaking world as a whole.

"Be"-deletion was actually the most recent manifestation of a sound change in progress for 5,000 years, the change responsible for "be"-contraction. In Indo-European, circa 3,000 B.C., word stress was variable: it could fall on any syllable. But the Indo-Europeans who migrated to Northern Europe and ultimately became the progenitors of Old English fixed word stress on first syllables. Four thousand years later, the French-Norman Conquest of England imposed the Romance languages' stress pattern, ultimately accelerating English's loss of stress from unstressed syllables and from monosyllabic function words such as unemphatic uses of "be"-forms. Renaissance English writing also provides examples of contraction, for example the merging of monosyllablic function words to yield both "'Tis" and "it's" for "it is." In the present day, as Labov argued, the sound change had extended from contraction to deletion of "be"-forms:

- Full: I am going, you are going, she is going, etc.
- Contraction: I'm going, you're going, she's going.
- Deletion: (In "I'm," nasal "m" resists deletion) you going, she going.

In the three age groups of Labov's male Harlem informants, "be"-deletion was conditioned by phonology and syntax. "Be"-deletion was especially favored when a "be"-form was followed by "going," rather than by, say, a noun phrase. "Going" was itself generally followed by a verb, as in a sentence from Labov's data such as, "he goin' try to get up." The "be"-form followed by "going" was thus a second consecutive auxiliary verb—which diminished the "be"-form's already minimal information value and word stress. Of all syntactic conditions favoring "be"-deletion, a preceding pronoun rather than a noun phrase had the greatest effect. A pronoun's referent usually occurs in the preceding discourse, so a pronoun carries no new information and is therefore vulnerable on semantic grounds to the loss of its stress.

When the effects are summed of a "be"-form's preceding and following environments, even a ritual insult like "Your mama's a Boston Indian" resists deletion because of the noun phrases preceding and following the "be"-contraction "'s." In contrast, "be"-forms preceded by pronouns and followed by "going" favored deletion, even if their clauses expressed highly charged information, as in "'Cause we, we gon' sneak under the turnstile."

But for Labov's informants, two *extra*-linguistic factors, conversational settings and speakers' identities—in particular, speakers' ages—produced the most dramatic "be"-deletion in style-shifting, shifts so extreme that in this discussion, among linguistic factors only data on the preceding pronoun need be discussed to show how dramatic the style shifts were.

Labov found that the preadolescents were more likely to delete "be" than to use the full or contracted forms—and in both individual and group conversation. Members of the Thunderbirds, for example, deleted at a rate of 51 percent when they spoke one-to-one with an interviewer, and 60 percent in group style.

The black adults were likely *not* to delete: their rates were 16 percent in individual style and 27 percent in group style.

The Oscar Brothers, however, deleted "be" 64 percent in group style—*more* often than the Thunderbirds—but only 15 percent in individual style—*less* often than the adults. The Oscar Brothers' use of "be" showed other dramatic shifts in contrast to those of the young adolescents and adults: in individual style, the Oscar brothers used the full form 25 percent of the time and contraction 60 percent. The adults used the full form only 4 percent of the time and the contracted form 80 percent. When the Oscar Brothers shifted into individual style, toward greater formality, not only did their control of deletion increase to match the adults' but they used the most formal full form six times more frequently than the adults. In short: when the Oscar Brothers spoke in the group, they spoke more like young adolescents than the preadolescents themselves. But when they spoke individually, they spoke more like adults than the adults!

But Labov's method did not enable him to explain *how* the Oscar Brothers style-shifted; it only allowed him to collocate his linguistic data with fine demographic and contextual distinctions. Labov could explain why the Oscar Brothers' patterns fit roughly between the other two: they comprised the middle age group. But the closest Labov came to an explanation of the *mechanism* of style-shifting was that it correlated with the degree of "attention . . . paid to speech" (*Language* 256–57). "Attention," however, does not explain why the Oscar Brothers' "be"-deletion rates diverge so dramatically between the two styles, nor why the other two groups do not style-shift more.

Any layman can explain the phenomenon, and in my History of English classes, many students do. "It's identification," they say. "They're outgrowing the kids' patterns, beginning to think and talk like adults, and that means talking like middle-class people in general."

"Identification" is a long-standing psychoanalytic concept, a stage in the process by which the child creates a less infantile part of his or her psyche on the models of his parents (Freud, *Interpretation* 150; "Dissolution"). Psychoanalysts would see the preadolescence of the Thunderbirds as the period of maximum peer loyalty, when a child's discontents with parents, teachers or older siblings are finally offset by the developing capacity to act independently. Psychoanalysts would also recognize the late adolescence of the Oscar Brothers as the period in which maximum peer solidarity wanes, and an even more independent adulthood begins.

In short, the style-shifting of Labov's informants can be explained by recognizing that rates of deletion and other linguistic variation in style-shifting connote important aspects of the style-shifter's identity, and that these identities change markedly in late adolescence. Labov's description of the peer groups shows how emotional these identities are. To sound like a preadolescent through high rates of "be"-deletion (and of the other variables)—especially in *individual* settings—is to identify with "the focal concerns of the groups['] . . . toughness, smartness, trouble, excitement, autonomy and fate" (*Language* 244). Lower rates of vernacular features express greater identification with mainstream adults. Labov demonstrated that the rates varied directly with individual speakers' popularity among other club-members *and* inversely with measures of academic success. Thus, the individual's choice of a speech style is the result of his or her *mediating* the existing community speech patterns as a personal stylistic *choice*.

Berthoff has warned against accepting recipes without understanding the theories that explain how they work (*Making* 19–59). The lack of a provision for mediation in structuralism can be addressed only at structuralism's roots, in terms of a definition of science. One definition appropriate for studying language was stated by Albert Einstein in "On the Method of Theoretical Physics":

A complete system of theoretical physics is made up of concepts, fundamental laws which are supposed to be valid for those concepts and conclusions to be reached by logical deduction. It is these conclusions which must correspond with our separate experiences; in any theoretical treatise their logical deduction occupies almost the whole book.

[The] fundamental concepts and postulates, which cannot be further reduced logically, form the essential part of a theory, which reason cannot touch. (265–66)

For Einstein, then, a science consists of (1) irreducible fundamental concepts and postulates, (2) logic, (3) observations, (4) conclusions. Applying these concepts to structuralism, we might accept that (4) the "conclusions" of research on language correspond to the "representations of reality" to which Einstein refers; (2) "logic" is the mode of argumentation, in syntactic research, for example, the formulation of test sentences which a given piece of theory can or cannot generate elegantly; (3) "observations" have been controversial in the past twenty years, sociolinguists like Labov questioning Chomsky's devotion to intuitions about language, critics like Berthoff emphasizing the relativity of all observation to the questions one is asking. Structuralism's problem with mediation is evident only in respect to the first of Einstein's four constituents, the irreducible fundamental concepts and postulates. Structuralism does not have a fundamental concept or postulate that introduces mediation into its approach to language.

Structuralism has two fundamental postulates, one formalist and the other conventionalist. The formalist postulate is simply that language always has form if one looks for it. Saussure specified form as paradigm and syntagm, Jakobson, as the axes of selection and combination. Chomsky focused on form when he discussed linguistic creativity, the infinite number of sentences that a language user can understand, as in this passage from *Language and Mind*:

the number of patterns underlying our normal use of language and corresponding to meaningful and easily comprehensible sentences in our language is orders of magnitude greater than the number of seconds in a lifetime. (12)

The conventionalist postulate is that language is the product of the speech community "convening" to define units of meaning and other structures for the sake of communicating. Saussure wrote, "Language . . . exists only by virtue of a sort of contract signed by the members of a community"

(14). Edward Sapir wrote, "Speech is a purely historical heritage of the group, the product of long-continued social usage" (4).

The conventionalist postulate has it that the primal conveners of English defined "be" in all of its inflections. Did they reconvene and write an amendment for contraction? Do they do so for every sound change? If so, do they add to the social contract the constraints on social class and context that Labov has shown to determine sound change? If sound changes occur gradually, as Labov has demonstrated, when and how often does the community reconvene? What about deletion—the null-copula? Are we to assume a convention by which the *lack* of a sign counts *as* a sign?

This *reductio* suggests that the conventionalist postulate does not have the resources to explain style-shifting, let alone the extreme pattern that the Oscar Brothers displayed in relation to the rest of the Harlem male community. Labov's account is filled with the "thick description" that Clifford Geertz recommends (Berthoff, *Reclaiming* 226–48), description of the club members' attitudes and practices regarding danger and fate, pigeon-racing and fighting, parents and friends. But such description "thickens" only the social convention. It neither introduces nor follows from a different fundamental postulate on mediation. "Thick description," with all its thickness, as it diverges from the spartan, empiricist style of much structuralist anthropology, provides evidence that mediation is taking place. But it does not bring mediation into structuralism.

In the absence of a provision for mediation, the conventionalist postulate creates a legacy of essay opportunities for skeptical philosophers and critics, phenomenologists and deconstructionists, who have only to call into question the so-called code resulting from the alleged convention of the purported speech-community. It creates openings for hermeneutic skepticism about the subjective bases of all observation and the observer's disruption of the object of observation, as if subjectivism and disruption were themselves undetermined and unknowable.

But the real problem with the conventionalist postulate, as Berthoff would say, is that the idea of a community convention prior to language use does not address the making of meaning, individuals' interpreting the existing language and giving it new meaning as they use it. Labov's data shows clearly that the language of the Harlem clubs' most popular members has the highest rates of nonstandard features, but structuralism cannot explain what every adolescent knows—that popularity has everything to do with imitation, linguistic or otherwise (241–92). Psychoanalysis, I would argue, explains "what every adolescent knows"—and what our most vexed students refuse to know.

II

Freud compared psychoanalysis to physics in respect to their reliance on inference from maximally simple postulates and observation. When he spoke of psychoanalysis' logical structure, he sounded very much like Einstein on physics. Psychoanalysis, Freud wrote in "On Narcissism,"

> will gladly content itself with nebulous, scarcely imaginable basic concepts, which it hopes to apprehend more clearly in the course of its development, or which it is even prepared to replace by others. For these ideas are not the foundation of science, upon which everything rests: that foundation is observation alone. They are not the bottom but the top of the whole structure, and they can be replaced and discarded without damaging it. (77)

Freud and his students have a correspondingly tough-minded term for "fundamental concepts and postulates": they speak of their "basic assumption." When they think about their discipline as a science—and they do so frequently—they "reduce," to use Einstein's term, the fundamental concepts to the basic assumption that underlies their entire effort. As the contemporary psychoanalyst Norman Reider states it, "The only absolutely necessary assumption for a psychoanalytic theory is the concept of psychic determinism and the continuity of psychic life" (Marmor 497).

"Psychic determinism" is the equivalent of the formalist postulate, an affirmation of the rationality of reality: it does not distinguish psychoanalysis from structuralism. It is "psychical continuity" that introduces something new: that a person's experience should be understood as coherent and connected. Should a person display meaningless behavior or suffer critical gaps in memory, the psychoanalytic basic assumption mandates that an explanation be sought.

The *locus classicus* for Reider's position is Freud's definition of the meaningfulness of the symptom in the *Introductory Lectures on Psycho-Analysis*: "Let us once more reach an agreement upon what is to be understood by the 'sense' of a psychical process. We mean nothing other by it than the intention it serves and its position in a psychical continuity" (40). Another *locus* is the opening of *The Interpretation of Dreams*:

> In the pages that follow I shall bring forward proof that there is a psychological technique which makes it possible to interpret dreams, and that, if that procedure is employed, every dream reveals itself as

a psychical structure which has a meaning and which can be inserted at an assignable point in the mental activities of waking life. (1)

Freud practiced neurology until he was forty. He had been trained in a very literal, physiological associationalism, a stimulus-response theory of animal nerve structure and function. Associationalism depicted the quantity of excitation produced by an organism's experience traveling through the nervous system toward motor discharge. Associationalism's basic principle was that the nervous system's function was to keep the level of excitation constant.

When Freud began to develop psychoanalysis, he adapted associationalism creatively, substituting thoughts and emotions for nerve tissue. His first psychoanalytic works, most notably the *Studies on Hysteria* written with Joseph Breuer between 1893 and 1895, explained hysterical symptoms as the shunting of excitations associated with painful memories into "symptomatic behavior." These symptoms expressed painful memories in distorted form, releasing energy associated with the memories without allowing them into consciousness.

Freud's second-period works, *The Interpretation of Dreams*, *The Psychopathology of Everyday Life*, and *Jokes and their Relation to the Unconscious*, written between 1900 and 1905, demonstrated the lawfulness of symptom formation. The basic assumption of psychical continuity emerged in Freud's effort to account for the energy transformed into symptoms through the logic and meaningfulness of the symptoms' distortions. Freud's famous concept of a "dynamic unconscious," which he discussed at length in the *Interpretation*, only made explicit that traumatic ideas could be removed from—and restored to—consciousness.

The concept of the ego was rudimentarily present in the associationalist *Project for a Scientific Psychology* (1887–1902) as the mechanism by which adult thinking controls excitations and defers gratification of desires in keeping with the demands imposed by reality (esp. 322ff). The *Studies* and especially the *Interpretation* also imply the ego: as the "censor" which keeps traumatic ideas from consciousness (and as a second censor which releases compromise versions once they have been sufficiently distorted).

But this model of the dynamic unconscious proved inadequate to Freud's growing understanding of child development. Although the *Interpretation* described dreams as expressing infantile wishes through regressive thought processes, it did not discuss the instinctual endowment with which children enter life, or the child's conflict with his parents over the regulation of his instincts.

Freud treated these developmental issues five years after the *Interpre-*

tation, in *Three Essays on the Theory of Sexuality*. He argued that the child modeled part of his or her psyche on the image of the disciplining parent, and that this part continued to judge the child as the conscience or superego. Only with further development was this conscience split again to create a mediating agency more sensitive to reality: the ego. Freud elaborated this concept of the ego in *Group Psychology and the Analysis of the Ego* (1921) and *The Ego and the Id* (1923).

It's necessary to disregard the commonplace meaning of ego as "narcissism," as in "he has a big ego." Psychoanalysis classifies narcissism as instinctual energy employed as self-love, or self-esteem. Nor should "ego" be understood as "self-image," which is not a dynamic concept and thus has a limited role in psychoanalysis.

Psychoanalysts would only chuckle to find the ego "discovered" as the mechanism of choice in language use, for no other agency could serve that function. Freud juxtaposed the ego as synthesizer and reality-observer to the id as the seat of instincts, and to the superego as the source of self-criticism. By definition, all behavior, regardless how instinctually-driven or conscientious, is the product of the ego's synthesis: analysts speak of, say, "id-derivatives" rather than of pure "id-expressions." Analysts never speak of a person *lacking* an ego, but rather of the ego's weakness or strength—its capacity to synthesize, the weight of demands which it can integrate, the degree of its autonomy in relation to particular demands. In particular, analysts consider whether or not a person's ego is tyrannized by his conscience.

Freud always spoke of the ego as a *body* ego—sensitive to reality from its grossest to its most refined aspects. We should therefore understand that a student's writing is only one of countless acts of synthesis performed every day. To the extent that the student recognizes that the elemental skills developed in writing can serve the rest of life, writing instruction is promoted.

Berthoff is right, then, to insist that interpretation is an ordinary activity. Freud's understanding of the ego implies that we should present composing to our students as continuous with their most successful integration of experience in ordinary life. We should understand that from a Freudian point of view the type of composition teaching that Berthoff has defined does nothing other than help students develop their egos' powers, and there may be no more valuable thing that a teacher can do.

Language was critical to Freud's conceptualization of the ego—and from the first. The *Project* argued that the possibility of associating a memory with a gratification becomes possible when the memory can be fixed to a word. Freud concluded that language "is the highest, securest form of cognitive thought-process" (374). He considered language a necessary condition of consciousness: "not until the sensory residues of verbal presentations had been linked to the internal processes [did] the latter themselves gradually became capable of being perceived" (*Totem and Taboo* 64). From Freud's perspective, teachers cannot be too emphatic about writing as a way of thinking: the writing of words, like the evolution of words, makes thought actual and manipulable.

Berthoff published in *Correspondences Four* my argument that it is unprofessional and dangerous to play therapist to our students—that in doing so we are not only acting unprofessionally and undermining our public identities as teachers, but actually colluding with our students' punitive superegos in splitting good from bad. But composition teachers are entitled to a psychoanalyst's awareness that every person manages conflict every day, in the best way he or she can. We are entitled to understand that the ego manages conflict from three types of demands: instinctual impulses, judgments of conscience, and considerations of reality.

Freud spoke of the ego as *sublimating* the instincts, transforming their undifferentiated emotional energy for the attainment of higher purposes, "higher" defined as the possibilities for success and pleasure afforded by the community and the non-human reality. The emergence of the superego and ego in late childhood is the first sublimation: in the rush of the infant's development, and under a good deal of parental consternation, he accepts his own thoughtful, cooperative action as an alternative to his infantile imperative that every wish be gratified.

Education should give the ego new ways to sublimate the instincts and manage conflict, to mediate its internal and external reality. But the mediating capacity of the ego is threatened by the superego. The ego emerges only as the extrication of a less critical attitude toward reality from the internalized parental conscience. The ego emerges tinged with parental criticism.

In his analysis of depression, "Mourning and Melancholia" (1917), Freud depicted most directly the superego's potential to overpower the ego. Faced with the loss or defection of a loved one, the ego is flooded not only with demands to adjust to a radically different reality but with its rage at the loss. But the supergo will not tolerate the ego's expressing such anger against the lost or unfaithful loved one. Instead, the superego substitutes the ego itself for the lost "object" as the target of the ego's wrath. Under the superego's direction, the ego criticizes itself with all the anger of its loss. The ego feels the result as feelings of worthlessness, lethargy, sleeplessness, self-hate, self-destructiveness, all dominated by the sense that "I" am contemptible.

Our students' tendency to defeat our teaching by working too literally or too slavishly derives from the continued interference of superego with ego's realistic and synthetic functions. There may be no clearer pedagogic example of the superego's directing the ego to attack itself than the response of a certain type of idealistic student to a truly unsatisfactory teacher. A less idealistic student will write off the teacher and the course; the idealistic student will make every mental contortion to excuse the teacher and assume the fault as his or her own. The superego of such a student holds the teacher above criticism. It must therefore override the ego's perception of reality. It does so by directing the ego to criticize itself. The greater the effort necessary for the student to deny the teacher's failings, the more intense must be the student's feelings of incompetence.

Whether or not structuralism has an interest in mediation, psychoanalysis does not need the full power of its basic assumption to explain the style-shifting of Labov's Harlem preadolescents. These youths express themselves quite directly. Their rates of "be"-deletion vary with other, more overt expressions of their personal solutions to the conflict between peer loyalty and adult authority. Labov showed, for example, that the preadolescents with the highest rates of nonstandard linguistic forms were, on the one hand, the most popular members of their clubs, and, on the other, had the worst records of school truancy and misbehavior. Their rates of "be"-deletion are direct products of the ego's mediating the values (to id, superego, and external reality) of peer loyalty in opposition to adult values. The Harlem preadolescents did not hide their sense of who they understood themselves to be. They displayed little of what the psychoanalytic basic assumption explains best: "inexplicable" gaps and "meaningless" behavior.

Composition teachers, however, encounter a good deal of seemingly meaningless behavior. Perhaps none is more vexing than that of the student who begins an assignment, finds his work "all wrong," tears it up, starts over, hates it again, and so on, and declares to us that he or she "just can't write."

In "Writing Without Confidence," I tried to show how the basic assumption and observation alone might help us to understand one type of problem student, the student who feels that his problem is that he "lacks confidence." With the assumption of a psychical continuity and the evidence of our teaching experience we can infer that such a student placed "success" and "failure" in stark opposition and then "failed" to prevent the real or fantasized punishment that accrues from loved ones or internal voices, punishment for "success." "I lack confidence," I argued, was a thinly camouflaged expression of "I need to disavow confidence so as not to succeed dangerously." The pedagogy for reducing the idealization of success is, I argued, to turn writing into modest practices which build strengths without raising conflict.

The concepts of the idealizing superego and the integrating, reality-testing ego were implicit in that discussion of the student lacking confidence, but it used only the basic assumption as a theoretical warrant. Because Freud derived id, ego, and superego from the basic assumption, we might employ them here as the assumption's corollaries.

Once again, a psychoanalyst could only chuckle: Anna Freud explained the student "who just can't write" in the chapter on "Restrictions of the Ego" in *The Ego and its Mechanisms of Defense* (93–105), the premier post-Freudian textbook of ego psychology. My discussion is hardly original, at most an exercise in using the assumption of psychical continuity with id-ego-and-superego.

We might first consider what stake each of Freud's three psychical agencies has in writing.

First, because external reality mandates the assignment, the ego is responsible for the student's awareness of the assignment. Conversely, as synthesizer of responses to reality, the ego is responsible for writers' "psychopathologies of everyday life": papers left at home, deadlines misunderstood or forgotten, not to mention "howlers" and other telling errors in the writing itself.

In play with language and ideas, the id achieves pleasure sublimated not far from sensuality. It may find the more sublimated pleasure of self-esteem from a successfully completed writing task. In short: there is no question that the id has a stake of gratification in writing.

Finally, the hostile criticism obviously expressed when one sheet of paper after another is crumpled and thrown on the floor can only emanate from conscience—superego. When the student mounds paper wads on the floor, psychoanalysis would say he is synthesizing responses to the varied demands upon him. But the synthesis is worse than niggardly to considerations of reality or to the wish for pleasure: to the id's and the ego's own interests, the ego's response is a dictatorial "No!" Until that 4:00 A.M. moment when considerations of reality finally panic the sleep deprived writer into writing a draft, the ego is generous only to the bullying conscience.

The writing teacher cannot know what particular edicts against writing the student's conscience delivers. But three general motives for superego censure have been described by psychoanalysis and can be applied to the student who "just can't write." The prohibited writing may symbolize instinctual gratification in general or some particular gratifications which the superego cannot abide. Or, if the student was nurtured to fail by adults who demeaned the student to boost their own self-esteem, conscience would regard success as a hostile act against the loved nurturer, the penalty for which is the loss of love. Or, contrastively, if the nurturer raised the student writer to believe that he is better than everyone else, completing an assignment might seem to the writer an unconscionably hostile act against classmates, if not everyone else.

Under any of these conditions, conscience would not allow the ego to progress on the writing task. The student who "just can't write" has gone one step further in fleeing not merely from a punishing showdown with the superego but from the danger signal of anxiety that the mere thought of the showdown provokes. The student's "just" tells everything: "just" means that whatever the potential gratifications, whatever the realistic demands, whatever the details of the actual work, the student will not *try*—or will try only so far as the most cursory keeping up of appearances. The student has experienced the superego's severity so uniformly that he *knows* that, should he put pen to paper, the superego will reject every fresh start. Where once the student suffered the brutality of his conscience, now the mere occasion for writing induces painful anxiety. When the defense is successful, the student who "just can't write" has no memory of the pain of either the superego's criticism or the anticipatory anxiety, and he or she may amaze us with cheerfulness and relaxation in discussing his or her profound failure. Freud explored this pattern of intensified defense in *Inhibitions, Symptoms and Anxiety*.

Composition teachers provide an invaluable service if they can install the "rule" of free writing as a sanctuary against the superego, to begin the composing process without self-criticism. But we must be realistic: if the student comes to us with a sufficiently harsh superego, it will veto the reasonable ego's acceptance of free writing, and the rationalizing ego will find an excuse why free writing doesn't work. One term later the student will find a new teacher to idealize and to whom to complain that he or she "can't write."

The student "who just can't write" is an extreme case. For the unimpeded student writer, the nature of the ego itself creates normal learning problems which need be addressed by pedagogy. Here are two suggestions:

First, the example of the Oscar Brothers suggests that the peer group is the adolescent's safe haven from adult criticism. Does the classroom return every student, regardless how mature, to early adolescence, with the teacher cast as a demanding parent? If so, will the empathetic teacher be inclined to lower the level of demand to fulfill the role of a *less* demanding parent? Instead, can the teacher employ the class in peer reviews and similar activities as an analogue to the Harlem preadolescents' clubs, to efface himself and reduce the student's tendency to project the superego's criticism into the classroom?

Second, that the ego's primary function is synthesis—and exclusion from the synthesis of alien material—has an extremely practical consequence: we can expect the most well-functioning students to reject new material until it is no longer new. It is striking how many of the ego's "defenses" which Anna Freud described are defenses against synthesis: for example, isolating, undoing, reaction-formation, denial of reality, and disavowal of one's thoughts and actions. Even among well-functioning students, the teacher must help the ego relax its defenses against the foreignness of new material. The teacher can do so by incremental repetition and by the establishment of continuity with other learning and the student's motives for learning.

It is only one step further—but beyond the scope of this essay—to realize why analytic writing must be difficult for students to learn: the synthetic nature of the ego suggests that we teach analysis as a special case of synthesis. None of this is surprising to anyone who has had the benefit of Ann Berthoff's work, who has traced her double helix of composing acts of mind, "continuous in all phases of the composing process," or heard her say that "if it doesn't happen all at once, it may not happen at all" (*Making* 6–12).

Works Cited

Berthoff, Ann E. *Forming/Thinking/Writing*. Portsmouth, NH: Boynton/Cook, 1982.

———. *The Making of Meaning*. Portsmouth, NH: Boynton/Cook, 1981.

———, ed. *Reclaiming the Imagination*. Portsmouth, NH: Boynton/Cook, 1984.

Bloomfield, Leonard. *Language*. New York: Holt, 1933.

Bruss, Neal H. "Writing Without Confidence." *Correspondences Four*. Portsmouth, NH: Boynton/Cook, nd.

Chomsky, Noam. *Aspects of a Theory of Syntax*. Cambridge, MA: MIT, 1965.

———. *Language and Mind*. 2nd enlarged edition. New York: Harcourt, 1972.

Einstein, Albert. *Ideas and Opinions*. Trans. Sonja Bargmann. New York: Dell, 1973.

Freud, Anna. *The Ego and the Mechanisms of Defense*. Rev. ed. The Writings of Anna Freud 2. New York: International Universities Press, 1966.

Freud, Sigmund. "The Dissolution of the Oedipus Complex." Trans. Joan Riviere. *The Standard Edition of the Complete Psychological Works* (hereafter, *SE*).

Gen. ed. James Strachey. 24 vols. London: Hogarth P and the Institute of Psycho-Analysis, 1953–1974. Vol. 19: 171–79.

————. *The Ego and the Id*. Trans. Joan Riviere. *SE*. Vol. 19: 1–66.

————. *Group Psychology and the Analysis of the Ego*. Trans. James Strachey. *SE*. Vol. 1: 65–143.

————. *Inhibitions, Symptoms and Anxiety*. Trans. Alix Strachey. *SE*. Vol. 20: 75–175.

————. *The Interpretation of Dreams*. Trans. James Strachey. *SE*. Vols. 4 and 5.

————. *Introductory Lectures on Psycho-Analysis*. Trans. James Strachey. *SE*. Vols. 15 and 16.

————. "Mourning and Melancholia." Trans. Joan Riviere. *SE*. Vol. 14: 239–60.

————. "On Narcissism: An Introduction." Trans. C. M. Baines. *SE*. Vol. 14: 67–102.

————. *New Introductory Lectures on Psycho-Analysis*. Trans. James Strachey. *SE*. Vol. 22: 1–182.

————. *Project for a Scientific Psychology*. Trans. James Strachey. *SE*. Vol. 1: 281–397.

————. *Three Essays on the Theory of Sexuality*. Trans. James Strachey. *SE*. Vol. 7: 123–245.

————. *Totem and Taboo*. Trans. James Strachey. *SE*. Vol. 13: vii–162.

Freud, Sigmund, and Josef Breuer. *Studies on Hysteria*. Trans. James Strachey and Alix Strachey. *SE*. Vol. 2.

Labov, William. *Language in the Inner City: Studies in the Black English Vernacular*. Philadelphia: U of Pennsylvania P, 1972.

————. *Sociolinguistic Patterns*. Philadelphia: U of Pennsylvania P, 1972.

Marmor, Judd. "Validation of Psychoanalytic Techniques." *Journal of the American Psychoanalytic Association* 3 (1955): 496–505.

Sapir, Edward. *Language*. New York: Harcourt, 1921.

Saussure, Ferdinand de. *Course in General Linguistics*. Trans. Wade Baskin. Eds. Charles Bally, Albert Sechehaye and Albert Reidlinger. New York: McGraw-Hill, 1959.

V

Wearing the Gaze of an Archaic Statue

The juggler in her suit of nerve
is eyes and hands. The rest of her
dangles soft-shoe below her shoulders,
relaxed, co-operating. She knows
that to toss things out is something
but not much, not important; is
for the sake of when, picturing
a ribboning like water spurting,
she is holding nothing.
She is on her own here;
she is not just letting go,
and her small touching skill is:
holding nothing.

Holding on, she is not a juggler.
She is you and me, hands full of things
she must practice juggling to get out from under.
She sets her feet and begins.
She smiles like Pomona, offering
3, a dozen, lifeless, bits & pieces she
can't get rid of; she presents them as
shapeliness and they lose weight.

The rhythm clarifies something, maybe her.
She settles back, a laughing fountain
pumping particles.
The order of motion emerges.
Up they loft one by one, she is tossing,
up, spheres, sticks, boxes, soft, metallic,

out with them she goes till her hands
close on nothing, are just
touched for the electric
seconds of netting the elements
with energy in air.
They drop, sprout, up, out, drop, up, & slowly
each touch makes her invisible save as
a phase of the great legislation
she proposes to obey.

MARIE PONSOT

18

The Lively Order
The Author's Authority and the Teacher as Monarch

ROSEMARY DEEN
Queens College, CUNY

The single writing class, its doors closed against the noise in the hall, works amidst the open problems of the society outside that door. We know that in the United States the school system rather than the class system, as in western Europe, initiates youths into the culture of their society. One of the demands on education in this country, therefore, is to become a better instrument of democracy. This keeps bringing into colleges the "nontraditional student," a steady source of anxiety.[1]

Anxiety arises for an ambiguous reason. Colleges are asked not only to be democratic, but to create democracy's professional elite. Yet colleges themselves find it hard to give status and professional recognition to writing teachers. Most writing courses are taught by "graduate students and other persons in non-tenurable positions" (Faigley 539). It's clear that there's a crisis of consciousness as well as a crisis of literacy. The situation brings ironically together in the writing class teachers and students with something in common that makes them both uneasy: the link of crisis and unsuccess.

Inside the writing classroom there are two local definitions of teaching/learning difficulties: the teacher's and the students'. As students see it, the problem is systematic. For one course you qualify by a test and failure. For another course, you qualify by success and then are taught your failures. From the students' perspective, in other words, the teacher is

part of a system of borders. Borders define you as someone you are not
familiar with. You become a "native," dependent on those who don't
know how to teach the person their instruments have identified.

From the teacher's perspective, certain students interfere, willfully or
haplessly, with class dialogue and work. They appear as the "third man."
In a dialogue, the "third man" is *static, noise, interference*, and the inter-
locutors unite to exclude him. The most charitable view is that certain
students are "unmotivated":

> What to do about universal education, mass education? One thing we
> have learned is that while we have the skills to produce literacy we are
> not doing it too well, because the nontraditional student for whom we
> have developed the skills doesn't seem to be motivated. (Hartman,
> Interview 69)

This formulation reveals the assumptions that are part of the problem.
Notice how powers are assigned to teachers, and lack of power—or motivation—to students.[2]

As I see it, the problem is first the lack of power in the student. Second,
and more serious, is the way the problem is located *within* the students.
I locate the problem within the teacher. The source of the students' lack
of power is the teacher.

The Alone Prolific: Entropy

In psycho-political terms, the writing class is a monarchy, the rule of
one. I realize that some teachers appear to abdicate and distribute their
power to "peer" groups, but the "peers" too often are one with the teacher
and do what teachers had done: talk, "critique," suggest improvements.
Politically and psychologically, the teacher is the party-in-power; students
are the party-out-of-power. A monarchy implies a perceptual relationship
in which the monarch's power is seen as god-like or in the *nature* of things:
"Is not God alone the Prolific?" (William Blake, *The Marriage of Heaven
and Hell*, Plate 16). A writing class is a monarchy with one source of
power, going in one direction, downstream—from teacher to students.
The party-in-power, the teacher, is the Alone Prolific.

Students are the party-out-of-power, the entropic body of the body
politic. The image of teacher "burn-out" suggests the class as an energy
sink. Energy drains away in a closed system. Whenever the teacher is the
Alone Prolific, or represents the academy as a closed community, students
are seen as having cognitive endowments and personal experience, but no
imaginable language and no literary repertory.

Problems begin with the way student differences are sorted out by the teacher's instruments: "diagnostic" tests leading to "remedial" classes. The names for these instruments seem to imply that students are not in a state of health, but the real power of the names is to suggest that the instruments are scientific. As Ann Berthoff would point out, the names are not so much scientific as technological: "brass instruments" (62–63). The teacher's need for a science-colored status and for the tools of a prior analysis make their student sort-out rapid and coarse.

The flow of power down from the teacher to the student continues in the relations between assignments and evaluation. Evaluation appears even before students write, embedded in assignments which sort out students' essays into those done right and those done wrong (Ponsot 203). Whenever *evaluation* is the teacher's response to students' essays, that response is projected as the writer's goal. Students are so well conditioned to this that their first remark in a conference is, "Tell me what my faults are," or "Tell me what you want." The teacher becomes significant as one source of the student's essay. It's as if Shakespeare had written his plays for strong editor Jonson, who returned them with instructions to blot a thousand lines—and told him which thousand. Not that Jonson might not be right, or that it was to Shakespeare's credit never to have blotted a line. But Shakespeare wrote, for better or worse, a large body of work that amply exceeds definition, by permissions he granted himself. He wrote on behalf of what he had in mind. If what he had in mind included audience response and author's profits, those represent evaluations he was free to interpret.

Teachers want to help students. But their position as the source brings power in a circle back to themselves. *They* set out to define the *writer's* problem. That establishes the curve. The writer's problem is to produce a better paper. That completes the circle back to the teacher who knows what *better* is. If the student's purpose is to write better, that means to write for the evaluation of the teacher. Then since the "new paradigm" is to work with students during "the writing process," the teacher becomes the strong editor or shadow-author, the one who has the author's authority. Here's a student interviewed two years after a writing course during which he was worked with, for one essay, through 19 pages of "rough draft" to get his key terms right. (He never did.) "I think it would be best to develop your own set [of terms] but 'cause you're trying to get a good grade you want to give them what they want. They might not want you using their ideas, but it seems like that's what they want . . . " (Bartholomae 130).

In his essay on revision in *Facts, Artifacts and Counterfacts*, Nicholas

Coles identifies two sources of revision: class discussion of the essay and the teacher's comments, but says only teacher's comments bring about "textual revision." He glances at one other possibility, what he calls "sequential revision," the effect of the incremental repetition built into the design of the course. It's odd that this doesn't bring about "textual revision," since the course is very well designed. Why isn't one of the goals of the course reached through the idea of the course embodied coherently in its ordered daily working? The answer seems to be that another principle comes in: the teacher's aim "to deliberately force a writer back into the chaos of his ideas . . . " (Bartholomae 191). This is a heroic or titanic principle. Its language would describe Milton's Satan as seen by Byron, but not darning a sock (Bruss). "Chaos" is said to do what design cannot. This discrepancy suggests how process-teaching fails to produce text or "textual revision" except by the intervention of the teacher-editor.

In the world of literary theory outside the classroom, there are live questions about the reception of texts. Michèle Barrett lays "failure to develop a theory of reading" to the fact that such a theory would have to confront the "problem of value," specifically, the "assumption that aesthetic judgment is independent of social and historical context," though we know that "refined details of aesthetic ranking [are] highly culturally specific . . . " (Eagleton 34). In a writing class untroubled by such theories of reading, the teacher simply directs power to the *problems*, the weaknesses of the writer. Naturally enough, the addition of the teacher's power augments those problems. Criticism entrains the teacher's other reading powers. Teacher power directed at making student essays *better* by teacher analysis reifies the personal and culturally specific values of the teacher. "But we can't get away from those!" Maybe not, but then it's imperative to give power to other centers of value. What do students need? Not at first to write better, but to write, from the start, on behalf of what they have in mind.[3]

As the party-out-of-power, students can hardly be seen to have anything in mind. And this is the teacher's real problem in a monarchy—the loss of power in the student. It affects teachers as Viviane Forrester, the French film-maker, says the loss of women's vision affects men: "We don't know what women's vision is." It is "what you don't see; it is withdrawn, concealed."

So what do men's eyes see? A crippled world, mutilated, deprived of women's vision. In fact men share our malaise, suffer from the same tragedy: the absence of women. (Eagleton 34–35)

So too with us teachers. We don't know what students' vision is. That vision is what we don't see. Students' lack of authority means their lack of authorship: of motivation or power, and signifies for the teacher: repression and entropy.

The Community of Differences: Energy

"Some will say, Is not God alone the Prolific? I answer, God only acts & Is, in existing beings or Men." Blake's answer locates the prolific power in "existing beings," in the Many. The Many form Blake's democratic community which Leonard Deen identifies as a community of differences:

> not the common denominator of our unique worlds of experience but the ordered structure of their totality, seen simultaneously from all the unique perspectives that make it up. (12)

An ordered structure seen simultaneously from all the unique perspectives that make it up: that is the writing class. Its structure is a structure of learning: knowledge, what the teacher knows. In a monarchy, the teacher's knowledge is "content," its explainable common denominator. But knowledge is order and is conveyed by form. In its root meanings and kin words, *order* suggests structure by images from weaving: *ordinis*, a line or row; *ordiri*, to warp; *exordiri* and *ordein*, to begin a web, to lay a warp. What we can grasp and remember is always structure. A competent teacher is the active agent of an inner order, the order of what s/he has in mind, conveyed to students in imaginable forms: the design of the course, the shape of assignments, the way of class working, and the reception of texts. This means, as Marie Ponsot says, that teachers structure the materials of the course—not students' responses. Students' responses can't be wrong—though they will all be different—because each student works by imagining the structure.

And will the student write anything of value, anything the teacher-reader can pay attention to? Each student, writing on behalf of what s/he has in mind, will write what we can take as literary art, will author writing that has priority over evaluation. This is the principle: "All writing is literary creation, unique and various, and can't be analyzed ahead of time. Analysis is the *re*-organizer; it cannot bring the body to life."[4]

Native Writing: "Raising It Right Up"

An ethnologist imagines the difference of other worlds and cultures. To imagine the difference makes scholarly work possible by enabling the scholar to put aside value judgments, which we know are socially and historically dependent. In the history of literature we can see what the levying of value judgments means: that it's precisely the *original* parts of writing we won't recognize. Any Blake critic knows parts of Blake he wouldn't have been able to keep his hands from if he had been Blake's editor. Emily Dickinson's early editors did not keep their hands from her text. Only scholarly editors have served the strikingly original author, because they, like historians, know that you don't tamper with the evidence.

Studying Native American literary texts, Karl Kroeber says that even "if we are inexperienced in Indian literatures, [we] are not innocent and unprejudiced readers" (2). In order to read such a text, he makes a critical hypothesis: "we have to hypothesize [this as] a work of art" (17). Then we can study and observe, and pay attention. There may be baffles, but once the reader is committed to the hypothesis of art, baffles call out reading skills. The hypothesis creates a point of view from which, as new observations are made, baffles are no longer "noise." Observations keep creating new points of view. "Noise" is reversed and added to the information.

Dennis Tedlock gives us the Zuni word *ana k'eyato'u*, what we call chant, and the Zuni call "raising it right up" (Kroeber 45). Chanting is the ritual equivalent of sustaining attention. Our task is to pay attention, observe how a text is written, instead of summing up our evaluations of it. Making observations raises it right up.

As an example, take the way Tedlock studies one version of the Zuni creation myth. He considers how the Word of the Sun-Father carried down to the moss people inviting them out into the light is a beginning Word, the beginning of a world. He thinks of Ricoeur's saying that hermeneutics reveals the "destination of discourse as projecting a world" (51), and he considers saying that the Father's Word projects the world. But he pauses. He looks more closely at the Zuni term that defines this Word: "*yulhahna: lha-* means important or even *too* important, too much, but the *-hna* on the end makes that negative and the *yu* on the front puts the word in the indeterminative: *yulhahna*, 'sort of not too important,' or the word is of 'indeterminate importance.' It is a word of *some* impor-tance, but perhaps not too much" (52). Tedlock might have simply taken Ricoeur's word, his authority. But observation showed him that "the word projects a world" suggests something "too inevitable." Indetermi-nacy—"sort of not too important"—was the key to reading the text. We don't know the value of indeterminacy. The hypothesis that the work is a work of art doesn't tell us whether the art is good or bad. But it does permit baffles to come into view, and the recognition of baffles encourages attention and literary observation. Textual attention raises it right up.

These ethnologists are much more tactful in interpretation, work more at observation than the average literary critic. They have rejected the hierarchy of Authority and Native implicit in the old anthropological distinction between "a telling *about*" the story and "a *doing* of" it, a position that limits the native to the *doing* and leaves the "commentary and interpretation entirely up to the ethnologist" (Kroeber 48). There is a similar distinction in writing classes where the student is *doing* the writing, and the teacher is *telling about* it. Tedlock places himself in the same body politic as his Native American authors by acknowledging their authority over their texts.

But aren't these texts different from the ones students create in Freshman English? Not in the way we receive them nor in the way that students, like all writers, create their own voice and language by writing. Like any other element in literature, language is not "out there" in home or street, neighborhood or culture. Lexicons and grammars are out there. But literature is the virtual language writers make out of their native languages. It's never the same as the common denominator of all the local languages. The most direct and economical way of developing one's own language is to develop it into literature. Ordinary language is always getting to be a language writers can think with by being made into flexible, open sentences, into pithy, elegant sentences, into images, and then being worked and worked again until it breaks into metaphor. Paying attention to how sentences work teaches writers to pay attention to thinking, to see that their sentences work as much to the point as possible. Working on the given language, the native tongue, by a shaping-writing is literary creation. Originated by a person, it is what Blake called "Original & Characteristical" (Erdman 654).

Writing, literary creation, means that the author originates the text, the texture, and in a special sense, creates the context. Broadly speaking, the author's context is her whole culture shown in the web of her feelings, perceptions, attentions, mental structures. In a narrow sense, however, the context of her writing is the whole body of her writing. A beginning writer, then, must first create her context as a matrix. The first writings are a matrix for the writer's consciousness. Without that, the writer will hardly experience authorship and recognize her authority. Gradually within that body of work, what the writer did, including the "mistakes," forms the writer's recognition of the significance of choice: the writer's own rules for writing well, her own repertory, her repeatable and un-mistake-able acts. So she builds the autonomy that enables a writer to continue to work and learn.

In the opus of a professional writer one sees pieces that are moments of rest, of consolidation, of experiment, along with things one wishes the author hadn't bothered to write. All of these were the necessary context for the perfected works. In the same way we can read, at the end of the semester, the folio of each student's written and rewritten work. We can see that early work we thought callow or tiresome may still seem so, but was also the writer's trial of an idea, the initial stroke of what turned out to be Original & Characteristical.

We have been talking about a crux, where intersecting points of view make the reality we see. When all the essays are written, they can be read backwards: *analytically*, or forwards: *developmentally*. While they are actually being written, they cannot be read "forwards" by the inexperienced writer. But they can be read with observant, literary, professional attention by a teacher, so as to make the "backwards" and "forwards" possible.

The Third Man

The single classroom sees itself as a local truth. Behind its doors, the teacher's dominance turns it into a monarchy of one voice. We need to consider the way in which the usual writing class is a talking class and works almost entirely orally.

The writing class becomes a discussion class because in it, as in every other class, reading has the priority. "Well, reading and writing are functions of each other," we say. "One involves the other." But that is simply a formula, in most cases, not a principle. A principle, a founding belief, is embedded in our assumptions and consistent practices. Here are the assumptions that yield priority to reading.

First, by "reading" teachers mean reading a *text*, and a *text* is almost by definition written by an author-not-a-student. Whatever the literary theory, the student essay cannot ordinarily be seen as a text: it has no dialogic, no sub-text, no plot nor emplotment, no structural dimension; there are no aporias to raise difficulties and spur further discoveries, no symbols and hence no hermeneutic keys; no fiction and hence no fictional modes; no narrative function and no achronological constraints; no world of discourse, no mimesis; there is no discordant concordance; no gender and genre, no writing the body, and not a jot of *jouissance*. Student writing has no textuality, in short, and cannot be "read." It can and must be "critiqued," however, and it comes into class occasionally to have its thinking difficulties analyzed or its model properties displayed. Second, writing assignments are based on reading: at one level, theses and subjects (topoi); or at another, "questions" to be discussed. Reading is also still being assigned as models for student writing.

To put reading first means beginning with all the powers and abilities of the teachers, and all the weaknesses and inabilities of the students to the fore.

But am I saying that *writing*, for students inexperienced in writing, represents their *strength*? Yes. Discussion based on reading is not an easier or a more successful mode of "composition" for students than writing. To begin with, writing puts the student in charge of timing. Time in writing is the space of leisure: composing and being composed, patience, second thoughts, and the freedom to be ordinary, non-agonistic. Writing is accessible, begins as an act of the hand.[5] The hand is the sign of ease, the knowledge that's been absorbed into the *soma*, the whole body, where obstructing self-consciousness drops away, and the person enters into habitual acts with energy, assurance, and pleasure.

When the writer is assigned a form or structure, s/he begins by originating the materials that realize that form. Working with form, what Marie Ponsot calls "generative structure" (R. Deen 5), students write directly out of their imagined perception of the form. Drawing on whatever materials the form calls for, they create significant material—and they can see its significance when they've written. The less the material has a self-evident, thematic or generalized significance, the more the writer *originates* its significance, its symbolic status: the meaning that language develops out of materials.

So to write in the terms I've described is to begin with success, with one's strengths. The only motivation integral or specific to work is success. It's important that in writing, *success* can be modestly defined. If I set out to write a sonnet, I succeed by writing one. It doesn't have to be a *good* sonnet. The student who sets out to write fifteen aphorisms by rewriting five sets of aphorisms succeeds by doing so. Success isn't necessarily to write an "A" expository essay, but to be able to produce the sufficient shape of assertion and evidence when asked to do so.

Success in talk or discussion is harder to see or define. Walter Ong, in a lifetime of scholarship on literature, rhetoric, and orality, identifies over and over the male-dominant, aggressive or agonistic mode of rhetoric: persuasion of reasoning or argument.[6] By "argument" I don't mean "going by the book" of logic, but discussion that puts a premium on *rationale*—thinking. It is usually strategic or polemical. That is, if you have no rebuttal, no counter-rationale, then you lose. Discussion is primarily oral: first in its assertive energy, its power to intersect or interrupt, its refusal to lose impetus by hesitation or deferral;[7] and second, in its timing, its power to "call the question."

"Thinking-writing" does not resemble oral discussion, oral rationale-thinking. Raymond Williams in "Notes on English Prose" describes an analytical traditional whose strengths "are in a special way, the strengths of literacy":

> . . . the composed page; the sense of time gained, time given; the mind working but also the mind prepared, in an exposition which assumes patience, reference, inspection, re-reading.(80)

It is not easy to see how class discussion in the writing class leads to, teaches, or engenders such literacy.

But someone protests, "My class is a dialogue. I listen to the Other." Some writing classes may be dialogues. Does this get us away from the monarchy of one voice? Does dialogue promote a community of differences?

"The most profound dialectical problem," says Michel Serres, "is not the problem of the Other, who is only a variety—or a variation—of the Same, it is the problem of the third man"(67). How is the Other only a variety of the Same? It's obvious when we consider that dialogue is the exchange of "reciprocal roles." That is, a dialogue is a speaker and an auditor exchanging roles. The "third man" in a dialogue is noise, static, interference (for which the French word is *le parasite*). Dialectic, says Serres,

> is a sort of game played by two interlocutors considered as united against the phenomena of interference. . . . These interlocutors are in no way opposed, as in the traditional conception of the dialectical game; on the contrary, they are on the same side . . . they battle together against noise. (66–67)

Psychologically dialogue is the exchange of roles.[8] In actual classrooms, dialogue goes on between the teacher and a group of adepts, while the back row is silent: daydreaming, indifferent, or hostile. The phenomena of interference are right there in the classroom: *"To hold a dialogue is to suppose a third man and to seek to exclude him . . . "* (67, Serres' emphasis).

Ultimately the third man is the empirical.[9] Dialogue works because of the recognition by both parties of abstract form. So *"the first effort to make communication in a dialogue successful is isomorphic to the effort to render a form independent of its empirical realization"* (69, Serres' emphasis). Abstract or ideal form is also the model of our address to students in the general language of test directions, assignments, and the voiceless language of textbooks, all of which seek to communicate, in a dialogue of teacher and taught, the ideal form of a generalization.

If we discard the model of the dialogue for the writing class, can we develop the model of the body politic beyond the monarchy, the closed system where energy flows irreversibly downstream? Obviously, we begin by keeping the "parasite," the third man. The writing teacher doesn't want to exclude the parasite because "the parasite invents something new. It intercepts energy and pays for it with information. It intercepts roast beef and pays for it with stories" (xxvii).[10] How? Serres looks at the origin of language in the living organism and at the question that information theory and thermodynamics ask, How does information gain against entropy? Since entropy is the condition of a closed system, an information system must be in some way an open system. The parasite, the unexcluded demon, opens the closed dialogue of the talking-writing class.

Information begins in biology. The number of chemical reactions in an organism is enormous:

> From a thermal and information point of view, these movements and transformations necessarily generate background noise. And this noise is certainly tremendous. (76)

Why don't we hear it?

> We are submerged to our necks, to our eyes, to our hair, in a furiously raging ocean. We are the voice of this hurricane, this thermal howl, and we do not even know it. (77)

Serres attempts to understand "this blindness, this deafness, or, as it is often said, this unconciousness. . . ."[11]

The organism functions on levels, but the levels are interlocking. At one level, the system mobilizes information and produces noise. At the next level, it integrates the information-background noise couple of the preceding level. How?

> [A] function, called ambiguity and resulting from noise, changes when the observer changes his point of observation. (78)

So far, we notice, there's no hierarchy or value judgment, simply "ambiguity."

> Its value depends on whether he is submerged in the first level or whether he examines the entire unit from the next level. In a certain

sense, the next level functions as a rectifier of noise. What was once an obstacle to all messages is reversed and added to the information. (78)

We approach an idea encountered before: the idea of unique worlds of experience as an ordered structure seen simultaneously from all the perspectives that make it up. Or the idea of studying the baffles in a native literature by observations until the baffles are added to our knowledge. If the writing class is a system of interlocking levels, and if the levels "always function as languages" (78), then the body politic of the writing class is a body of languages.

The writer operates on one level, mobilizing information and producing noise. S/he cannot hear the noise. But at the next level, the level of the observers listening to the essay, the noise is reversed and added to the information. What, from the teacher's view, is "senseless din," the problems of the writer's essay, is "made meaningful by the series of rectifiers" (80). It is not a case of the teacher's consciousness being better, finer, more rectified, better languaged than the student's. It is that meaning comes from the *series*, many sets of observations representing many points of view.[12]

We accept the parasite, noise, the third man, then, because he invents something new. When integrated, he enables the system to pass from a simple to a complex level: "what was supposed to interfere begins constructing; obstacles combine to organize; noise becomes dialect" (80).

Value judgments on students' writing—offered as information—are really the retention of static from an earlier level. It is static; teachers attempt to pass it on as information. To edit students' writing is like trying to return the unrectified noise to the first level and make the producer hear it. This undoes the complexity the system has just achieved. It is de-energizing, entropic. The parasite has intercepted the roast beef and not paid with stories or wit. He has become the churl, the refuser of festivity. It would be a mistake to invite him to dinner. The teacher cannot return noise to the earlier level except destructively, by reverting to political power. And the reversion to hierarchy destroys the language community.

The community of differences is energetic because it puts differences to work; it is realistic in a simple way about what its members have in common. "But," someone says, "differences taken this way leave out the quality and even the amount of what teachers know. They *do* know more, are more sophisticated, have more self-understanding, more capacity for analysis." Probably true. But the limitations of a class and a course mean that the more teachers try to "motivate," control and direct (even through surrogate "peers"), to edit, and to impose rewriting as a way of making writing *better*, the more they pay for control with loss of consciousness.[13] Students' language includes their lives, and their language can be made into literature: parable or wit, history or discourse, by being imagined through writing. Literature is the student writer's power, literary power.

Teaching begins with the image of an intent which the teacher can name for herself but not for others. S/he cannot directly hand over what s/he knows to others, as if knowledge were a set of objects. As objects, knowledge weighs too much. Students cannot conceive these forms as the teacher conceives them. But when the teacher "presents them as / shapeliness . . . they lose weight. . . ."[14] What s/he knows is not things, heavy with explanation, but a lively order, forms. By means of forms, the teacher's knowledge passes to the students.

In Blake's dialectic, the idea of the Alone Prolific is confronted by the idea of unique worlds. But in a community of differences, unique worlds of experience are or will seem incommensurable. We seem closed from one another, inconceivable. But not unimaginable. We "must therefore imagine the difference . . ." (L. Deen 43). And by *imagine*, of course, I mean something mundane, Susanne Langer's imagining as human image-making, allied to symbol and language-making:[15] our capacity for the virtual. Imagination is the way most persons participate in a democracy. As a monarchy the writing class is a single kingdom, the "city of communication maximally purged of noise" (Serres 68). As a democracy of differences (Ponsot 203), a writing class is a world of writers all at work. Imagining is work, "active energy—the body of the body politic . . ." (L. Deen 34).

Writing anything, teaching anything, is a lofting, a sustained action of awareness and keeping awareness in act as it patterns, tracks relationships, subjects and objects, weight, distance, by an almost electric grasp, release, and impulse. Though it sounds like magic, it's knowledge, skill, patience to put elements into play, the input of energy by a touch that lets go, to keep order alive.

Notes

1. Anxiety governs descriptions of the nontraditional student, as here: "students whose problems are grounded in massive cultural deficiencies that require extensive reading and studying as well as practice in writing if they are to be remedied." (From a talk given by Robert Scholes to the CUNY Association of

Writing Supervisors [CAWS], October 24, 1985). The suppressed metaphor of hemorrhaging makes it sound as though a transfusion rather than an education is what is needed.

2. David Bartholomae and Anthony Petrosky in a concerned discussion of nontraditional students see their *language* as the problem, the seal of their out-of-power condition: "it is something in the margin, belonging neither here nor there and preventing their participation as speakers with place, privilege or authority" (4).

3. A phrase synthesized from Marie Ponsot's chapter in *Beat Not the Poor Desk*, "Rewriting," which is the single most comprehensive, yet succinct and knowledgeable account of rewriting.

4. A remark of Leonard Deen's in conversation. I've used it before, in *The Common Sense*.

5. See Susanne Langer on the hand as a sense organ: " . . . the human hand is a complex organ in which the distribution of sensory nerves and the extremely refined musculature coincide, as they do in our eyes and ears, to implement perception. . . . " In fact, the "sensibility of the hand is not only high, but epicritical . . . " (*Mind* 2:257).

6. "The orality and concomitant agonistic mentality of early human culture persist in the Western literate, academic tradition . . . " (Ong 125, 122–28 *passim*).

7. " . . . it is clear that reading and writing constitute an intensification of 'delay time' . . . " (Hartman, *Pieces* 172). Answering the question "What can the humanities, and literary study in particular, contribute to a society in which 'communication' is the operative ideal?" Hartman answers, "mainly doubt and delay . . . " (182). "The drive for meaning," Hartman says—and this is especially pertinent to the classroom—"is as compulsive as a blood sport. But the humanities . . . [work] within and against that drive, by displacing our attention from the act of possession to the interval, the delight in aesthetic play, the freedom to interpret what is arbitrary yet must be given meaning" (180).

8. Dialogue, of course, is not limited to two people: *dia*- ("through" or "among") is not to be confused with *dis* ("twice" or "double").

9. Abstract form is not the inexact square or diagonal Socrates drew in the sand, but its ideal form. By evoking the ideal form "I eliminate the empirical, I dematerialize reasoning . . . in a single blow, we eliminate hearing and noise, vision and failed drawing; in a single blow, we conceive the form and we understand each other" (69–70). Serres' ironic parallels show the cost of "dematerializing" reasoning: we lose hearing along with noise, and vision along with failed drawing.

10. The reference here is to the French edition. The phrase occurs on page 36 of the English edition, but the translation is not very good.

11. "Everything occurs," says Serres, making the connection explicit, "as if Freud, who started from energy models of thermodynamics, had intuited, by a dynamics of language, the subsequent development of thermodynamics into information theory" (82).

12. To pay attention is to gain consciousness, to learn, but also to relinquish the center of attention—or the position upstream, at the source.

13. In a system where the unconscious of writers is taken into account (and

analyzed) but not that of the teacher, writers have no autonomy, and neither has the teacher. Serres says that when the issue is communication, "There is only one type of knowledge and it is always linked to an observer submerged in a system or its proximity. And this observer is structured exactly like what he observes" (83). So teachers can give up their special knowledge and become "one of the gang" they are teaching; or merely give up their special authority and submerge what they know in designs and forms that can be learned inductively.

14. See the poem "Wearing the Gaze of an Archaic Statue," on page 211 of this volume.

15. "The process of . . . making reality conceivable, memorable, and sometimes even predictable, is a process of imagination" (*Problems* 71). Imagination is "the source of all insight and true beliefs. Imagination is probably the oldest mental trait that is typically human—older than discursive reason; it is probably the common source of dream, reason, religion, and all true general observation" (70).

Works Cited

Bartholomae, David, and Anthony R. Petrosky. *Facts, Artifacts and Counterfacts*. Portsmouth, NH: Boynton/Cook, 1986.

Berthoff, Ann E. *The Making of Meaning*. Portsmouth, NH: Boynton/Cook, 1981.

Bruss, Neal. A reply in *Correspondences One*. Portsmouth, NH: Boynton/Cook, nd.

Deen, Leonard W. *Conversing in Paradise: Poetic Genius and Identity-As-Community in Blake's Los*. Columbia: U Missouri P, 1983.

Deen, Rosemary, and Marie Ponsot. *The Common Sense*. Portsmouth, NH: Boynton/Cook, 1985.

Eagleton, Mary, ed. *Feminist Literary Theory*. Oxford and New York: Basil Blackwell, 1986.

Erdman, David V., ed. *The Complete Poetry and Prose of William Blake*. Berkeley: U of California P, 1982.

Faigley, Lester. "Competing Theories of Process: A Critique and a Proposal." *College English* 48 (1986): 527–42.

Hartman, Geoffrey H. *Easy Pieces*. New York: Columbia UP, 1985.

———. Interview. *A Recent Imagining: Interview with Harold Bloom, Geoffrey Hartman, J. Hillis Miller, Paul de Man*. Robert Moynihan. Hamden, CT.: Archon Books, 1986.

Kroeber, Karl, ed. *Traditional American Indian Literatures*. Lincoln: U Nebraska P, 1981.

Langer, Susanne K. *Mind: An Essay on Human Feeling*. 3 vols. Baltimore: The Johns Hopkins UP, 1982. Vol 2.

———. *Problems of Art*. New York: Charles Scribner's Sons, 1957.

Ong, Walter J. *Fighting For Life: Contest, Sexuality, and Consciousness*. Ithaca: Cornell UP, 1981.

Ponsot, Marie, and Rosemary Deen. *Beat Not the Poor Desk*. Portsmouth, NH: Boynton/Cook, 1982.

Serres, Michel. *Hermes: Literature, Science, Philosophy.* Baltimore: The Johns Hopkins UP, 1982.

————. *The Parasite.* Trans. Lawrence R. Schehr. Baltimore: The Johns Hopkins UP, 1982.

Williams, Raymond. *Writing In Society.* London: Verso, 1986.

19

How to Write
Like Gertrude Stein

PHILIP M. KEITH
St. Cloud State University

Any experience with a shelf of composition textbooks demonstrates
immediately how thoroughly dominant is the concern with "functional
writing," with writing, that is, as an instrument for something else. Most
texts seem basically in sympathy with the notion that has been identified
with E. D. Hirsch, Jr. that efficiency is a kind of primary end in writing.
Hirsch's *The Philosophy of Composition* brings a Darwinian weight to an
historical argument that writing has developed as an instrument for efficient communication, and that, for students to get into "the system,"
they need to be able to communicate their thoughts as clearly and effi-
ciently as possible. This means, for writing teachers who take this way
of defining things seriously—Hirsch himself seems to have recently backed
away from such applications—learning to write means in the main learning
to master the use of such stylistic devices as parallelism and repetition,
devices that make it easier for a reader to read what has been written.

Obviously, it would be foolish to deny the value of such techniques.
It is certainly useful to learn to lay out the structure of a paragraph or
essay in the opening sentences, to avoid over-burdening the reader's capacity to order and remember detail, to use sentence structures and punc-
tuation that clarify rather than obscure relationships. But a serious
pedagogical problem arises when such skill is seen as the totality of writing
skill at the expense of seeing writing as an invitation for a reader to make

meaning. An effective pedagogy of writing must work at all levels of writing proficiency, and that means providing language experiences that test the construing faculties of the reader as a way of strengthening the capacities of the mind to conceptualize through language. That explore meaning relations as well as meaning. That are calisthenic for the reader and aim at reflexivity or even opacity of style, rather than transparency.

Notable versions of this style are sixteenth- and seventeenth-century writings in the Ciceronian manner, and more recently, in the writing of Gertrude Stein. In this essay, I am exploring some dimensions of a notion put forward by Marshall McLuhan in *The Gutenberg Galaxy*, that Gertrude Stein's significance lies in her being a model for the theory and practice of this sort of writing, and that the knowledge and method she has made available in her writing in *How to Write* and other works normally relegated to a Steinian *Obscurata* can be useful for teachers concerned with the nature and development of reading and writing abilities.

My account begins with a day when I was following Ann Berthoff's advice and using some writing classes as a research laboratory. For my experiment, I took into two classes, one in freshman composition, the other in writing and rhetorical theory for graduate and advanced undergraduate students, a passage from Stein's essay titled "Forensics" in *How to Write*:

> Will he ask them why she chose this. If they do he will be disappointed in her being so withdrawn and reminded and when will two meet one. The necessity. Further. Should hurry be advantageous more in coming than in going in adding and following. Should he be they worship welling. Their emotion welled up but admittedly they were admiring.
>
> Forensics are plainly a determination.
>
> Does and do all include obstinacy.
>
> Particularly for pleasure in clarity.
>
> She makes hours.
>
> Well what do you believe. Do you believe in ease in understanding. Do you believe in favors in accomplishment. Do you believe that they regard with forbearance their increase of rectification nor do they they bewilder and but whether in fancy they charge them and consistently they are better without followers. They should be charity without call. No noise makes tranquility a burden with help and a trouble to them to end well. Very well I thank you is why they were generous. Think forensically. How I doubt.
>
> It is more than a pleasure to dream more than a pleasure. To dream.

Were he to manage to whom would there be an obligation to oblige.
(389)

Both groups saw the passage as a farce. They read the fragments as implying that the writer did not know her grammar and they saw the lack of question marks as signs of either illiteracy or infantile rebelliousness. One student in each class made a half-hearted defense of a "poetic" quality in the passage—specifically in the sentences about the pleasure of dreaming in the penultimate paragraph. However, the intensity of the students' unanimous conviction that the writing here was plainly "wrong" came from the fact that Stein was playing fast and loose with features that are often seen with something approaching hysteria as "basic" elements of writing, the formal orthographic conventions that have become something like rules of the syntax of writing for many readers and most writing teachers. But even though the students in both classes predictably had difficulty seeing Stein's purpose in writing, they were quite capable of seeing a good deal of what was going on, of seeing that the logic of error has expressive possibilities as well as the logic of correctness.

I took the passage into the freshman composition class as a lark, wanting to see how, after taking two required quarters of composition, the students would respond to a writer who was systematically and strategically breaking basic rules that they had been putting considerable effort into mastering. I asked them what an English composition teacher might say about these sentences. One student noted that the writer didn't know how to use the period, especially in the first and second sentences. Another student whimsically observed that not only was the third sentence a sentence fragment, but a paragraph fragment as well. We chuckled over Stein's making "forensics" a plural in the fourth sentence—until we actually checked the *New World Dictionary* and found that she was right. Another student noticed the redundancy in the second sentence and suggested that everything after the first "dream" should be deleted. Another student suggested as an alternative to such radical surgery that we might put a comma after the first "dream" and drop the period after the second "pleasure."

I asked if these two last revisions made the statement true. "No," someone said, "it may not be a pleasure to dream if you're having a nightmare." The original is truer because it talks about the pleasure of dreaming pleasure. Furthermore, the misuse of the period and the resulting suspension of grammatical closure has the effect of making the sentence more representative of the dream experience.

They were beginning to see how it might be useful to think of grammar

and mechanics more as resources in the system than as rules or maxims
to be followed, and even how one might command some special power
as a user of language-acts when one can work with rules in this way.

The upper level class was invited in an optional assignment to edit the
Stein passage according to the basic principles Hirsch proposes in *The
Philosophy of Composition* as the essence of traditional textbook practice:
maximize contextual constraints at the beginning of a piece of discourse,
and limit burden on short-term memory by using parallelism, quick
syntactic closure, thematic tags and explicit transitions. I was trying to
provide an opportunity for them to see some limitations in his analysis.
Only one student managed to get through even the first paragraph, and
then the task simply became impossible even for her:

> Will he ask why? If so, she will withdraw and he will be disappointed
> they are no longer one. Necessity compels him to try. He wonders if
> rushing in will be advantageous, or if leaving the matter alone would
> be best. They would be worshipping each other, not sitting apart.
> Their emotion welled up as they eyed each other.

She seems to have quit in some irritation, commenting in her written
reflection:

> I cannot go futher with the Stein piece. It is not that I am afraid of
> saying the wrong thing. I cannot interpret such a piece without any
> contextual information. I do not feel that there is anything to be gained
> from such an exercise. It seems to be a ridiculous task.

The bothersome question she was implicitly raising was how much we
know what we know when we read. In one sense, the Stein paragraph is
nonsense language, if only because of her pleasure in using pronouns that
have no antecedents. And yet, the translation does represent meaning that
is in Stein's writing, in some special "potential" way. As in Lewis Carroll's
"Jabberwocky" the syntactic structure projects a meaning: certain kinds
of things are happening to certain kinds of things in certain kinds of
ways. Stein's structures, if we can call them that, are more than syntactic,
though syntax is a basic instrument of their making and shaping.

The student's translation has reduced Stein's meaning-relations to a
single genre—pop-romantic (drug store) fiction. She spotted the lack of
contextual information in the passage, but she also unconsciously dra-
matized in her translation how contextualizing is a driving reflex in the
reader/writer. The strength of this reflex is clearest in her version of the
first sentence where she changes "Will he ask them why she chose this."

into "Will he ask why?" The original sentence is a study in pronoun categories as an occasion for meanings to be made, an exercise, you might say, in populating a world. The student collapses all that into a question of motive. With the second sentence, she found "If so [i.e., if he does ask her], he will be disappointed they are no longer one" in Stein's more rococo "If so [what?] he will be disappointed in her being so withdrawn [she had been before, but apparently it hadn't disappointed him then] and reminded [it is unclear whether he or she is being reminded] and when will two meet one." (This sounds like getting together for a social drink, and since three is a crowd according to the most generally accepted social convention, none of my student's projected "deep communion" seems likely here.) Stein subverts conventions of meaning to throw readers back on an intensified experience of their own reading processes and ultimately to challenge the expectation that meaning is merely referential.

Predictably, my student's line of interpretive revision hits a snag with Stein's second paragraph, "Forensics are plainly a determination." In her romantic fiction, the idea of forensics, loosely translated as "formal speaking or argument" is "plainly" out of place. But Stein is reminding us that all language operations are broadly formal, are a determination, and finally require an effort—even if habit has made the effort largely unconscious. It may take some dialectical effort to make a "worship" of "welling" into a matter of planned argument, but it is well worth the effort, for without such effort in reading, the intricate weaving of language, thought and feeling in Stein's writing and the subtle possibilities of language that Stein has made available will escape us.

In the last part of this essay I will make an effort to place the activity of Stein's writing and of our reading it into a broader philosophical perspective. This experiment showed Stein as a strategic breaker of rules and conventions, as a challenger of cultural conventions of writing that limit considerations of writing as a resource for experience and thought. It would be nice to be able to say just what has been constructed when such rule-breaking dialectic is at work in writing.

Stein criticism has made some effort to answer this question. In particular, Michael J. Hoffman has seen Stein's writing activity through the philosophical screen of William James, under whom Stein studied and for whom she had a great admiration. Hoffman argues that a rhetorical motive for Stein was James' notion of abstraction as a basis of consciousness and language. Simply put, Stein seems heavily influenced by James' sense that mind works through a kind of abstracting attention paid to experience. By abstraction, James means the process of focusing on a particular feature or part of an experience of a thing, and letting that stand for the whole (28). This may help explain Stein's attraction to abstraction in the art of Picasso and Matisse, but it doesn't help very much in cracking the operational code of such anasyntax as we find in the passage on forensics. Hoffman points out, though, that Stein was clearly influenced by James' discussion of grammar and language as controlled by learned conventions, and her reaction, in Hoffman's view, is to write by systematically breaking these conventions (213–14). He does not, however, go on to answer the question of what she manages to construct for us to construe when she writes that way.

A clearer answer to that question comes up when we examine the relation between Stein's experimenting and the work of another of Stein's mentors, or what she calls "geniuses" in *The Autobiography of Alice B. Toklas*, Alfred North Whitehead. The Whitehead work that addresses the general problems of knowing and expressing in a way most applicable to Stein is *Modes of Thought*, especially the section that was the series of lectures he gave at Wellesley College in 1929, where he undertook to discuss some of the assumptions that underlie philosophical activity. Whitehead was a forthright critic of the limitations of theories of language that are based too narrowly on simple notions of empirical referentiality, on approaches to language that see its purpose as a mere conveyer of information, and hence as an instrument whose value lies in its transparency rather than its own processes. Whitehead calls the notion of "matter of fact" "the triumph of the abstractive intellect," and he argues that knowing something means not knowing it as a fact, the aim of empiricism, but knowing it as a process. Clearly, when one works from this assumption, one knows things like trees and love not from data alone but from the process of interpreting it, the process of meaning-making. Under this system, what becomes important is not the *what* that one is writing about, but the *process* of writing itself. Writing is no longer a telescope trained on objects out there, but is in itself the laboratory in which knowledge is generated by processes of focus, balance and expansion. Stein's writing is that sort of place.

For Whitehead, any theory or fact is *composed*, controlled through choices according to what is perceived as *important*. This control by choice is the basis for *understanding* which underlies expression, which leads to a definition of perspectives, all of which are sequenced in a process that works from *datum* through *form* and *transition* to *issue*. The data I sense in a pebble are composed according to choices I make concerning such matters as use or need, and that process of composition precedes understanding which in itself precedes the opportunity to use the pebble for expression. My expression with the pebble defines perspectives, which may lead to the issue of the pebble, say into a photograph or shepherd's slingshot. Whitehead focuses on knowledge knowable only through process because, in synchrony with Stein, he sees the mentality of mankind and the language of mankind as having created each other (40–41). And he sees the development of western philosophy as "hampered by the tacit presupposition of the necessity of static spatio-temporal, and physical forms of order" (88).

Whitehead also pushes us to see writing as "situational" rather than a matter of form and fact in two important respects. He observes that "the data of our experience are of two kinds. They can be analyzed into realized matter of fact and into potentialities for matter of fact" (94). Clearly, the latter form of analysis he finds more interesting than the former. He also speaks of the relation between the individual expression and the perceiving of that expression by society in a way particularly pertinent to Stein when he observes that "Nothing is more interesting to watch than the emotional disturbance produced by any unusual disturbance of the forms of process" (95). In my classes Stein's writing constituted precisely that sort of "disturbance in the forms of process." The intent of the Stein passage, rather like the intent of much of her writing, is to provoke in the reader an enhanced awareness of the broad processes of construing and constructing language. However, one needs to start from a somewhat broader perspective than my student did in order to get the full force of the passage.

Whitehead describes "importance" as "an aspect of feeling whereby a perspective will be imposed upon the universe of things felt" (11). If one takes the "Forensics" paragraph as a kind of mini-universe of things felt, then an alternative to seeing it as an expression of romantic emotion would be to see it under its title, as an effort to say what forensics are, to involve the reader in understanding forensics as a process that goes beyond such definitions as "formal argument," "formal speaking," or "judicial persuasion." The passage is a universe of reasonably discrete sentences and phrase-compositions that interact by association and implication.

The first sentence after the first paragraph, "Forensics are plainly a determination" interacts in this way with the noun-phrase "the necessity" above, and with the two sentences below, "Think forensically. How I doubt." Throughout, this passage is concerned with persuasion and disappointment. Sub-areas of meaning or expression are "sympathy," "understanding," "accomplishment," "forbearance," "charity," "clarity," "pleasure," "obligation," and "generosity." Anyone who has read Aristotle's *Rhetoric* with any care would know that all bear a relationship to forensic rhetoric. Stein's sentences pass through this universe of poten-

tialities like a particle through a cloud chamber, or in Whitehead's res-
onant phrasing, as "data for feeling diffused in the environment."

When reading—when *really* reading—this passage, we hear voices that
speak out of highly charged situations, but situations now somewhat more
complex than the emotional environments of romantic novels. The first
sentence, "Will he ask them why she chose this" is composition by
reference error, a kind of socio-babble in which the denial of any reference
point refers us to intimate knowledge of the mutability of pronoun reference. The second sentence moves into the freshman composition error
of the mixed construction as a principle of composing—"If they do, . . .
will he be disappointed . . . and reminded and when will two meet one."
This condition as defined by "If" is labeled in the following sentence "a
necessity." Then "Further," in an Alice-in-Wonderlandian sort of way,
leads our focus back to "hurry" and an emotional consummation.

So then, forensics are indeed plainly a determination that spans a
spectrum of expression between reacting to obstinacy and giving pleasure
in clarity. The sentences here illustrate this, and even in my incomplete
reading, do involve a "making of hours." Such analyses as this illustrate
Stein's interest in the relation between logic and aesthetics that Whitehead
calls "one of the undeveloped topics of philosophy" (60).

The second of the two extended paragraphs in the passage shifts from
narrative into direct address in an almost Whitmanlike manner. The voices
challenge us most insistently in the long third sentence—"Do you believe
that they regard with forbearance their increase of rectification nor do
they they bewilder and but whether in fancy they change then and consistently they are better without flowers"—an even more rococo version of
normal Steinian compositional practice. It sounds coherent enough if you
are not quite paying attention, but when you are, it drives you to a frenzy
of construing procedures that will provide the continuity between the
structures headed by "Do you believe . . . ," "nor do they . . . ," and "but
whether. . . . " The craft in the sentence-composing lies in its self-consciousness about normal "not-quite-paying-attention procedures."

Stein's primary aim here seems to me to be pedagogical as well as belle-
tristic. Reading her puts the reader in a reading workshop or a reading
lab, and the dream analogy as it is developed in the penultimate sentence
is a wonderful metaphor for such a reading experience with its process-
generating and process-focusing circularity. Gertrude Stein should have
a lot to say to teachers of basic reading and writing when her work is
effectively tapped for that sort of application. That is why I look forward
to seeing chapters in future freshman composition texts on how to write
like Gertrude Stein.

Works Cited

Hirsch, E. D., Jr. *The Philosophy of Composition*. Chicago: U Chicago P, 1977.

Hoffman, Michael J. *The Development of Abstractionism in the Writings of Gertrude Stein*. Philadelphia: U Pennsylvania P, 1965.

Stein, Gertrude. *How to Write*. New York: Dover, 1975.

Whitehead, Alfred North. *Modes of Thought*. New York: Macmillan, 1968.

20

Reclaiming Digression

SANDRA SCHOR
Queens College, CUNY

We readers are travelers in good faith. We set out like Young Goodman Brown, of two minds, on the one hand tempted by our daring into the unknown territory of a book, and at the same time faithfully expecting to come back home without getting lost. Along the way we apply good-reader habits, traversing the whole by tracking our way across the linked elements. The reader expects that parts *will* cohere, since none of us survives as a reader unless we can go on. In short, the reader-in-good-faith expects to meet, not the devil, but a writer-in-good-faith. Yet our plan is always paradoxical because the adventurous reader secretly hopes for the unexpected appearance of that devil, imagination—what Bruner has called "effective surprise" ("Creativity" 18–23). Surprise is a sign that the imagination has intervened to steer us off the expected path, though whether the writer's or the reader's creativity is responsible for our willingly going astray remains moot, susceptibility to digresssion existing of course in both.

Thus the first hallmark of digression is its exceptionality. Something along the formally composed, carefully networked route of discourse takes hold of our attention, attracting us not by how adroitly it contributes to the development of the argument, for it is rarely an element of argumentation, but by how powerfully it arrests us in its own form, its own point, its own argument within an argument. Imagination is evident

238

when we devilishly wander off to enjoy an element for its own sake and not for its immediate service to the larger work. Yet our readers' survival kit soon has us make less of it. We are challenged to make the usual sense of it, to treat it like just another quarter mile of text, to throw across a bridge no matter how makeshift.

To counter exceptionality, our unexceptional, routine skills as readers speed to our aid: we seek to establish bridges of form and meaning; to see causal connections; to reconcile unrelated elements; to construe a whole where subversive elements sabotage completeness; to reread an ambushed inference in the preceding paragraph; to undo an implication of contrast, so strong, perhaps, as to appear adventitious until we reread and recognize that the bedrock of similarities breeds the stoutest contrasts.

Everyone knows the masters of digression: Sterne, Trollope, Frost, Woolf, Swift, Montaigne, to name a few. Ah, we say, in his essay "On Cannibals" Montaigne digresses when he considers the deviousness of men of intelligence who, although they observe things more carefully, also

> comment on them; and to establish and substantiate their interpretation, they cannot refrain from altering the facts a little. They never present things just as they are but twist and disguise them to conform to the point of view from which they have seen them; and to gain credence for their opinion and make it attractive, they do not mind adding something of their own, or extending and amplifying.

Hence, he suggests, we need as informant "either a very truthful man, or one so ignorant that he has not material with which to construct false theories and make them credible, a man wedded to no idea." The man who reports to Montaigne on the region in Brazil where cannibalism exists is precisely such an ignorant—and eminently trustworthy—man. Montaigne understands that he has made a lengthier than necessary detour; he is not so much establishing the credibility of his informant as he is aggressively seizing this point in his narrative to advise us about the credibility of all informants. For generalizing is an act of aggression. In fact, the connection between *di*gression and *ag*gression is often more than incidental; every digression violates the reader's habit and intent, at the same time that it fulfills the possibility of a rendezvous with the devil. Montaigne makes his exit from the digression unmistakable: "Now, to return to my argument" (108). At this point he introduces the central concern of his essay, which is that "we all call barbarous anything that is contrary to our own habits," carefully pointing out that the man "wedded to no idea" has with his own eyes seen that *corpses* are eaten. Then he reasons with us that roasting and eating a body already dead is far less barbarous than the sixteenth-century practice "to roast it by degrees, and then give it to be trampled and eaten by dogs and swine," especially "under the cloak of piety and religion" (113).

How quickly, if at all, are we obliged to notice that our resilient attention has been led astray by an imaginative act? We trust Montaigne and read through the essay, our global response to the work owing as much to his impertinent digressions as to his central argument. Our response to the work of Montaigne is to both its logical and sub-logical elements; they combine to enlarge our respect for his enterprise (Haswell 406). Rather than denounce him as duplicitous, we relish his irrepressible mind, a mind incapable of reducing digressive thoughts to shadows falling across the main path, but which is instead driven to erecting digressive episodes in their entirety as landmarks. They call forth counter landmarks of the reader, which sprout up as a result of the reader's deviousness, antic thoroughness, individuality, concession, skepticism, openness, and charm—mirror images of the writer's own. In another sense, digression reveals the writer in that it re-creates the imagination of the writer in the reader.

In Hegelian terms the pleasure of art is born twice, once in the spirit of the artist and again in the spectator; Hegel says in his lectures on the Philosophy of Art that it is "essentially a question, an address to a responding breast, a call to the heart and spirit" (qtd. in Wallace 383). The experienced reader is therefore the flexible, imaginative reader who through digressive adventures enlarges his or her capacity to make meaning. The digression works "against" the form in the same way that a porch leans against a building for support, the broad, solid structure of the whole strengthening and embracing the appendage. But for the reader the digression has a good many more privileges. More than a literary veranda, it serves as a door, opening a way for the reader to enter the main edifice, linking the elemental nondiscursive and the orderly discursive. It belongs, in its quirky subversiveness, even more than does the mainstream of the work, to both spectator's and artist's imagination. Ann Berthoff saves *imagination* "to name only the nondiscursive," and therefore agreeably uses it as the speculative instrument it is (67). Digression, as we know it, is precisely that, the speculative instrument of a speculative instrument.

As teachers, we are promoters of the speculative, for that is our calling, and we call to our service that other, even greater, instrument that speculates finely for the imagination, the dream. Dreams occur almost spitefully, as do digressions, without transitions or expressed logical relations. Freud has shown how dreams disguise what is important; the *manifest* dream makes a remote connection or a blurred connection to the *latent* dream content (168, *passim*). The writer's power like the dreamer's comes out of the unconscious, that dangerous, devilish, Hawthornian terrain. Profound psychic connections require intense work if they are to be uncovered. The first revision of a draft of writing often calls for "digression-work," just as the interpretation of a dream calls for "dream-work"; now the composition teacher, not the therapist, recognizing the gaps that exist between digressions and the "latent" content of a student's essay, questions the writer in such a way as to elicit connections and reconcile inconsistencies. The manifest dream, like the digression, "does not express logical relations. . . . It has no 'but,' 'therefore,' 'because,' or 'if' " (Fromm 71), and the pedagogic analogy to performing the "work" of the imagination applies; I have watched students discovering their unexpressed connections (Schor, "Revising: The Writer's Need" 116–24), and I sense that the same kind of energy that interprets a dream integrates a digression. A hot observation, an intensely felt qualification, a surprising juxtaposition of indwelling thoughts that resists logical connection, some previously held knowledge that impinges on a recent event either supporting or abusing the connection—these come to the aid of the reader's unconscious desire for art, the unconscious willingness to become the "responding breast."

The writer of the digression (a figure similar to the one Fromm calls the dreamer/spectator in a dream) (24–33) is often indifferent to the dislocations of logic and unembarrassed by his own theatricality. Readers are willing to be held in this embedded drama if the writer's narrative is only good enough to hold them. Digressors, like dreamers, have something of the exhibitionist about them; here is where censorship is cut away at the knees, for the reader, also like the spectator/dreamer, is no censor. The reader is greedy and willing to look with both eyes at whatever relationship comes his or her way.

What then *is* a digression? The digression is in itself an imaginative act. In the tradition of romance, digressive episodes make more urgent claims on the hero and on ourselves than the quest itself. Digression, even in speculative non-fiction prose, is dangerous, pleasurable, narcissistic. It unsettles the reader. It creates a new coherence by risking the available one for a limitless aside. In fiction it displaces the fictive world (we will deal with that notion again later). In both, digression is the outcome of rhetorical drives, easily tolerated in an oral tradition, to arrest and apprehend ideas hitherto unconnectable, an acting out of an unconscious indiscretion that is a kind of exhilarating free fall in an otherwise determined universe.

But digression is not error. It is not a substitute for what is proper or correct, like a slip of the tongue, but a supplement to what is whole and correct. Does it then become part of the whole or does it stand outside of the whole? Do elements laid side by side without connectors, or those in Samuel Johnson's words "yoked together by violence," end asunder, or do those privileged by imagination drift finally and permanently into an embrace thus forever to remain in the reader's mind? If the metaphysical poets are any indication, Johnson's position notwithstanding, we have long since allowed the "violent" elements of a conceit to cool into art. Using Johnson's criterion of naturalness, we ask: Is the digression far-fetched? Is it labored? Yet, digression is not metaphor. Metaphor can surprise us, he says in his dispute with the metaphysical poets, but it must be natural (22–31). Metaphor at its peak is so natural as to be necessary. It does not interrupt. It hurls the idea forward with its suddenly concrete and exact rendering. Its appeal is at once to intellect and feeling. Digression creates a rupture in the discourse for other discourse; that is, it is non-discursive but in a wholly discursive way. It has a natural, though not a necessary, relationship and is characterized chiefly by its detachableness rather than by its far-fetchedness and remoteness from the text, though they may exist. Finally, though it need not intensify feeling or appear miraculous as metaphor does, if a digression is not in itself interesting, it is nothing.

One would think that the threat of detachment were enough of a risk to discourage writers from digressing. And some are discouraged. In a discussion of digression in *Beowulf*, Adrien Bonjour says a digression "must have an element inappropriate or irrelevant to the main narrative." "An episode," he says, "is a moment which forms a real whole and yet is merged in the main narrative." A digression (his example is the passage on Hygelac) is "an adjunction and generally entails a sudden break in the narrative" (xiii). But true digressors digress, willy-nilly, for digressions speak their language: digressors are disclaimers, confessors, ironists, cynics, mind-changers, and especially reporters of facts. Consider, for example, "truth" breaking into Robert Frost's poem "Birches" "with all her matter-of-fact about the ice-storm." Here is Frost's voice at its most accurate. A desire to make room for reality in the imaginative world is sufficient to justify digression. Mary McCarthy's essay "The Fact in Fiction" proposes that the inclusion of fact is not merely desirable; it is the stamp of the novel.

The distinctive mark of the novel is its concern with the actual world, the world of fact, of the verifiable, of figures, even, and statistics. If I point to Jane Austen, Dickens, Balzac, George Eliot, Tolstoy, Dostoevsky, the Melville of *Moby Dick*, Proust, the Joyce of *Ulysses*, Dreiser, Faulkner, it will be admitted that they are all novelists and that, different as they are from a formal point of view, they have one thing in common: a deep love of fact, of the empiric element in experience. Most of the great novels contain blocks and lumps of fact— refractory lumps in the porridge of the story. [Some readers] skip these "boring parts" to get on with the story, and in America a branch of publishing specializes in shortened versions of novels—"cut for greater reading speed." Descriptions and facts are eliminated, and only the pure story, as it were the scenario, is left. But a novel that was only a scenario would not be a novel at all.

Are we to understand, at its simplest, that anything tangential to the narrative is digressive? Think of *Moby Dick* without the chapter on "whiteness," *The Magic Mountain* without the passages on tuberculosis (McCarthy 250–51); or even Updike's *Roger's Version* without the opposing worlds of academic theology and computing.

As telling as McCarthy's essay is about "fact," it is just as telling about what we have been calling digression. Digression, with its sneer, arrogance, assertion of fact, forthrightness, nostalgia, and compulsiveness of the writer to reveal what she or he knows, uncovers reality as the writer yields to it. As I noted earlier, digression displaces the fictive world by nudging it into the real world. In Julian Barnes' novel *Flaubert's Parrot*, his factual "digressions" about Flaubert re-enact the narrator's marriage and his forays into biography. In the end, one must reread the work in order finally to put to rest the notion that biographical "digressions" interrupt the novel and affirm instead that we have been reading a complex and imaginatively constructed novel. Interruption and digression bring forward the imagination and displace our assumptions about the world of discourse.

If digressions belong to the whole work rather than stand outside of it, what is it that connects digressions to the main text? Can a given digression be slipped in anywhere? Do digressions generate an ironic comment on the text? In what manner are they detachable? In a discussion of medieval rhetoric and its link to sermons, I was amused to read that in Cicero's *Rhetoric*, "the 9th ornament is Digression, which is equivalent to Transition. It occurs when one proceeds artistically from one part to another. A reader of Cicero's *Rhetoric* can see that this is improperly called digression. If digression is considered as something incidental, it does not belong in a sermon. But the digression which we are discussing here consists of a certain skillful connecting of two principal statements by verbal and real concordance" (Murphy 353). Perhaps the connection between digression and transition runs deeper than Murphy's passage suggests. Cicero apparently has grasped the notion that the intention of a digressing writer is to connect parts through apparent deviations from the main trajectory, deviations that often deepen and extend the argument and provide a new understanding.

Digressive material finds its way in because the shape of the whole is constantly changing, owing to the persistence of free association, or the insurgence of unexpected and idiosyncratic similarity, or black/white contrast, or dozens of other unconscious seductions. The less structured a work, the greater our license as writers to digress and as readers to overlook displacement. Sub-logical connectors tie digression to the mainstream of the work. Strictly logical material has a greater freedom of movement within a work. If the parts are logical, logic and not order holds the parts. Recent research into cohesion shows that ties between parts also exist between remote sections of a text and are not necessarily limited to adjacent parts (Bamberg 418). Remoteness introduces the role of memory into the issue of digression. Remoteness refers not only to the remoteness of living experience and linguistic experience of the reader, but to "the way in which during the reading the reader keeps alive what he has already elicited from the text. At any point, he brings a state of mind, a penumbra of 'memories' of what has preceded, ready to be activated by what follows, and providing the context from which further meaning will be derived. Awareness—more or less explicit—of repetitions, echoes, resonances, repercussions, linkages, cumulative effects, contrasts, or surprises is the mnemonic matrix for the structuring of emotion, idea, situation, character, plot—in short, for the evocation for a work of art. . . . For the experienced reader, much of this has become automatic, carried on through a continuing flow of responses, syntheses, readjustment, and assimilation. Under such pressure, the *irrelevant or confusing referents for the verbal symbols evidently often are ignored or are not permitted to rise into consciousness*" (Rosenblatt 57–58, emphasis mine). In other words, according to Rosenblatt, the experienced reader suppresses irrelevancies. I grant a greater degree of skill than does Rosenblatt to the experienced reader, who under the spell of an interesting writer is not at all passive, but drives collaboratively through material supplying relationships where none are explicitly stated and parlaying verbal impediments into literary possibility. The good reader does not get lost, for digressions, work of the devil though they appear, suspend the narrative; they elevate it, adding a steeliness to the stretched span, increasing the tensile strength of good discourse.

Consider that phenomenon known as the Zeigarnik Effect, named for the Russian psychologist who held that tasks interrupted are more likely to be completed and remembered than tasks not interrupted, especially when these tasks have a clearly felt structure (Bruner, *Toward a Theory* 119; Schor, "Alternatives" 48–51). Zeigarnik's psychological proposition refers to readers as well as to writers. The digressions in a well-focused piece of writing are not merely tolerated; they lend memorability and excitement to a work precisely because the reader is driven to overcome the digression from which he or she longs to return to the trajectory of the writer. It is another case of "plot as desire . . . prolonging the detour and more effectively preparing the final discharge" (Brooks 139).

But perhaps best of all, digressions have their own intrinsic value, memorable for what they impart and for the romantic drama that they stage between their own heady extravagance and the decipherment of the main text. Good digressive activity is inherently satisfying, but at the same time it creates two possibilities: first, digression destabilizes the narrative, driving writer and/or reader back to complete the text within the shape of the original structure, which has already taken hold; or, second, digression is a significant part of composing; it is embedded in the shape of what is being written, thereby changing it and offering both writer and reader a new coherence.

Still, as teachers we know that digressions have liabilities for the inexperienced writer. Liabilities often arise, not out of the failure of the digression, though that may occur, but out of the writer's inadequacy to render the reader committed to finishing the work. In the case of an experienced reader, when a digression undermines the unity of a piece, either the writer has lost his or her sense of proportion, or the intrinsic value of the digression outweighs the value of the main text. Confusion and distraction in the reader are attributed to weakness in the main narrative more than to the "flaw" of digressing. The writer must weigh such questions as these: Is the digressive passage too long, i.e., is it out of proportion to the scale of the whole work? Do I need to exit from the digression under a prominent transition? Does the tone or style of the passage conflict with those of the main narrative? If the digression is a kind of illustration, is it gratuitous, repetitive? Is the writer's thought pattern more visible than the argument itself? Would the reader's perception be significantly altered were the digression omitted? Or, to ask the question another way, does the digression fail to produce harmonious resonances?

Does it fail to create a reciprocity of pressures by means of which words influence each other, floating like Chagall figures to breathe imagination into the whole work?

How, finally, can digressions widen our contributions as composition teachers? In those kinds of writing that are speculative and reflective (Hairston 445), we expect the student's speculations to go beyond the rigors of form just as we expect them to go beyond the rigors of topic. The teacher sees into first drafts with special scrutiny and hope (Schor, "Revising: The Writer's Need" 123) for here is where the unconscious with its powerful span always operating, raises up a student paper, and here is where the teacher reclaims digression and its surpassing possibilities.

Works Cited

Bamberg, Betty. "What Makes a Text Coherent?" *College Composition and Communication* 34 (1983): 417–29.

Barnes, Julian. *Flaubert's Parrot*. London: Jonathan Cape, 1984.

Berthoff, Ann E. *The Making of Meaning*. Portsmouth, NH: Boynton/Cook, 1981.

Bonjour, Adrien. Preface. *Digressions in Beowulf*. By Bonjour. Oxford: Blackwell, 1950. i–xvi.

Brooks, Peter. *Reading for the Plot*. New York: Knopf, 1984.

Bruner, Jerome S. "The Conditions of Creativity." *On Knowing: Essays for the Left Hand*. Cambridge: Belknap P of Harvard UP, 1962.

———. *Toward a Theory of Instruction*. Cambridge: Belknap P of Harvard UP, 1967.

Freud, Sigmund. *The Interpretation of Dreams*. New York: Avon, 1965.

Fromm, Erich. *The Forgotten Language*. New York: Rinehart, 1951.

Frost, Robert. "Birches." *Poetry and Prose*. Ed. Edward Connery Lathem and Lawrence Thompson. New York: Holt, 1972. 54–56.

Hairston, Maxine. "Different Products, Different Processes: A Theory About Writing." *College Composition and Communication* 37 (1986): 442–52.

Haswell, Richard H. "Organization of Impromptu Essays." *College Composition and Communication* 37 (1986): 402–15.

Johnson, Samuel. *Lives of the Poets*. Ed. George Birkbeck Hill. New York: Octagon, 1967.

Kinneavy, James L. *A Theory of Discourse*. New York: Norton, 1971.

Montaigne, Michel de. *Essays*. Trans. J. M. Cohen. Harmondsworth: Penguin, 1958.

Murphy, James J. *Rhetoric in the Middle Ages*. Berkeley: U of California P, 1974.

Rosenblatt, Louise M. *The Reader, the Text, the Poem*. Carbondale: Southern Illinois UP, 1978.

Schor, Sandra. "Alternatives to Revising: The Proleptic Grasp." *Journal of Basic Writing* 6 (1987): 48–54.

————. "Revising: The Writer's Need to Invent and Express Relationships." *The Writer's Mind.* Ed. Janice N. Hays, *et al.* Urbana: NCTE, 1983.

Wal[lace], W[illiam] and [Sir] J[ames] B. Ba[illie]. "Hegelian Philosophy." *Encyclopedia Britannica.* 1957.

21

Romancing
the Prose

LOUISE Z. SMITH
University of Massachusetts, Boston

As you recall from our tale always already in progress, a shipwrecked man washes up on an island. He scans the seaward horizon but finds it as empty as his memory. All he knows is that the name-tag on his shirt reads Hector Scribbly. No islander recognizes him. "I must have come from across the sea," he surmises. In time he learns the language, goes to graduate school, writes his Ph.D. thesis on Chaucer, lands a job teaching mostly writing, and becomes comfortably assimilated. Still, he likes to walk on the beach. From his doctoral seminar in Anglo-Saxon, he knows that the hero-on-the-beach (to whom something shining, maybe a sail or a helmet, appears at the beginning or conclusion of a journey) is an archetypal figure of decision and discovery. Maybe on the beach he too will see something shining with import, something to remind him why he left home.

One day the castaway finds on the sand a bottle containing a message (Walker Percy tells this part of the story). The next day, another arrives. Eventually, hundreds of bottles wash up on the beach, and the castaway naturally wants to know three things: *where* they came from (their *author*ity); what their author's *intended meaning* was; and *how to sort* them so his island culture can understand and, perhaps, use them. He tries out various taxonomies—analytic and synthetic sentences, island news and news from across the sea, and so on.

When not sorting the bottled messages, Scribbly thinks about his teaching. Knowing the fragility of memory, he decides to keep a running account of his pedagogy. He buys a firmly bound black-and-white speckled notebook (to which Percy did not have access) and fills its pages, front and back, all the way to the edges with meticulous records. The writing classes aren't going well. Following tradition, he has assigned essays by Swift and Tuchman, Eisely and Didion, as models of rhetoric and style, as sources of information and important themes, as chances to practice interpretation. Most of all, he hopes the essays will foster students' writing and make them lifelong readers. He writes in his notebook, "My freshmen don't seem to know much about even recent events. Interpreting professionals' writing can't help but widen their horizons." Day after day, though, he finds himself doing most of the talking: teaching means telling Right Meanings. Given the powerful readings he's explicated, his students write surprisingly flat, cautious papers. "Is this what you wanted?" they bleat. Scribbly imagines himself roaring, "NO!" But instead he just writes on too many essays, "C+—interesting paper." At first the students seem just shy, then lazy, finally vacant. To keep his mind from being dulled, he plunges ahead with his research. But as he tries to sort the bottled messages, he begins to see his student writers as castaways. "Time for a walk on the beach," he sighs.

After staring for a long time at the cold, blank horizon, Scribbly writes in his notebook that, like himself, his students read messages from unknown authors writing from distant cultures to be read by unintended readers. These cultures seem so distant that, while the students do not exactly lose their memories, they set them aside as somehow inadequate for interpreting the professionals' essays. "After all," he writes, "these essays weren't written particularly for *student* readers—never mind writers—any more than the bottled messages were written for *me*. My castaways read through a glass darkly, wondering how many messages a bottle contains and how to extract, decipher, sort, and use them. Like me, they wonder, 'Do we—will we ever—Get It?' "

"Getting It," Scribbly knows, is the only reason for reading they have been taught: to extract the information and the chain of argument, to cultivate the well-stocked mind and gain cultural literacy. "Fine!" thinks Scribbly, who rests better knowing that the island's nuclear power plant crews can read their manuals for facts and can recite emergency procedures. Besides, he seldom uses lectures as chances to show off his erudition or his wit in refuting students' interpretations, infrequent as they are. What little he has time to explain to them, they jolly well need to "get." Yet, the realization nags him. His primary intention—that interpretation of professionals' essays foster the students' *writing*—remains as remote as home.

"Reading to recite subverts learning to write!" Scribbly puts down in his notebook:

> It places readers outside the text, makes them approach reading as a linear hunt for the product. In their "consistency building" (NB: term from bottled message #387 signed "Iser"), they disregard inconsistencies that could distract them from "the point" or mess up the "proof" they're trying to construct. They identify an essay's thesis and plod paragraph by paragraph, noting transitions, definitions, and evidence—attending to all the elements without ever asking, "What's this for?" Then they test its validity (which they always confuse with "truth" and "practibility"). They never see, of course, the processes by which the author wrested it into Being, never see reading *as writing*.

Catching his own gaze in the mirror, he admits that he too read this way in school. By transcribing scholars' commentaries, memorizing translations (lexical equivalents), and reciting the opening lines of *Beowulf* in an oral exam, he had passed Anglo-Saxon with an "A." He had deliberately chosen a dissertation topic ("New Light on Chaucer's *Astrolabe*: Somer, Lynne, and the Hanseatic League") so obscure that virtually nobody could refute his claims and had discarded whatever might disrupt his proof. But now those Right Meanings he had learned and proven ages ago seem different from the meanings—the rigors of the storm-darkened sea, the Wanderer's longing for companions in the meadhall—that begin to come home to him, when gazing out to sea the castaway glimpses the monster-infested horizon of poets who sang when the earth was still flat.

"Why," he asks himself, "should my explications of reading affect my students' writing any differently from the way the Anglo-Saxon experts' explications of *Beowulf* or each other's commentaries affected mine? Their subtle, polished explications daunted me! Awed by the finished product, I no more used that reading *as writing*—as a risky venture filled with obstacles, choices and surprises—than my students use Swift's or Eiseley's essays *as writing!* I'll think about that some more."

Meanwhile, his occasional literature courses go better. He covers lots of material; he is tweedily learned; his literary anecdotes charm: he gives a good show. But students seldom question his interpretations, and their responses to "Write a well-organized essay on *Antigone* as an example of Aristotelian tragedy" are numbingly similar. No students suggest their own topics. Papers using terms he's used in class ("the unities," "*hamartia*") seem to show that some students, at least, know what's going

on. These papers get good grades. One writer mentions that even the
Soviet Constitution forbids "persecution on religious grounds." "That's
relevant!" chortles Scribbly. But at her paper conference, she seems surprisingly unable to explain *why* such persecution is wrong and finally
blurts out, "Oh, I guess you shouldn't act that way near a church."
Religious grounds. Churchyard. In a flash, he Gets It: a person can *sound*
like she understands a concept without understanding it at all. (Some
weeks later, he finds a bottled message saying that "parrotlike repetition
of words" may be "covering up a vacuum" where the understanding of
the "corresponding concepts" belongs [Vygotsky 83].) He scrawls in his
notebook,

> Lucky Robinson Crusoe with only one parrot to listen to! How could
> anyone who had done the reading so totally miss the point? And how
> many others are missing it too? And what makes me think anybody is
> doing the reading anyhow? I am nothing but a TV set!

Slamming his office door, Scribbly strides out of Mead Hall intending
never to return.

Walking, and watching the waves, he calms down. His hunch is that
it's not TV but *schooling* itself that teaches people not to read and write.
Students sentenced to copy some rule 500 times survive by playing with
vertical stripes of non-writing ("I I I will will will not not not dog dog
dog— — —ear ear ear pages pages pages . . . I I I will" etc.). The school's
reading is too often done to meet the school's needs: tests (and papers
that function as tests). For better or worse, students on this island value
the "right" jogging shoes, academic major, football team, and candidate,
but (after the test) the Right Meaning of *Lycidas* is not a big item for
them. Since tests reward whoever knows facts, students learn that knowing
is less important than knowing about. When Scribbly asks a question,
they avoid eye contact, certain that within fifteen seconds (as his throat
tightens up in its thirst for words), he will answer it. Since his pseudo-
Socratic monologues *tell* the Right Meanings, why should they read?
Crouching over his notebook, Scribbly writes lightly now in pencil,

> Am I so different? Convinced I'd never be learned enough or theoret-
> ically double-jointed enough to find Right Meanings on my own, I
> transcribed the scholars' views. Now (due to my committee work and
> all those freshman essays) I barely skim. At the Chair's party, I lam-
> basted Biff Scrawley's new book on Neo-realism without having read
> it, and everyone nodded in assent except that smirking DeTrop, who
> couldn't ride every avant-garde ripple if he had the bottled messages

hanging around his neck! And when I *do* read, I'm not so much using common sense to give the author's argument a chance as I am searching for holes, or at least dents that I can bend further out of shape, anything to provide leverage for a "Letter to the Editor." If students read for "consistency building," I read for "inconsistency building," read in bad faith.

Scribbly muses that these could be embarrassing statements and wonders if he should hide, if not shred, his notebook. He also wonders now why his own lifelong motivation for reading—to understand how who did what and why, to see how and why that might matter to him, and, now, to pass that interest along to his students for their reading beyond the classroom—counts for so little in schooling and in the professional writing he does.

Valuing a single, "valid" Right Meaning over a more multiplicitous Understanding, using Kantian *a priori* rules to separate the Author's one intended and unchanging meaning in a work from its unintended and changing Significance to readers—these now seem to Scribbly the root of all his evils. A hierarchy of readers (like the judicial hierarchy that, under legal pragmatism, legitimizes interpretations of law) *could* validate historical interpretations, were its existence not denied (in a bottled message [Hirsch 250], though other messages—about "bungled meanings" in freshman essays [Hirsch 233] and the naïveté of not recognizing that *"all men in a culture do not share the same general perspective on life"* or "speak the same idiom" [Hirsch 257]—weaken this denial and lay the groundwork for the "cultural literacy" movement.) But Scribbly knows that on *his* island such a hierarchy does exist (and may exist elsewhere). Through the years, its pre-eminent theorists—Wimsatt, Frye, Trilling, Ransome—enunciate infallible (in their day) decrees, each entailing its priesthood of New Critics, Formalists, and so on. The more pluralistic decrees urge the congregation to read, re-read, talk and write about meaning; theirs is a hierarchy of Understandings. But the hierarchy of Right Meaning depends upon proximity to validity (and demolition of all competing meanings); its congregation can only await The Answer. Scribbly pictures himself tied upon the Boethian Wheel of Fortune: it rises, he basks momentarily in Strong Probability if not Perfect Validity, but then there's nothing to re-read or talk over, nowhere to go but down and down to silence, and worse yet, to the monotonous ride back up to the unchanging and already-known Right Meaning. Logically, the more Right Meanings are validated, the more literature turns into *fact*, the less reason people will have to read!

As overwork and despair mount, Scribbly hides out, spending more and more time pacing the beach, so preoccupied he even lets some bottles lie uncollected. What if he, Hector Scribbly, were to know all Right Meanings? "Professional omnipotence, my students'—and Washington's!—adulation, my own late-night TV show, *Rightline*—all, all would be mine!" But the vision quickly fades. "Worth, and adulation, and press. That's all, that's all, that's all, that's all," mumbles Scribbly Agonistes. "I'd be bored." Ironically, his lifetime collection of Right Meanings is worse than useless: as long as he purveys them, they will prevent students from questioning, from talking and writing their speculative answers, from reading for themselves. Now Scribbly understands bottled message #512 that reads, "*students can read only as well as they can write*" (Slevin in Berthoff qtd., "I. A. Richards" 52). If he can't get them to write—and apparently he can't—then he can't get them to read better either. His whole professional life seems washed up.

He vows to walk straight into the ocean and disappear. If the notebook he tapes to his chest is ever found, it will be unreadable and unburnable too, like Shelley's heart. Let them all wonder what it might have said: they'd never explicate his life or his text! Savoring his final moments in the sun, he notices bobbing toward shore a large bottle containing a very bright object. Strange! It couldn't hurt to read just one more message. As he removes the wide cork, into his hand falls an immense and perfect butterfly mounted on a card bearing the lines,

So halt' ich's endlich denn in meinen Händen,
Und nenn' es in gewissem Sinne mein

which he haltingly translates, "So I hold it finally in my hands / And call it in certain senses 'mine.'" The card also reads, "recited by Stein to Marlowe, *Lord Jim*, Ch. 20." For the first time, Scribbly recognizes a bottled message, one he knows by heart, so to speak, not only from having re-read this favorite novel, but also as if the romance of his own life opens his Understanding. Always, he now recalls, it was the pursuit, not the lifeless butterflies taxonomized in their glass cases, that brought Stein happiness. "No wonder students respect my collection without thrilling to the pursuit of meaning, knowing they'll never be more than spectators before Right Meanings snared, taxonomized and encased in glass," thinks Scribbly. He whispers Stein's words, "I took long journeys and underwent great privations; I had dreamed of him in my sleep, and here suddenly I had him in my fingers—for myself!" The frail and beautiful wings quiver faintly, as if Scribbly's breath for an instant calls back to life that gorgeous object of Stein's dreams. Dreams! "A man that is born falls into a dream like a man who falls into the sea," murmurs Scribbly, repeating Stein's words he had memorized:

> If he tries to climb out into the air as inexperienced people endeavour to do, he drowns—*nicht wahr?* . . . No! I tell you! The way is to the destructive element submit yourself, and with the exertions of your hands and feet in the water make the deep, deep sea keep you up. So if you ask me—how to be?

"Submit," muses Scribbly. The proponents of Right Meanings have feared linguistic, hence literary, indeterminacy as a destructive element. They have tried to "climb out" by dividing Meaning from Significance, then claiming to "validate" Meaning. But what if we submit to indivisibility and to indeterminacy? What if we recognize "validity" as the death of literature into fact and of readers into second-hand owners? By submitting to indeterminacy, readers—swimmers in texts—will have reason to exert themselves in experiencing and understanding language, to keep on reading—and writing—all their lives.

But during the night Scribbly's courage ebbs. Might he not go on as before, the good showman, the dogged taxonomist—only now living in bad faith? At dawn, he soberly gathers some of the neglected messages. One (#223 Burke, "Dialectician's Hymn" 447–50) contains these lines:

> Let the Word be dialectic with the Way—
> Whichever the print
> The other the imprint.

Scribbly understands that Burke, instead of drowning while pondering which is supreme, the Word or the Way, Kantian *Logos* or Hegelian *Erlebnis, declares* them interchangeably print or imprint: *Let* them be dialectic! The declaration saves Burke from "the mania of the One"—the Right Meaning, thinks Scribbly—and "the delirium of the Many." In the same way that a novel's title *names* its events and the events *enact* its title, so the Word is a "Great Synecdoche," the Way a "Grand Tautology." "Beside Burke's imprint on the sand, Friday's seems insignificant," rejoices Scribbly, gathering up all the messages and, most tenderly, the butterfly, and striding home as the sun bursts over the horizon.

Let there be writing and reading, all in good faith! As he untapes the notebook from his chest, he guesses that re-reading it might help him figure out how to practice his faith. Odd that he's never re-read it before. He soon wishes he had not written his pages so full. He, who had always filled the wide margins of students' papers with comments, had left himself no room to write. "My intended meaning seemed so clear, complete, and

Right there'd be nothing more to say," he mutters. Somebody, he thinks, ought to invent a dialectical notebook. Rummaging in a bottom drawer, he finds a long forgotten package of tissue pages gummed narrowly along one side, the kind he had inserted over each page of Klaeber's *Beowulf* so he could write his meticulous translations without marring his text. Fastening these along the binding of the speckled notebook takes a long time. Not quite ready to re-read, he places the butterfly on his desk, where the late afternoon sun shining through its wings colors the tissue pages. Later by lamplight he fills them with his reflections as he re-reads the original text lying beneath. Then he sleeps, dreamlessly.

Next morning he first thinks of the bottled message he'd found yesterday, right where he must have stuck it long ago between the pages of his notebook (instead of filing it methodically with the others). It must somehow have seemed to belong to him, rather than to his research project:

> Nothing is so purely the trace of the mind as writing, but also nothing is so dependent on the understanding mind. In its deciphering and interpretation a miracle takes place: the transformation of something strange and dead into a total simultaneity and familiarity. This is like nothing else that has come down to us from the past. The remnants of the life of the past, . . . are weather-beaten by the storms of time that have swept over them, whereas a written tradition, when deciphered and read, is to such an extent pure mind that it speaks to us as if in the present. That is why the capacity to read, to understand what is written, is like a secret art, even a magic that looses and binds us. In it time and space seem to be suspended. The man who is able to read what has been handed down in writing testifies to and achieves the sheer presence of the past. (#90 Gadamer, *Truth and Method* 145)

In the notebook, Scribbly had written, "Beware mumbo-jumbo that illicitly installs the reader's present in the Author's context, thus obfuscating intended meaning!" But last night on the tissue overleaf he'd said, "If writing depends on the understanding mind and on re-presenting (I mean making the past present again), then readers can read immediately. The more we read, building our hierarchy on ways of re-experiencing words, the more intimately we'll *fuse* (think about what "fuse" means???) the author's past with our present. Interpreting will not be Validating but Understanding, and the Meanings will be *for* us."

In the as-yet unsortable "Misc.—G" file, Scribbly finds more messages from Gadamer: recitation "is closed to the sudden idea" (497); translation figures forth Understanding (346–51); the present does not comprise a "fixed set of opinions and evaluations," nor can the past be distinguished

from the present as if it were a "fixed ground" (272–73). " 'Ground'
again," Scribbly muses; "Every word seems to have its own horizon."
Perhaps, he thinks, the puzzling term "fuse" might have come from this
message about "fusion": "There is no more an isolated horizon of the
present than there are historical horizons. Understanding, rather, is always
the fusion of these horizons which we imagine to exist by themselves"
(273). Maybe the term stuck in his mind because of his walks on the
beach, where the seaward horizon, cold and blank, seemed a rigid, eternal
barrier between himself and home. The meaning of "fusion of horizons,"
though, seems deliberately opaque. If Gadamer had only chosen a phrase
like "harmony of ages," Scribbly could easily imagine voices of two eras
blending, like Mozart's with Händel's. "In my experience, horizons appear
and disappear with the sun but simply do not fuse. What mediating term
can I use to understand Gadamer?" wonders Scribbly.

In hot pursuit, Scribbly sorts the messages in his (surprisingly thick)
file on "Horizons." Some are two-dimensional (like the flat line between
sky and sea): a work's "inner" and "outer" horizons (Hirsch 224); the
"horizon" as an abstractly defined limit (Burke 9); the teacher's "destination" in imparting a concept (Schor 103)—to Scribbly this seems to
mean "point"; the "resymbolization" of a work into one's psychic horizon
(Bleich 97–99). These won't do: they flatten the experience of reading into
a silhouette, like the figures following Death across the horizon in *The
Seventh Seal*. More promising messages were three-dimensional: "Rhetoric," whose "horizon [is] nothing less than the field of discursive *practices*
in society as a whole" particularly viewed as "*forms* of power and performance" (Eagleton 205, emphasis added) might help explain "fusion of
horizons." Both the reader's and the work's "horizons" seem to include
three dimensions: a viewpoint, some objects within a field, and a context
surrounding the field.

"Fusion" must not, he thinks, mean welding edges together (like halves
of a buoy, rings in a figure eight, or balls on a pawnbroker's sign). In
nature, Scribbly has never seen this "fusion": oil and water remain too
separable, clouds and rainbows too diffusive, a mirror reflection too exactly
oriented toward the object. "Fusion" does not mean naive assimilation of
reader into work or work into reader. Instead it emphasizes the *differences*
among the viewpoints, the fields, and the contexts of each. "Maybe I
could call it," thinks Scribbly, "a continuing audit of meaning," a back-
and-forthness between the reader's horizon and work's. "Audit" impels
Scribbly again toward music, but he knows he can't speak of "resonance,"
partly because Gadamer chose otherwise and partly because the puzzling
phrase "fusion of horizons," like the puzzling experience it expresses, both

seeks and resists resolution, thus creating energy (as Peirce knew when he explained the "triadicity" of metaphor). "The phrase *should* have no Right Meaning!" Scribbly exclaims, striking his brow. "It should never dwindle to a slogan plastered across textbooks as other once useful phrases (like "writing as a mode of learning") have been." Instead, its meanings *happen*, living and changing in the exertions of readers and writers as they submit to language.

"From now on," Scribbly vows, "we'll romance the prose!" He imagines that he and his students will slay pseudo-Socratic monologues and reading in bad faith. They'll set free a truly reciprocal dialectic in which both questioner(s) and answerer(s)—be they person(s) or text(s)—can introduce questions at any point (Gadamer 330). Together they'll leap (following Stein's philosophy) into the midst of a text, submit to it *as writing* and let reciprocal questioning buoy them up. They'll experience reading as a game that plays its players as they play it, differently in each playing, its significances an incentive for them to grow more and more literate. The old motto of the Hanseatic League, "It is necessary to sail the seven seas; it is not necessary to live," not only urges stoicism but, as Scribbly suddenly realizes, affirms that Doing takes care of Being, just as Burke's Way enacts the Word. A sailor need not ask, "What is the meaning of Life that I should live it?" His Life, in its sailing, takes care of itself, enacts its Meaning. So for a reader, Meaning, in its continuing fusing of horizons, takes care of itself.

Now Scribbly anticipates classes that will be adventures, risky and unpredictable. While he pries loose students' deathgrip on "reading to recite," he'll be letting go of his step-by-step lesson plans, virtuoso performances and feats of detecting (well, actually repeating, he reminds himself) Right Meanings, and his entitlement to having the last word. Scribbly's hierarchy of readers (where admittedly his greater experience as a writer and reader usually, but not necessarily, places him higher than most of his students), will depend not upon proximity to Right Meanings but on resourcefulness in maintaining open horizons for re-experiencing reading. His adrenalin is really flowing now.

They will begin with middles, he resolves, not like the epic poets who began reciting *in medias res* but already knew the whole story, but like Henry James' observer "upon whom nothing is lost." Laying aside the official textbook, he asks Penny Squire (his work-study student) to ditto a paragraph she chooses randomly from any book in the Mead Hall library. On Monday, he and his students find themselves castaways in a strange text. He says they'll all write observations about it. The students write things like, "The point is . . . " or "It flowed." Nobody Gets It—the text or the notion of observing as opposed to proving or evaluating. As Scribbly realizes, they suspect he actually knows the source, and they resent his secret knowledge of its Right Meanings. "They're well schooled," he has to admit. So, with sweaty palms, he asks a student to read aloud a "middle" paragraph from any book in her bookbag. He writes on the board the reciprocal questions it asks him and he asks it: he lets them catch him in the act of thinking, in the play of reading. Next time a student volunteers this unidentified "middle" paragraph:

> The assumption is that the Grand Canyon is a remarkably interesting and beautiful place and that if it had a certain value P for Cárdenas, the same value P may be transmitted to any number of sightseers— just as Banting's discovery of insulin can be transmitted to any number of diabetics. A counterinfluence is at work, however, and it would be nearer the truth to say that if the place is seen by a million sight- seers, a single sightseer does not receive value P but a millionth part of value P.

They ask: "Who assumes?" "Who is Cárdenas?" "Why express aesthetic value as mathematical?" "Why say 'discovery' (instead of 'insulin') is 'transmitted'?" "What truth?" While Scribbly tries to keep quiet, the text questions them: "Whose assumptions count and how? Whose don't?" "Who cares if Cárdenas is an explorer from Spain or from the Bronx?" "Why does 'nearer the truth' sound odd in a math context?" Next they write some plausible answers. As Scribbly had speculated about "fusion of horizons," they speculate about "value P" and other puzzles. Then, asking themselves "What could I make with this?" they write a paragraph that could precede or follow what they have so far. Many invent identities for Cárdenas, some consider how "sights" are transmitted and received or why people "sightsee," some compare geographic and scientific "dis- covery": the variety shows there are lots of meanings. When they finally write a larger essay including somewhere the given "middle" paragraph and their short elaborations, nobody bleats, "Is this what you wanted?" and no two essays are alike!

Afterwards, when the student provides the whole essay, Percy's "The Loss of the Creature" (of all things), they see how the paragraph fits into his meditations on how expectations too firmly fixed limit one's percep- tions. But Percy's meaning does not become "right" and their meanings "wrong." All their Words and Ways meet dialectically in a fusion of horizons. The next "middle" is picked from a student essay. With lit- erature classes, Scribbly avoids "big" middle scenes: no heroes on beaches, no Wordsworth rowing on Ullswater, no Isabel Archer glimpsing Madame

Merle *tête-à-tête* with Gilbert Osmond, but instead any line, then its enclosing scene, then chapter. Readers will naturally turn to the first (if not the last) page as soon as they can, but his deliberately *un*natural exercise has shown them a way to use reading *as writing*, to glimpse what viewpoints, fields, and contexts might constitute the horizons of the text-as-writing and the text-as-reading, what choices the writer and reader did make and could make in their efforts at fusing horizons.

Scribbly decides to share his pedagogy with fellow writing teachers at the Four Seas Conference. "But if I tell about the butterfly and the bottled messages, if I read from my tissued notebook DeTrop will smirk," he acknowledges. So, to Authorize his experience, he bones up on theories of all kinds. His paper teems with footnotes proving he's done the home-work and "Gets It," proving beyond doubt that romancing the prose is not a crackpot idea. But when he demonstrates how to teach *as writing* the Grand Canyon paragraph, his colleagues find in it so many unanswered questions that they fall to bemoaning the many "flaws" in the student's writing (what professional would write so oddly?) and before he can explain, a gong proclaims it is the next speaker's turn. In the discussion period, he is an outcast.

Back on the beach, Scribbly calls his Four Seas performance what it was: bad faith. "After what I've learned, how could I do that?" he moans. He should have trusted, trusted the bottled messages, his processes of understanding them, his notebook and his teaching, his listeners' good faith efforts to fuse their horizons with his. And next time he would! Somewhere across the seas, a new generation of teachers had begun think-ing about speculative writing (McCord) and reading (Bialostosky). He would set sail and find them, share tales of fortune and fusion. Strength-ened in trust by their comradeship in like pursuits, he would return in good faith to Mead Hall, knowing that "home" is not some point on a distant horizon but always already around him in language.

As a token of his return, he decides to leave behind the beginnings of the story he will later dare to tell. In his new loose-leaf notebook, he begins (in indelible ink, with versos blank), "Savoring my final moments in the sun, I noticed bobbing toward shore a large bottle containing a very bright object. . . . "

The following readings, bookmarked and annotated, were found on Pro-fessor Scribbly's desk (but the butterfly was gone):

Berthoff, Ann E. "I. A. Richards." In *Traditions of Inquiry*. Ed. John Brereton. New York: Oxford UP, 1986. 50–80.

Bialostosky, Don H. "Dialogics as an Art of Discourse in Literary Criticism." *PMLA* 101 (1986): 788–97.

Bleich, David. *Subjective Criticism*. Baltimore: The Johns Hopkins UP, 1978.

Burke, Kenneth. *The Philosophy of Literary Form: Studies in Symbolic Action*. Berkeley: U of California P, 1941.

Eagleton, Terry. *Literary Theory: An Introduction*. Minneapolis: U of Minnesota P, 1983.

Hirsch, E. D., Jr. *Validity in Interpretation*. New Haven: Yale UP, 1967.

Iser, Wolfgang. *The Act of Reading: A Theory of Aesthetic Response*. Baltimore: The Johns Hopkins UP, 1978. 107–34.

McCord, Phyllis Frus. "Reading Nonfiction in Composition Courses: From Theory to Practice." *College English* 47 (1985): 747–60.

Percy, Walker. *The Message in the Bottle*. New York: Farrar, Straus, & Giroux, 1954. 119–49.

Shor, Ira and Paulo Freire. *A Pedagogy for Liberation: Dialogues on Transforming Education*. South Hadley, MA: Bergin and Garvey, 1987.

Vygotsky, Lev. *Thought and Language*. Ed. Eugenia Hanfmann. Trans. Gertrude Vakar. Cambridge: MIT Press, 1962.

Contributors

David Bartholomae teaches English at the University of Pittsburgh, where he directs the Ph.D. Program in Composition. He is co-author of *Facts, Artifacts, and Counterfacts*, co-editor of an anthology, *Ways of Reading*, and author of many articles on composition and rhetoric.

Lil Brannon teaches English at the State University of New York at Albany, where she directs the Writing Center. She is co-author of *Writers Writing*, co-author with C. H. Knoblauch of *Rhetorical Traditions and the Teaching of Writing*, and author of articles on deafness education, writing centers, and composition theory.

John Brereton teaches English at the University of Massachusetts at Boston. He is the author of a rhetoric text, *A Plan for Writing*, and a reader, *Themes for College Writers*. He has also edited *Traditions of Inquiry*.

Neal Bruss teaches English and linguistics at the University of Massachusetts at Boston. He has published articles on relationships between linguistics, literature, and psychoanalysis and is completing a book on Freud's interpretive method.

John Clifford teaches English at the University of North Carolina at Wilmington, where he also directs the Writing Program. He has edited *Modern American Prose* and has published articles on ideology and discourse, rhetorical criticism, and reading and writing theory.

Pat D'Arcy is County English Advisor for the primary and secondary schools of Wiltshire, UK.

Rosemary Deen teaches English at Queens College, City University of New York, and is poetry editor for *Commonweal*. With Marie Ponsot, she is co-author of *Beat Not the Poor Desk,* which received the MLA's Mina Shaughnessy Award, and of *The Common Sense*. She is writing two books, one on the teaching of literature and the other a collection of her own poems.

Angela G. Dorenkamp teaches English at Assumption College, where she directs the Writing Program. She is co-editor of *Images of Women in American Popular Culture* and has authored articles on Coleridge, Marvell, and Jonson, and on writing in general.

Judith Goleman teaches English at the University of Massachusetts at Boston. She has published articles on social dialectics in the writing classroom and on the language theory of Bakhtin in relation to sequenced writing assignments.

Robert M. Holland, Jr., teaches English at the University of Akron, where he was Director of Composition. He has published articles on Piaget and writing assignments, subjective criticism, and responding to students' writing.

Paul Kameen teaches English at the University of Pittsburgh, where he is Associate Director of Composition. He is the author of articles on rhetorical theory, poetics, and pedagogy. He is now working on a project entitled *Metaphor, Meditation, and Method*.

Philip M. Keith teaches English at St. Cloud State University in Minnesota, where he was Composition Director. He is assistant editor of *Rhetoric Society Quarterly* and author of articles on Burke and on composition pedagogy.

C. H. Knoblauch teaches English at the State University of New York at Albany, where he formerly directed the Writing Program and now is consultant to the Writing Intensive Program. He has published articles on rhetoric, composition theory, and eighteenth-century British literature and, with Lil Brannon, is co-author of *Rhetorical Traditions and the Teaching of Writing*.

Eleanor Kutz teaches English at the University of Massachusetts at Boston, where she directed the Freshman Studies Program, a program designed to introduce underprepared students to the principles that underlie academic inquiry through research-based seminars. She is the author of articles on medieval narrative, ethnography and writing, and linguistics and the teaching of writing.

Marie Ponsot teaches English at Queens College, City University of New York. She is co-author with Rosemary Deen of *Beat Not the Poor Desk* and *The Common Sense.* She is author of three books of poems, *True Minds, Admit Impediment,* and *The Green Dark.*

Ann Raimes teaches writing to ESL and graduate students at Hunter College, City University of New York. She is the author of *Focus on Composition, Techniques in Teaching Writing,* and *Exploring Through Writing: A Process Approach to ESL Composition*, and of articles on ESL writing, approaches to language teaching, materials and methodology, and writing-across-the-curriculum.

Hephzibah Roskelly teaches English at the University of Massachusetts at Boston. She has published articles on basic writing and on the relationship between reading and writing.

Mariolina Salvatori teaches in the Literature, Composition, and Basic Reading and Writing Programs at the University of Pittsburgh. She has published articles on aging, ethnic literature, Gadamer, and reading and writing relationships. She is working on a book on pedagogy.

Sandra Schor teaches English at Queens College, City University of New York, where she directed the Composition Program. She is co-author of the *Random House Guide to Writing* and the *Borzoi Handbook for Writers* and has published articles on revising and on relations between translating and composing. She is author of many short stories and poems.

James F. Slevin chairs the English Department and directs the Writing Across the Curriculum Program at Georgetown University. He is author of articles on relationships between rhetorical and literary theory and on current conflicts in the profession of English Studies and is working on a book called *The Writing of English Studies.*

Louise Z. Smith teaches English at the University of Massachusetts at Boston, where she directs the Freshman Composition and Writing Tutor Programs. She is co-author of *The Practical Tutor* and has published articles on writing-across-the-curriculum, the teaching of writing, and British and Continental Romanticism.

Susan Wells teaches English at Temple University. She is the author of *The Dialectics of Representation* and is completing a book on narrative and exposition in the natural and social sciences.

Vivian Zamel teaches English as a Second Language and graduate courses in Applied Linguistics at the University of Massachusetts at Boston, where she directs the ESL Program. She has published articles on ESL composing processes and ESL writing pedagogy.